THE SHADOW OF THE MINE

THE SHADOW
OF THE MINE

Coal and the End of Industrial Britain

Huw Beynon and Ray Hudson

VERSO

London • New York

First published by Verso 2021
© Huw Beynon and Ray Hudson 2021

1 3 5 7 9 10 8 6 4 2

Verso
UK: 6 Meard Street, London W1F 0EG
US: 20 Jay Street, Suite 1010, Brooklyn, NY 11201
versobooks.com

Verso is the imprint of New Left Books

ISBN-13: 978-1-83976-155-3
ISBN-13: 978-1-83976-156-0 (UK EBK)
ISBN-13: 978-1-83976-157-7 (US EBK)

British Library Cataloguing in Publication Data
A catalogue record for this book is available from the British Library

Library of Congress Cataloging-in-Publication Data
Library of Congress Control Number: 2020948743

Typeset in Adobe Garamond Pro by Hewer Text UK Ltd, Edinburgh
Printed and bound by CPI Group (UK) Ltd, Croydon CR0 4YY

Contents

List of Maps

List of Tables and Figures

Tables

Figures

Map 1. Coalfields in Britain

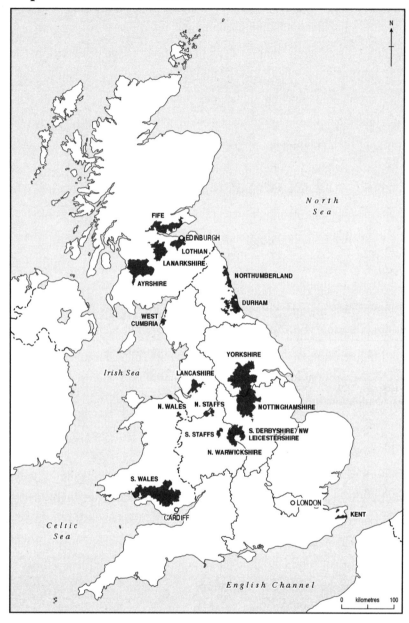

Map 2. Durham

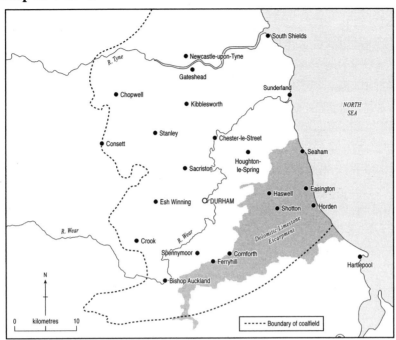

Map 3. South Wales

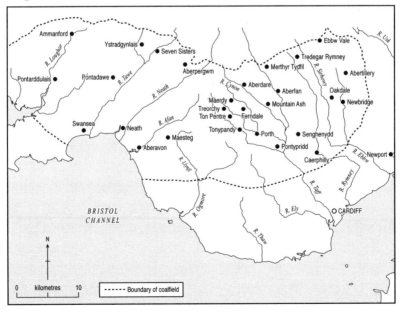

Every little boy's ambition in my valley was to become a miner. There was the arrogant strut of the lords of the coalface who stand on street corners and look at the posh people that passed with hostile eyes; insulting them with cold looks because they were the kings of the underworld.

Richard Burton, *The Dick Cavett Show*, 1980

Introduction

This is a book about the coalfields of Durham and South Wales, and the people who live there. We have come to know these areas well over the years, keeping up many contacts and friendships. This has brought home to us the need for a sympathetic historical account of how life has changed in these communities. Our aim is to explain why Britain's coalfields, once significant centres of industrial production and political influence, became marginalised, and to explore the ways in which the state has played a central role in their declining fortunes.

These concerns were brought into sharp relief at the time of the 2016 Brexit referendum, when Durham and South Wales both voted strongly in favour of leaving the European Union. In the days and weeks that followed, the referendum's outcome was greeted with incredulity, and often presented as the mutiny of the old and the uneducated – a Peasant's Revolt – or an outburst of nostalgia for a time when Britain was Great. It seemed to us, on the other hand, that in the coalfields at least, the Leave vote was a case of a forgotten people striking back. Coalfield politics came back into the spotlight in the General Election of 2019, Brexit once more at issue, as large numbers of Labour seats in old industrial and mining areas, including in Durham, turned to Boris Johnson's Conservatives. It was a cataclysmic event, and one which suggested that historical working-class identities have been eroded.

In her 2016 investigation of surging support for the Tea Party Republican right among economically disadvantaged white voters in the USA, the sociologist Arlie Hochschild argued for the need 'to know others from the inside, to see reality through their eyes, to understand the links between life, feeling and politics', and to trace the 'deep story' that sits behind the day-to-day anger and political rhetoric.[1] At this time in Britain there is a similar need to trace the 'deep story' of a disenfranchised working class, and to tell it through the voices of those whose communities have been taken apart piece by piece.

In attempting this, we have chosen the case of the coalminers. Before the First World War, Durham and South Wales were Britain's leading coal-exporting regions, with a dominant position in the global trade. In South Wales there was pride in the dry steam coal mined from its central valleys, which powered the ships of the British fleet. *Times* journalist Ivor Thomas commented in 1934:

> It is no exaggeration to say that the Industrial Revolution was founded upon coal, and without coal Great Britain's remarkable industrial advance in the nineteenth century would not have been possible. On sea and land, coal for a century and a half knew no rival.[2]

As George Orwell emphasised in *The Road to Wigan Pier* three years later,

> The machines that keep us alive, and the machines that make machines, are all directly or indirectly dependent upon coal. In the metabolism of the Western world the coalminer is second in importance only to the man who ploughs the soil.[3]

He marvelled at the endurance of the miners. How easy it was to forget that 'their lamp-lit world down there is as necessary to the daylight world above as the root is to the flower'.[4]

Like the man who ploughed the soil, the coalminer lived and worked away from the towns and cities. Whereas factories were associated with an urban way of life, the mines were located within distinct *coalfields*, where miners were easily the dominant occupational group. It was a world apart. In his autobiography, the Durham miners' leader John Wilson recalled a miner who visited London in the 1860s and, on announcing that he was a pitman, was greeted with incredulity, and marched around the public house to be observed. The onlookers were surprised that he walked upright, having previously believed that miners 'could only walk in a doubled-up posture owing to the cramped conditions of their work and their continued residence underground.'[5] Such beliefs persisted well into the twentieth century. During the Second World War, children from London were lodged in the mining villages of South Wales as evacuees from the Blitz. Every mining village, or so it seems, had at least one account of a child who expressed surprise at seeing miners above ground. As in the nineteenth century, there existed a widely held view that miners lived in underground caves.

The combination of social separation and arduous work performed by men alone, in difficult and often dangerous conditions, were important elements of a paradoxical occupational culture amongst the miners. 'More than most men,' observed social scientist Mark Benney from a Durham mining village in 1946, the miners had a sense of the past.

> Their fathers and grandfathers had been miners, and had talked of their craft . . . and out of the long evenings of pit talk reaching back through generations had developed something like a tribal memory.[6]

Similarly, as Tony Hall, later Lord Hall, director general of the BBC, noted in his book *King Coal: Miners, Coal and Britain's Industrial Future* (1981), the miners 'will describe at length the horrors and the hardship of mining.'

They will encourage and even plead with their sons to find another job. Yet at the same time there can be no other group that would fight as hard for their traditions, collieries and industry.[7]

Some of the 'tribal memory' was composed of local genealogies; other parts were made up of accounts of trade union struggles, of leaders good and bad, of owners and of managers. The Labour Party also had a role to play, for remarkably, it was in these isolated coalfield areas that the Party found the heartland of its support. Durham and South Wales became synonymous with a 'Labourist' form of politics, one held together – at times uneasily – by the separate but supposedly complementary interests of the trade unions and the Party. Miners' leaders from Durham and South Wales were pivotal to national coalmining trade union-ism, including at the time of the 1926 General Strike and the 1944 formation of the National Union of Mineworkers, while six leaders of the Labour Party have represented constituencies in these areas: Keir Hardie, Ramsay MacDonald, James Callaghan, Michael Foot, Neil Kinnock and Tony Blair.

Coal and the coalminers therefore seem a good subject for our long story. In the cultural sphere, life on our chosen coalfields has been documented in myriad ways. Two of the greatest novels of A. J. Cronin, *The Stars Look Down* (1935) and *The Citadel* (1937), are set in and around them, in the fictional towns of Sleescale and Drineffy respectively. The latter work, based on his experiences as a doctor at the Tredegar Medical Aid Society organised by the miners to provide free healthcare, was one of the inspirations for the NHS. Both novels were made into films, swiftly followed by Richard Llewellyn's somewhat inferior *How Green Was My Valley*, which won the Oscar for Best Picture in 1942. The coalfields returned to the public mind in the post-war years, indelibly associated with a series of industrial disasters, including, in 1966, the collapse of a waste tip over the school and village of Aberfan.

The 1970s and 1980s brought major strikes. The first two seemed to shift the balance of power in the land, and led to a change of government. The third lasted a year and ended in defeat. This defeat affected everyone, not just those in the mining areas, where pits closed at a rapid rate. People would say, 'if the miners can't do it, nobody can' – such was their hard-won reputation for solidarity and determined struggle. The Leeds writer Bernard Hare, for example, reflected in 2006 that:

> I wasn't born into the underclass – it didn't exist when I was born – but my whole family sort of plopped into it after the Miners' Strike in 1984–85. Before that we felt that we were part of something, a community, a great nation with a great history. After that, we knew that we were redundant, rubbish, nothing . . . Our communities crumbled, people lost hope and felt betrayed.[8]

If anything, the sense of betrayal and abandonment has increased since then. The hopes for transformation and renewal under a Blair government were unfulfilled. Jobs were increasingly scarce, underpaid and temporary, putting both Durham and South Wales near the bottom of the national wages league as the gap between them and the South East widened, and creating a growing sense that these areas had been deliberately left behind, their young people recruited to fight in wars of no purpose in the Middle East. Within both areas there was a mismatch between the logics and sentiments of the old industrial economy and the upbeat post-industrial future promised by New Labour's 'Cool Britannia', with its emphasis on markets, branding, innovation and globalisation. The financial crash brought this to an end, and the pain that followed rubbed salt into the wounds.

In the two coalfields, as in many other deindustrialised places throughout the UK, the world had changed almost beyond recognition. Many people increasingly felt that their concerns and interests were being ignored by politicians of all parties and that Westminster was blind or perhaps just indifferent to what was happening in the rest of the country. As a consequence, the past increasingly came to be remembered as a more meaningful time, when industrial areas counted for something, when people stuck together, when they had clout and when other people took notice. By unpicking the transformation of these two thoroughly industrialised and deeply politicised areas into deindustrialised backwaters, we can begin to understand the anger that exploded into the 2016 referendum and 2019 general election, and which continues to bubble under the surface of British politics in the 2020s. The historian Edward Thompson stressed the importance of rescuing the defeated, the silenced and the dispossessed from the 'enormous condescension of posterity'.[9] This concern is even more appropriate nowadays, when condescension and hypocrisy are in plentiful supply and when there is a pressing need to answer the question, 'whatever happened to the miners?'.

CHAPTER ONE

Two Coalfields, Two Labour Traditions

We older ones can go back to a time when there were number 1,
2, 3 and 4 pits open in Maerdy, number 5 pit in Ferndale,
number 9 pit in Tylorstown . . . there was a pit in every town. The
hooter would sound at 11 o'clock and you would know that that
was the end of the third lesson of the day. The pits then dominated
the valleys. They dominated the community completely.

Terry Williams, Maerdy, 1999

For centuries the economies of South Wales and Durham were
synonymous with coal mining. Durham was part of the Great
Northern Coalfield, which from the sixteenth century produced
coal on an increasing scale, reaching its high point at the beginning of the twentieth. Coal mining in South Wales began much
later, developing very rapidly from the 1880s. Most of the coal
was shipped from Cardiff and sold through its Coal Exchange,
where the first ever million-pound cheque was signed and paid
over for a coal shipment in 1904. Mining fed into the railways,
into steel production, into engineering – and in the North East,
into shipyards and the chemical industry as well – placing both
regions at the centre of a single-fuel industrial economy.

Here, among the furnaces and coal mines, workers organised.
Their unions were political, focusing attention on the need for

proper state regulation of the industry. To this end the miners supported the Liberal Party against the Tories, and then provided the core support for the embryonic Labour Party. In 1900 Labour leader Keir Hardie was elected by the constituency of Merthyr Tydfil, becoming one of the Party's first two MPs. In these places, the ability of workers to organise themselves effectively in the mines – and, above ground, to build complex political machines, networked across their coal-based economies – came to shape the mass social democratic politics that emerged in Britain in the first half of the twentieth century.

Deep Legacies

Though they have many similarities, Durham and South Wales developed in quite different ways. Coal mining had its earliest expansion on the Great Northern – the 'historic' – Coalfield, with aristocratic landowners deeply involved in the trade (later diversifying into industrial production and finance). Pre-capitalist rural practices of tied labour were incorporated into the sector as it grew. Miners were tied to their employers through an annual bond, placing unfree labour at the heart of the area's industrial economy. This continued until annulled by an Act of Parliament in 1872 under pressure from the newly formed Durham Miners' Association (DMA). Miners were provided with houses free of charge as part of their wages, along with coal to heat their homes. The 'fuel allowance' became generally incorporated across the industry, but company housing was much more restricted and unusual in South Wales, where miners either rented privately or became homeowners through the formation of savings clubs. In Durham, therefore, coal mining enclosed the workers' lives even more fully than it did in South Wales. There coal became dominated by modern firms that amalgamated and developed into large multi-entity combines – allowing access to social institutions beyond the industry.[1]

Geology created other differences between the areas. In Durham, the coal seams to the west lay relatively near to the surface, while those to the east are concealed under a deep layer of the Magnesian limestone and extend beyond the coast under the sea. As a consequence, deep mining began in the west of the county and moved eastward as techniques improved, leaving redundant mines in its wake. In South Wales, the coal measures lie in an oval-shaped formation with sharply incised river valleys cutting across them from north to south, often exposing seams to drift mines, with the shafts of the deep mines driven into the valley floors. Unlike in Durham, there was no systematic spatial shift in the locus of coal production; rather, many centres emerged at around the same time, in each of the twenty valleys that stretch from the Ebbw Fach in the east, across to the Taff, Cynon and Rhondda in the central coalfield, and then to Neath and the Loughor valley of the western anthracite belt.

Geology also connects the two coalfields, however. Contrary to popular belief, coal is not a homogeneous material. Produced through powerful geological processes, its makeup varies, and this is expressed as a rank order, from one (anthracite, the most valuable) to nine (lignite, the least). Durham and South Wales produced some of the highest-ranked coals in the world. The coals of Durham belonged to the third and fourth ranks, which made them eminently suitable for making coke; the same was true of the coals of the eastern valleys of South Wales. Superior 201 coals were found in the central valleys of Glamorgan: the Taff, Cynon and Rhondda. Referred to as 'dry steam', these coals are exceptional in their capacity to burn cleanly without smoke and were in great demand, particularly for powering the boilers of steam-driven naval ships. Further to the west was an anthracite belt of 101 coals, made of pure carbon and hard as diamonds: producing great heat with little smoke, they were a popular source of domestic heating and also drove the locomotives of the Great Western Railway, enhancing their reputation for speed and cleanliness. As a consequence, and in their different ways, Durham and South Wales became regions that propelled the development of British industrial capitalism.

Yet the coals, valuable as they were, were often located in very thin seams and could be difficult to extract. Miners endured a harsh regime of heavy physical labour in often perilous conditions. The men working the Garw seam in South Wales and the Victoria and Brockwell in West Durham did so with a pick and shovel while lying on their sides, often in water. The high methane content of these coals made them prone to explosion, and there was extensive loss of life through innumerable 'disasters'. One occurred at the West Stanley colliery in 1909, when 168 men and boys were killed. Another, even more calamitous, took the lives of 439 miners at the Universal colliery in Senghenydd four years later. Events like these, focusing attention on the need for adequate ventilation of the mines and full safety procedures, help explain the political nature of mining trade unionism and its concern with state regulation of the industry.

The Miners, United?

Focused locally on the branch, or 'lodge', the trade union was the main organising point within a mining village, dealing with industrial, social and political issues. Trade unionism took on particular regional characteristics in Britain's coalfields. The Durham Miners' Association (DMA) was established in 1869, its members united in their opposition to the annual bond. This, together with the experience of disharmony and failure in the past, influenced the creation of a highly centralised county union – something that would remain a principal aspect of its character. In contrast, the South Wales Miners' Federation (SWMF) was founded much later, out of a number of independent local unions, after the failed 'six month strike' in 1898. Local autonomy was written into the constitution, and repeated attempts to alter the rules in favour of greater centralisation foundered.

The significance of these differences in structure can be seen in the methods used to elect full-time officials. In both areas there were normally five such officeholders: the president, general secretary and three others, termed agents. In Durham, elections were decided by lodge vote rather than individual ballot, with each lodge being allocated a quota of votes (up to six) dependent on the number of members (up to 700). This method seriously disadvantaged the more militant lodges of the large east-coast collieries that employed up to 3,000 miners. Furthermore, the all-important positions of president and general secretary never went to ballot. In Durham, all elections were for the position of agent, the successful candidate moving up the hierarchy over time as people retired. This was justified as a way of ensuring that the most senior positions were occupied by men who had had an extended induction into all the activities and commitments of the union. It also provided a safety valve for the organisation, preventing newcomers from making radical changes.

Other differences between the regions stemmed from the ways in which the work in the mine was organised. In Durham, miners at a young age commenced underground as putters, involved in the haulage of coal from the faces to the shaft.[2] In time they progressed to being hewers, working in pairs of marras (mates) on two short shifts of seven hours to dig out the coal, while the putters worked on one longer shift of ten or eleven hours. This occupational progression, with the mature men in the best-paid jobs, led to the DMA being seen as 'the hewers' union' and contributed to the skilled men (at that time the blacksmiths, boilersmiths, masons, horseshoers and their various apprentices and labourers) breaking away to form their own union, the Durham Colliery Mechanics' Association.[3] Finally, the miners in Durham retained customary practices, significantly in relation to the allocation of workplaces, where a lottery system known as cavilling, a practice that dated back to the nineteenth century, was retained into the contemporary period.[4]

The arrangements in South Wales offered a contrast. There was no cavilling, and the cutting and hauling of coal were arranged as separate modes of progression for young miners. As a consequence the face workers had a less powerful presence than in Durham, and all grades worked the same shift patterns. It was found that in 1906, hewers in Durham worked an average shift of six hours and forty-nine minutes, while in South Wales the colliers in Monmouthshire worked for nine hours and fifty-seven minutes. Wages differed too, both between the regions and within each and, given the use of piece rates, earnings were affected by geology and the problem of working in 'abnormal places' (which were not actually uncommon in either area).

Variations in working conditions and remuneration were tempered to some extent in Durham through cavilling (the law of chance) and conciliation, which allowed reference to wages within the range of a 'county average'. Nevertheless, these were the sorts of issues that the Miners' Federation of Great Britain, loosely coordinating the several district coalfield unions, aimed to resolve through national agreements. Durham's hewers were reluctant to join the MFGB. When they finally did, in 1907, the Great Northern stood alongside South Wales as a numerically dominant Area in the campaign for an eight-hour day and a minimum wage.[5]

The density of miners and manual workers in the coalfield districts meant that, with the advent of a universal parliamentary franchise, these areas were in a powerful position in national elections. Both the DMA and the SWMF were effective in influencing the selection of candidates and in organising their support, initially for the Liberal Party, with officials including William Abraham and John Wilson themselves sitting in Parliament as Lib–Lab members alongside some of the coal owners. In Durham over many decades, the presumption of a necessary unity of interest between owner and miner had produced an elaborate system of conciliation and compromise which Wilson defended in his resistance to joining the MFGB. He was even more staunch in his opposition to the fledging Labour Party, so that while Abraham prudently took the Labour whip in 1910, Wilson never did. In his words:

> I went into the House as a thorough believer in and supporter of Mr Gladstone and the Liberal Party in general politics. From that I have never swerved. That is my political creed now [1909] and without a shadow of doubt it will remain.[6]

But his time had passed, and through skilful campaigning, the group of Independent Labour Party (ILP) activists was set to replace him. In the general election of 1918, the MFGB put forward a total of fifty-one candidates, of whom twenty-four were elected: two in Durham and five in South Wales. The leading socialist thinker and Oxford academic G. D. H. Cole, a strong supporter of guild socialism, saw this as evidence that Labour was 'overwhelmingly a trade union party', adding that 'half of the trade union representation was drawn from a single union'.[7] Across both coalfields Conservative candidates – coal owners or those allied closely with them – were defeated by checkweighmen and agents from the miners' unions. This pattern was to continue, emphasising the political nature of the miners' trade union, which saw industrial class struggle played out through parliamentary processes.

Coal Mining and Domestic Labour

Despite the differences in shift patterns and working arrangements between the coalminers of Durham and South Wales, they shared the reality of a job that was dirty, arduous and dangerous. It was widely understood that given the option of alternative employment, men would not choose to go down the mine. This, together with the remoteness of many of the mining locations, helps to explain how mining villages in both areas became separated from other forms of work and influences. In Durham, where mining had gestated over centuries, the labour force had developed through generations. The employers' language reflected this pattern, with talk of 'mining stock' and their own 'breed' of pitmen, sometimes expanded through 'imports' from their other landed estates.[8]

In South Wales, where coal production grew apace, employers had to recruit widely, resulting in a workforce of migrants drawn from the Welsh countryside, and later from the Welsh borders and the West Country. At the turn of the century there was a large influx of mine workers from Spain.[9] Such patterns of recruitment were not unusual and can be seen in the reconstruction of the coal mines in Belgium after 1945 and also across the history of gold and coal mining in South Africa. In each of these cases, however, the employers found it necessary to provide dormitory facilities to accommodate and feed the miners, with spaces to wash and to clean their clothing. In South Wales, as in Durham, these services (the care of the mine workers and their children, the provision of hot baths and meals, the continual washing of work clothes) were provided by women in the home. In this way the villages of the coalfields were made up of mining families whose routines were geared to the rhythms of the mine. In complex households, women were known to sleep in a chair, so as to cater for the needs of their husband and sons as they left for work on different shifts, to return at different times tired, dirty and hungry. In times of disaster, the photographic record shows women standing at the pit head, anxiously waiting for news of loved ones.

So, although each region had its own distinctive mining culture, many (perhaps most) features of the miners' working and domestic lives were similar in Durham and South Wales. Of these similarities, the strict division of labour based on gender, with women's domestic labours supporting production in the mine, is perhaps the most significant. So complete and extensive was this division that it deserves to be central to our understanding of the coalfields, with the women and men both incorporated into 'a coal mining regime of production'.[10]

While excluded from working underground, the women of the coalfield played a central part in supporting coalmining through their intense domestic labour. This contribution was unrecognised in the wage paid to the miner, disguising women's labour as 'unproductive' and also formally condoning the power of men within the family, local communities and the labour movement. This important positioning of women in the home was assisted in great part by the comparative absence of available paid employment for them in these areas. While sons went underground, daughters went 'into service', working as maids for the middle and upper classes in Cardiff and Newcastle and across the south of England. Often returning to marry, they brought with them an understanding of the world beyond the coalfield.

While there was a strict division of labour based on gender within the coal mining regime of production, it would be wrong to assume that women were restricted to domestic labour alone. Many of them played an active part in the chapels, and in the formation and development of the cooperative stores that thrived in the villages. Women were also active protesters at times of food price increases and during strikes, especially in 1926, and they often played a critical role in the reorganisation of food provisions and in demonstrating against and shaming strike breakers. In these and other ways the social arrangements that underpinned the economy of these areas drew the women directly into the world of the mine.

Coalfield Landscapes

At the high point of the coal industry, when 'coal was King', its presence was unmistakable, its mark upon the local landscapes indelible. It could be seen in the web of railway lines that carried the coal to the coasts and to the steel mills and other local industries, in the ubiquitous winding gears – the 'pulley wheels' – of the mines, and of course in the distinctive settlement pattern of terraces surrounding them, which housed the miners and their families.

In Durham, in the small villages in the western valleys and also in the larger newer settlements near the east coast, red brick – typically made from clay deposits dug up from sinking the shafts and from around the coal seams – dominated. At Easington Colliery and Horden the company constructed terraced houses, all made of the same brick, forming parallel numbered streets on a grid pattern – First Street, Second Street and so on. In South Wales the pattern was quite different. Here, rows of houses built of local sandstone clung like ribbons to the steep sides of the valleys. What both had in common was the link that existed between the village and the mine. Ned Cowen in Durham recalls, 'The clock for the village was the pit buzzer. Very few people had clocks those days. The pit buzzer was blown at the start and finish of every shift. This warned the womenfolk to prepare the meal.'[11]

The hooter and the sounds of the mine are a constant in accounts of life in these villages and townships. Lewis Jones' classic novel *Cwmardy: The Story of a Welsh Mining Village* (1937), begins with miner Jim Roberts and his young son Len surveying 'the splendour of the mountain landscape' and its 'tranquil serenity' above the village before turning to travel home down into the valley where they encounter a 'changing panorama':

> their bodies tingling to the palpitating throb of the pit engines that came to them from below. Its vibrant rhythm broke through the air with the monotonous regularity of a ticking clock.[12]

Coal, mined underground and then washed on the surface, produced large amounts of waste, which was, most often, collected in local spoil heaps or tips that scarred the landscape around the mine or up the valley sides. In the 1930s, on his

English Journey, J. B. Priestley encountered the pit heap at Shotton in East Durham.

> Imagine then a village consisting of a few shops, a public-house, and a clutter of dirty little houses, all at the base of what looked at first like an active volcano. This volcano was the notorious Shotton 'tip', literally a man-made smoking hill. From its peak ran a colossal aerial flight to the pithead far below. It had a few satellite pyramids, mere dwarfs compared with this giant; and down one of them a very dirty little boy was tobogganing. The 'tip' itself towered to the sky and its vast dark bulk, steaming and smoking at various levels, blotted out all the landscape at the back of the village. Its lowest slope was only a few yards from the miserable cluster of houses. One seemed to be looking at a Gibraltar made of coal dust and slag.[13]

The Shotton tip may have been exceptional in size, but it was not unique. Many such were scattered across Durham. In South Wales, given the constrictions on the valley floors, much of the waste was moved by aerial buckets up onto the tops of the mountainsides above the villages, creating a unique topographical mix of natural and man-made elevations. The account of Shotton is, however, unusual in that the village is a single street, made up only of houses, shops and a pub. More commonly the mining villages in both areas were larger than this and would have contained more than one chapel, as well as a cooperative store and (certainly in Durham) a working men's club. Each of these buildings was paid for and funded by the combined efforts of the local inhabitants, the men and women of the village. In South Wales it has been estimated that a chapel opened every week at the middle of the nineteenth century.[14] There, the size of the mining villages and the density of social life around the mine eased the transmission of nonconformity from its rural origins and provided the basis for religious worship and social organisation. The chapels also produced the first tranche of trade union leaders in both areas, giving them the opportunity to develop their oratorical skills: it was here that they 'first found the language and art to express their antagonisms to grim conditions and injustices'.[15]

In addition to the chapels, miners in both areas set up their own meeting halls and libraries, with the miners' institutes in South Wales being described as 'the greatest network of cultural institutions created by working people anywhere in the world'.[16] At a time when there was no public library provision of any kind in the county of Glamorgan, these libraries filled a void. After the passing of the Mining Industry Act of 1920 by the coalition government of Lloyd George, miners' halls were to be paid for from a Miners' Welfare Fund established under the Act and funded by payments from the employers of a penny per ton of coal mined. When Tory MPs asked why it was that the mine owners, unlike other employers, were being taxed, they were informed by the Secretary of Mines, William Bridgeman, that 'I do not look on it as taxation, but rather as a benefit'.[17] The Act, in establishing the fund to support the 'social well-being, recreation, and living' of coalminers, was an attempt to help the coal owners to reduce tension in places which were – in so many ways – like no other. The fund survived the years of crisis that followed and was used to construct many hundreds of welfare halls that became pivotal local institutions, seemingly permanent and commanding features of the coalmining landscape. Run by joint committees, the mining unions embraced these new centres, seeing the important role they could play in the political and social structure of the village, and often struggled with the employers over their administration.

These institutions, clear markers of a powerful working-class culture, are perhaps the most significant features of mining trade unionism. Historically, the coalminers were establishing themselves as an occupation of some substance. Although ostensibly unskilled, the miners had great capabilities, not just in the dangerous work of winning coal underground but also in social and political organisation, building local communities around institutions of their own creation. The miners' welfare halls became integral to these communities and, alongside the chapels, cooperative stores and clubs, sat near the pit heads that dominated the mining villages of the two areas.

Strikes and Struggle

The first two decades of the twentieth century were turbulent ones on the coalfields, all associated with the huge expansion of coal production; by 1911, fully two-thirds of the Welsh population were concentrated in the mining counties of Glamorgan and Monmouthshire. Ten years later, the census recorded that one-third of Wales's entire male labour force worked in the mines and quarries. The Rhondda Valley's population grew from 24,000 in the 1870s to 100,000 by 1895 and 150,000 by 1911. In Durham the expansion took place in new mines sunk alongside the east coast, and here the growth of villages such as Easington was just as remarkable.

A long dispute at the Cambrian Combine (in which 'abnormal places' were an issue) produced rioting in Tonypandy in 1910, occasioning the deployment of troops.[18] The following year, concerned to build support in their struggle with the employers, miners from South Wales travelled as delegates to open discussions with miners in Durham. They were frowned on by Durham officials but well received by the lodges.[19] In the midst of a move to centralise the SWMF, a series of meetings was held across the South Wales coalfield producing a discussion document, *The Miners' Next Step*: this became the most eloquent testimony to revolutionary syndicalism in Britain, resolute in its opposition to the 'outworn policy' of conciliation and its commitment to rethinking questions of leadership. Influenced by daily experience and also by argument and debate in Ruskin College, some ideas expressed in the document had a major impact in Durham, most specifically references to the use of direct action and the need for change within the trade union.[20] The successful national strike in 1912 had a further galvanising effect, not least by revealing the political isolation of the coal owners as a class. In an attempt to resolve the dispute, the Liberal prime minister, Herbert Asquith, called a conference involving twenty-three coal owners and nineteen members of the MFGB executive. After three days of fruitless discussion, Asquith settled in favour of the miners through an Act of Parliament, leading a senior figure at the Board of Trade to refer to the coal owners as being 'extraordinary ignorant of all that has been happening in the miners' movement'.[21]

A further strike in South Wales in 1915 obliged the British state to take emergency wartime control of the industry. This benefited the miners considerably, and made them keenly aware of the importance of coal to the war economy, and of the potential power that came with it. The measure also put long-term nationalisation on the agenda of several official inquiries.[22] Against the backdrop of the Bolshevik Revolution in Russia, the village of Maerdy – home to Arthur Horner and Noah Ablett, leading author of *The Miners' Next Step* – became known as 'little Moscow'.[23] In Durham, the village of Chopwell under lodge delegate Will Lawther also took that name, its lodge banner emblazoned with images of Marx, Lenin and Keir Hardie. Another red village, Wardley, had its own Lenin in the shape of checkweighman George Harvey.[24]

In 1919, as trade union membership peaked on both coalfields, with almost all miners – certainly those working underground – enrolled as members, A. J. Cook was elected agent in the Rhondda Valley.[25] He was soon joined by another Marxist, S. O. Davies, as agent for Dowlais. Together with Ablett, they made a formidable trio visibly at odds with the established 'moderate' style of leadership. Cook was quite exceptional. Having developed an oratorical style in the chapel, his speeches were full of passionate emphasis on the importance of the rank and file, of trade union power and impending revolutionary change.

All this was tested when the Lloyd George government returned the industry to the hands of the owners on 31 March 1921. The owners locked out a million workers when the latter refused to accept a 50 per cent reduction in wages. The MFGB relied on support from the steel and transport unions as part of a triple alliance. But on 15 April, 'Black Friday', the support fell away and the miners were isolated and defeated. Cook was tried in Swansea on various charges of incitement, intimidation and unlawful assembly. Found guilty and sentenced to two months hard labour, he was handcuffed and, in a piece of symbolic violence, chained together with five others, including Arthur Horner who would later provide an account of their journey by passenger train to Cardiff and the jail.[26]

Victory and Defeat

The twenties were hard years for the miners, with South Wales and Durham especially badly hit. The rigid adherence by all governments – Liberal, Conservative, Labour – to the gold standard seriously weakened coal's position in the export market, with consequent struggles over wage reductions and unemployment.[27] Sporadic conflict continued until, in 1926, the coal owners returned with demands for more wage cuts and a lengthening of the working day, once again locking the miners out. By this time, Cook, who had been on the executive of the MFGB in 1921 and was admired for his activities during that dispute, had been elected general secretary. His appointment was widely decried within the Labour Party, where Beatrice Webb's description of him as an 'inspired idiot' was often repeated. Party leader Ramsay MacDonald was more detailed in his dislike, seeing Cook as a man 'utterly incompetent in his job and with enough vanity to go around the whole of our Empire'.[28]

But Cook had support among the miners. In 1925, obdurate in his refusal to accept the employers' terms, with the support of the Trade Union Congress (TUC) he had forced Stanley Baldwin's government to intervene and subsidise existing wage levels until 1 May 1926. This victory – it became known as 'Red Friday' – was, however, a line in the sand. Speaking at Crook in Durham, Cook reminded his audience of what Baldwin had said to him: 'You have had us this time: next we will be prepared.' Lord Londonderry was more direct: 'Whatever it may cost in blood and treasure,' he said, 'we shall find that the trade unions will be smashed from top to bottom.'[29]

When the subsidy expired, hostilities resumed. For a short period of seven days, the MFGB was supported by a general strike organised by the TUC. The miners stayed on strike for another seven months. It was an enormous struggle, in which the institutions of the mining villages (lodge, cooperative store, chapel) came together with the families to sustain one other. In Durham, local councils of action took charge, with little or no involvement by the official DMA structure.[30] Will Lawther took a central role in the effort, along with the Chopwell Lodge, and he was imprisoned with Harry Bolton for, amongst other things, 'police intimidation' and establishing a 'reign of terror' in the district. When their trial took place, several thousand people marched to the court in Gateshead singing 'The Red Flag'.[31]

Left to fight alone, the MFGB executive decided after seven months that resistance should end (in spite of lodge votes in South Wales and Durham to the contrary), and that each of the Area unions should negotiate its own terms for a return to work. In South Wales the Area executive met on 25 November to obtain the agreement of members to enter into negotiations with the employers. When news of the impending ballot became known,

The rush to the pits in South Wales . . . became serious. The result of the ballot vote of the men . . . was 50,815 for and 27,291 against. The SWMF had become a ghost. After a strike lasting from May 1 to November 30, some 70,000 had deserted. Many of the local leaders were in prison for picketing. The long struggle had broken the spirit and sapped the energy of the active elements . . . The SWMF entered the fight as an army and ended it as a rabble. This was not fighting it was a massacre.[32]

In Durham, the rules of the DMA allowed the officials to commence negotiations without needing members' permission. When the terms were put to the ballot they were rejected (33,916 for, 48,435 against) but without the necessary two-thirds majority required at that time. The hewers were particularly incensed by the increase in the length of their working day. Their intransigence gained them some compensation, but like the rest they returned to work resentful. In the words of W. P. Richardson, DMA general secretary:

The miners are on the bottom and have been compelled to accept dictated and unjust terms. The miners will rise again and will remember . . . The victors of today will live to regret their unjust treatment to the miners.[33]

The strike had broken down first in the Nottingham Area, and this was to have far-reaching consequences. Nottingham differed substantially from the exporting coalfields of Durham and South Wales, and in the decade that led up to the strike there were many in the Nottingham Miners' Association (NMA) who opposed developments taking place within the MFGB.[34] Here many of the miners lived in and around urban centres such as Nottingham and Mansfield, commuting to the mines while their wives and daughters worked in the local hosiery textile factories. This weakened the link between the mine and local community. The work was also organised in a different way, with the use of subcontractors (butties) who then hired the miners. These butties 'seemed a kind of middle class amongst the miners'.[35] The weak lodge structure allowed the butties to obtain an oligarchic control over the NMA, with policies of 'ultra moderation'. This situation was exacerbated by the sinking of new mines. The butties were actively involved in undermining the strike, with one of them, George Spencer, described by Arthur Cook as 'a black-leg of the worst order'.[36] A new union was formed, the Nottingham Miners' Industrial Union, which operated alongside the NMA in mines that became increasingly non-union.[37]

Attempts were made to spread non-political trade unionism to the other coalfields, with some success in South Wales, where the SWMF faced an ongoing battle with the encroachment of the new South Wales Miners' Industrial Union (SWMIU), supported by a number of the coal companies. The staggered opening of mines after the dispute allowed for the vetting of recruits, and the Ocean Coal Company amongst others used this process as a way of filtering out SWMF men. More dramatic was the opening of a new colliery by the Taff Merthyr Company at Bedlinog with the purpose of recognising the newly formed Union. In spite of the propaganda inflating its number of branches, it is doubtful if SWMIU membership ever exceeded 6,000 and it never seriously challenged the dominance of the Federation. It was fought and defeated by a highly imaginative campaign involving committees of rank-and-file miners across the coalfield, with sit-down strikes as well as community ostracism of SWMIU men.[38]

In the aftermath of 1926, Cook was marginalised within the TUC. The coalminers' trade union was severely weakened, even virtually destroyed, as a fighting force for over a decade. In South Wales, experienced and militant trade unionists such as Will Paynter were blacklisted and forced out of work.[39] Those who had held out the longest were the most likely to find their labour unwanted at a time when victimisation was rife.[40] In Durham, even Kibblesworth, known as a 'moderate' village, saw strike leaders and supporters blacklisted. Dick Beavis started at the Dean and Chapter Colliery in Spennymoor in 1928 as a boy of fourteen. He recalls how:

It was private enterprise then in its most ruthless form . . . As a kid I used to think that there ought to be police down the pit to see some of the things that went on . . . You were penalised from going down to coming out . . . To me you were nothing else but wage slaves.[41]

One year after the strike had ended, the Conservative prime minister Stanley Baldwin visited the Cwm Colliery after fifty miners were killed in an explosion. He had given many assurances to the miners' leaders as part of the settlement of the 1926 strike. These included a promise that there would be no black-listing of union activists and that the government would put pressure on the coal owners to behave more sympathetically towards the trade union. None of these promises was kept, and at the colliery he was 'hooted and jeered at by a large body of miners and their wives who were waiting at the pit head for news of the entombed men'.[42]

Labour Politics

Something of the anger expressed on that day energised support to remove Baldwin in the election of 1929. Labour emerged from the poll as the largest party, and Ramsay MacDonald formed a government despite lacking an overall majority. In Durham and South Wales, every constituency returned a Labour MP. MacDonald had replaced the Fabian Sidney Webb as the candidate for Seaham and was returned with an enormous major-ity. In South Wales, Aneurin Bevan, a miner from Tredegar, was elected by his local Ebbw Vale constituency. The election seemed finally to have resolved the national political conflicts of the twenties in favour of the Labour Party and the working classes.[43]

Through its 'Labour and the nation' programme, developed in opposition, the Party pledged to 'take every step in its power' to ensure that unemployment benefits were 'humane and adequate'. The programme also raised the possibility of the nationalisation of the coal industry 'with the utmost rapidity that circumstances allow'. After the Wall Street Crash, however, the MacDonald administration proved incapable of reconciling financial ortho-doxy with its manifesto promises or the views of the trade union movement. On 24 August 1931, MacDonald met with the King and became the head of a Conservative-dominated national government. He was joined by only three of the Cabinet, all of whom were expelled from the Labour Party, resulting in another general election on 27 October. The result was disastrous for Labour, and its representation in Westminster would have been virtually wiped out were it not for coalminers' votes. Remarkably, given the circumstances, the Party's support *increased* in South Wales, where the bitterness of the defeat in 1926 still festered and the campaigning against non-political unionism had had an exhilarating effect, so much so that in Rhondda West the Labour vote rose by 20 per cent over its 1929 level. The story in the other constituencies was similar, if not quite as dramatic, with four seats returning Labour candidates unopposed. The employers seemed to have left the field.

The situation in Durham was very different. Labour's repre-sentation collapsed, returning just two of its MPs, Jack Lawson and Joe Batey, while the overall vote fell by 10 per cent. Here, the employers were highly engaged and a pact had been struck between the Conservatives and Liberals to leave each other unchallenged in four seats. This made all the difference in a vote that Peter Lee, who had taken over as DMA general secretary after Richardson's early death, described as 'the worst-fought election of modern times for abuse and misrepresentation'.[44] Undoubtedly the fact that Ramsay MacDonald was standing for election as a National Labour candidate in Seaham caused confu-sion and divided loyalties. Still, the difference with South Wales (where in the post-war period no Conservative represented mining seats) is remarkable, and a testament to the radicalism of the Valleys and the deep impact made by the SWMF during the brutal conflicts there in the twenties.

Table 1. General election results, number of MPs, 1918–35

Durham

	1918	1929	1931	1935
Labour	4	10	2	10
Liberal	4		3	
Conservative	2		4	
National Labour			1*	

*Ramsay MacDonald

South Wales

	1918	1929	1931	1935
Labour	7	13	13	13
Liberal	6			

Distressed Areas

What followed in the aftermath of the 1931 election was a protracted period of unemployment, which deeply affected both Durham and South Wales. When Pilgrim Trust researchers visited Crook in 1936, they recorded that 71 per cent of unemployed miners had been out of work for over five years. In Merthyr Tydfil and the Rhondda Valley, there were similar findings.[45] Overall, they found that 123 in every 1,000 coalminers had been out of work for over a year, a figure that contrasted remarkably with those for new industries like car manufacture, where only 10 in 1,000 were so affected. This discrepancy had a significant consequence. While it was accepted, belatedly, that conditions on the coalfields were critical, unemployment there came to be seen as a *regional* rather than a national problem. The political focus turned to underpinning regional economies through unemployment and welfare provision. The coalfields shifted from the centre of the capitalist economy to peripheral areas, secondary to the new manufacturing belts emerging around London. Once identified with hard work and industry, they and their people were now treated as pathological.

A Special Areas Act was passed in 1934 with the purpose of encouraging capital to move to the stricken coalfields. Placed in the hands of Neville Chamberlain, it was predictably weak in conception and execution. Under the Act, commissioners responsible to the minister of labour were provided with a fund of £2 million to facilitate 'the economic development or social improvement of the areas'. Critics deemed this totally inadequate, with Bevan describing the initiative as 'an idle and empty farce'.[46] The commissioners were able to establish some new industrial estates, including Treforest in South Wales and Team Valley in Gateshead. They also encouraged the Richard Thomas steel company to move to Bevan's constituency in South Wales, and (more mould-breaking) secured the relocation of Polikoff's clothing factory from the East End of London to employ young women workers at Ynyswen near Treorchy in the Rhondda.[47] However, the overall impact of these policies on employment and the conditions of life in the coal districts was minimal.

The unforgiving national politics of the 1930s strengthened an oppositional left current within both the MFSW and the DMA. In South Wales Arthur Horner won the election for president of the union after Jim Griffiths was elected to Parliament in 1936. Another Communist, Will Paynter, was elected as agent soon after. In Durham, Will Lawther became an agent in 1935, joined by Sam Watson in 1936. At delegate meetings of the MFGB, Nina Fishman recalled how 'no right-wing miners' leader attempted to counter the passionate oratory of South Walian communists nor that of the left-wing representatives from Durham, Sammy Watson and Will Lawther'. At the MFGB conference in 1937, against the backdrop of the Spanish Civil War, these two coalfields came together to propose a number of motions favouring a united front between the Labour and Communist Parties. One of the Durham motions noted that there were 'thirty-six delegates attending our Council who are members of the Communist Party ... they are the most disciplined in our movement and have worked very hard for a number of years in fighting the cause of the worker.'[48]

The motion was narrowly defeated, but the political unity between Durham and South Wales was progressive and genuine. A greater war against fascism loomed on the horizon, one that was to be far-reaching in its consequences for the miners, returning the mines to full production, putting nationalisation back on the agenda and bringing the Soviet Union and international politics into the very heart of their new national union.

CHAPTER TWO

State Ownership

When they nationalised the industry, they didn't just nationalise the mines, they nationalised the men as well.
Jackie McAuliffe, Boldon Colliery, 1980

As the Second World War approached and the armaments industry increased production, the miners returned from the dole queue and the means test to work underground from Monday through to Saturday. Although they were earning money for the first time in many years, the organisation of the war economy meant that there was nothing to spend it on. This contributed in Will Lawther's view to 'a mood of sullen resentment and anger on the coalfield'. Almost 60 per cent of miners were at some time involved in disputes leading to strike action. These were usually local to a particular mine or colliery, where class antagonisms remained, accentuated by memories of the thirties and by a deep sense of exclusion. Easington Colliery in Durham was particularly turbulent and gained a national reputation as 'the ca'canny pit', derived from the Scots term meaning 'proceed warily'. It became associated with worker resistance and various strategies aimed at deliberately restricting output and effort.

Between 1939 and 1945, 47 per cent of all recorded stoppages resulting from unofficial strike activity took place in the coal mines, and the industry accounted for 56 per cent of all days lost through strikes. In many cases these strikes stemmed from what Arthur Horner, president of the SWMF, referred to as 'years of the most drab and sordid existence with nothing to do and nowhere to go except work'.[1] But they also touched on bigger things. While the trade unions were prepared to support the war effort, they were also concerned to ensure that government involvement in the industry (through the Essential Work Order) both delivered a guaranteed working week and exercised control over the behaviour of employers, preventing them from taking advantage of the situation. At the Penrhiwceiber Colliery, which was taken over by Powell Duffryn in 1943, a new system of payment was introduced, accompanied by the withdrawal of some allowances, causing men to fall below the minimum wage. The subsequent strike, which spread to other collieries, repre-sented, in Horner's words, 'the opportunity to express all the grievances that existed, especially in Powell Duffryn Collieries', and reflected resentment at the high-handed approach of its managers. This was the context for the election of 1945, which the wartime prime minister Winston Churchill was expected to win for the Tory Party. Such an outcome was eagerly anticipated by the coal companies, and in both Durham and South Wales plans were being drawn up for a new period of private enterprise. However, Clement Attlee led the Labour Party to a massive victory, with landslide majorities for the Labour candidates in both areas. It was a vote for change and hope, but change didn't come overnight.

The coal owners were implacably opposed to nationalisation and had drawn up their own plan for the future of the industry. Dismayed by the election result they 'first capitulated then precipitately accepted compulsion and Emanuel Shinwell's nationalisation scheme in 1945, with its surprisingly generous compensation terms'.[2] This generosity to the owners of a techno-logically backward industry, and the fact that the profitable mining engineering and machinery sector was left in private hands, caused considerable resentment. Powell Duffryn was among the companies that benefited twice from the nationalisation process. Having been compensated for the loss of its mining assets, it was also to profit from selling machinery to the new state enterprise.[3]

Coal was a vital ingredient in the plan for post war reconstruction, and the new government was concerned to see coal production increase and rates of absenteeism cut back. There was a view that the promise of nationalisation would be sufficient, in itself, to achieve this aim. This was strongly felt in Durham where the new general secretary Sam Watson demanded a pledge from his members to work all possible shifts, to cease strike action and to operate with maximum cooperation with management.[4] This had little impact, however, with ca'canny continuing and the miners at Wingate colliery accused of restricting output in order to improve their wages.[5] Nationalisation in itself was proving no incentive, with little found in the published Bill that would directly improve the conditions of the workers.[6] At the first post-war Durham Miners Gala in 1946 the speech from Hugh Dalton, the chancellor, on the topic was 'received in stony silence'[7].

In response, the NUM produced its *Miners' Charter*, a list of clear demands aimed at improving the working and living conditions of its members. These included a call for a five day week without loss of pay, a guarantee on wage levels relative to other industries and the establishment of holiday pay. When these proposals were put to a cabinet meeting by Emanual Shinwell in June 1946 they were met with disquiet, for fear that they could lead to even further loss of production. However it was clear that without the support of the NUM things would be difficult, and the *Charter* was agreed. It was the new union's first victory. But the pressure of production would remain one of its biggest problems.

On 1 January 1947 the coal industry was formally taken into public ownership, to be run 'on behalf of the people' by the National Coal Board (NCB). In doing so, the state took control of all the mines, houses and land previously owned by the coal companies. This keynote nationalisation sat at the centre of policies to extend the influence of the state in a new social democratic post-war settlement. On vesting day, at Horden Colliery in Durham, the lodge secretary and the manager came together in a ceremony in which a hatchet was buried at the base of the flagpole carrying the new NCB flag. Despite the profound symbolism of this moment, the remorseless need for labour in the mine continued unchecked. As one man put it: 'the flag went up the pole alright, but it was all the same for us – we went down the shaft'.

Siamese Twins

For the miners' trade union representatives and their MPs in the House of Commons, recognition of the National Union of Mineworkers within the 1946 Coal Industry Nationalisation Act was crucial: it established the NUM within a new system of negotiation and conciliation. In practice, the union was also directly involved in constructing the formal apparatus of the National Coal Board, with nationalisation bringing coal owner, mine manager and union official together as administrators of the industry. 'The Board', as it became known, called upon the support and assistance of a trade union which itself had been formed just two years earlier, the product of an amalgamation conference held in Nottingham in 1944. To many people involved in the industry it seemed that the union and the Board were 'like Siamese twins' – conjoined from birth. As time went on, the analogy would take on a deeper significance.

The first director of industrial relations at the NCB was Ebby Edwards from Northumberland. Edwards had been general secretary for the MFGB since 1932, and believed deeply in the need for a genuinely *national* union to take the place of this loosely federated MFGB. Previous attempts to establish such a union had foundered, as regional groupings and local interests created divisions among the miners. The 1944 conference was therefore a major achievement for Edwards, affirming his beliefs and vindicating his commitment to national collective bargaining. He was initially elected as the NUM's first general secretary, to widespread acclaim. That he was persuaded to leave this post (the expression of his life's work as a trade unionist) within a year to take up a position at the National Coal Board says much about the ways in which nationalisation was understood – the more so as this pattern of recruitment operated throughout the structure of the new organisation. In every coalfield, leading trade unionists resigned their positions and took office in the labour relations and welfare departments of the NCB.

In contrast, NCB production managers were recruited from the old private coal companies. In South Wales, managers from Powell Duffryn and the Ocean Company dominated, and it did not escape notice that the national head of the NCB, Viscount Hyndley, had been managing director of Powell Duffryn for fifteen years. Meanwhile H. O. R. Hindley, a former director general of the British Air Commission, became chairman of the NCB's Northern Division, covering Durham, with a former director of the South Derwent Coal Company as his deputy. The other key positions, the production and finance directors, went to men who had previously held senior positions in the Londonderry Collieries and Pease and Partners.

The transformation of the DMA, SWMF and other district unions into constituent Areas of the new national union wasn't a complete one, with many Areas retaining some of the rules relating to local practices, while groups such as the Durham Colliery Mechanics' Association retained their independent identities and held a seat on the National Executive Committee. As this implies, the new union contained within it strong elements of its federated past, and had to accommodate very different regional political traditions. The task of holding together this potentially fragile alliance fell upon the national leadership drawn from Durham and South Wales. Will Lawther of Chopwell became the NUM's inaugural president, and Arthur Horner of Maerdy its general secretary. These two men from 'little Moscow' villages – Horner a member of the Communist Party – shared deeply ingrained memories of the twenties and thirties, and were determined that the NUM and the NCB should not fail. Each received advice and support from powerful figures within their home Areas, notably Sam Watson in Durham and Will Paynter (who would later succeed Horner as general secretary) in South Wales.

Despite their common history, the relationship between president and general secretary was often tense.[8] Lawther, along with Watson, had swung to the anti-communist right, deeply influenced by the politics of the Cold War and US involvement in Western Europe through the Marshall Plan.[9] Their home Areas, once of a similar mind, became opposing wings of moderate and radical opinion within the union, and Paynter and Watson would remain at the centre of events through the critical decades of the fifties and sixties.

In his autobiography, *My Generation*, Paynter identified himself with 'the age group which was too young to have soldiered in the First World War from 1914 to 1918 but old enough to have been employed in industry during the post-war violent struggles of 1921 and 1926'.[10] Watson was also clearly part of that group. Slightly older (he was born at the end of the nineteenth century), he too had begun working underground as a young boy, and was drawn into the activities of the lodge and eventually, in 1936, into trade union office in Durham. His career, however, was unmarked by the direct action and violence that Paynter experienced at the hands of the police in South Wales, where he served two spells in jail, before being taken to court and sacked from his position as checkweighman at the Cymmer Colliery in 1930. An active member of the Communist Party, Paynter spent the rest of the decade blacklisted. In 1937 he joined the International Brigade to fight with the Republican forces in the Spanish Civil War before being elected as a miners' agent in 1939. It was often said of him that he was a miner and trade unionist first, and a member of the Communist Party second. The opposite could have been said of Watson, who with similar deep roots in mining seemed to put the Labour Party first, especially when it was in government.

The new social arrangements, and support of men like these from the right and left wings of the NUM, took the new state corporation through the difficult years of fuel shortage which accompanied post-war reconstruction. In the 1950s the NCB's appointment of James Bowman (previously general secretary of the Northumberland Miners and vice-president of the NUM), as national chairman sealed the social structure of the corporation – so much so that recalcitrant miners on unofficial strike were often told by their union officials that they were simply striking against themselves, for 'the chairman of the Board is a miner'. In this they were affirming what Arthur Horner had told miners' delegates at their 1948 conference: they had to get away from this 'class approach towards management'. Siamese twins indeed. So powerfully were union and management interwoven that after 1957 – when the dependence upon coal dramatically declined – it was to Alf Robens, Labour MP for Blyth in Northumberland and shadow minister of labour, that the Conservative Harold Macmillan government turned for Bowman's successor.

While these changes in the administration of mining were quite dramatic, and the trade union was more secure, in the coal mines themselves control of production remained with managers – often the same people who had been in charge during the years of private ownership. Nationalisation and the establishment of the union had altered the balance of power in the pit and controlled much of the bullying and high-handed behaviour that had typified labour relations in the industry for decades. In the years that immediately followed, weekly wages were considerably increased from the war years' minimum, gains that were slowly eroded after 1956. However, in 1960, when John Rex coordinated a discussion in Yorkshire and asked miners if the men in the pits felt that it was *their* industry, the responses were clear:

No, no. I don't think so ... it's simply changed its name.
Otherwise there's the same staff, the same everything. I think
that that's the experience throughout the collieries. The men
feel that the bosses are the same, although there has been this
change.[11]

In the twenty years that followed vesting day, the complex
cultural apparatus which underpinned the nationalised corporation solidified into a significant political bureaucracy. It adminis-
tered the industry, regulated industrial disputes and coordinated
production. It ramped the industry up, then closed half of it
down. In doing so, it drew upon the industry's roots within the
politics of the coalfield localities and also within the culture and
daily lives of the coalminers and their families.

Production, Production, Production

During the early years of nationalisation, the National Coal
Board was operating as a coal monopoly within a single-fuel
economy at the centre of a reformed capitalist economy. It was
faced with the task of upgrading an industry that had decayed
under private enterprise. The 1945 report of a technical committee chaired by mining engineer Sir Charles Reid was particularly
damning of the deficiencies that needed to be dealt with if the
industry was to be brought to the standard of the mines in West
Germany. At the same time there was pressure to increase coal
production. Lord Ezra, later a chairman of the NCB, recalled
that 'Between 1947 and 1957 the pressure was on us to produce
all the coal we possibly could ... at meetings the question
constantly put to us was, 'can't you invest faster, can't you produce
more coal?'

Across those years coal production increased from 193 to 227
million tonnes through some important changes in the social
and technical organisation of production. Coal was mostly

mined by teams of men on longwall faces using hand tools, aided by pneumatic picks, explosives and undercutting machines. Often these faces were linked to a conveyor-based haulage system which involved considerable amounts of shovelling. In some mines the traditional bord-and-pillar system still operated, with haulage based upon tubs or drams pulled by men and ponies.[12] This problem of moving the cut coal to the surface had been identified by Reid as the 'greatest single technical cause' of low output per man-shift (OMS). He stressed the need for the underground layout of the pits to be completely reorganised, along with improvements in mine ventilation and the extensive introduction of electricity underground. In these circumstances, only a small proportion of new investment went into the mechanisation of actual coal cutting. This was not helped by the fact that West German mines led in this field, with machines designed to cut soft coal in high, unfaulted seams – conditions not found in South Wales or Durham. Still, the shift to longwall mining continued, and Arthur Askew, who worked in the Ballarat seam at the Wooley Colliery near Crook in Durham, remembered how it changed his experience of pit work:

> It was too much crawling and too much dust. I used to go about fifty yards before I got to the open hole. It was too much dust when it was face work, and there was too much dust windy picking [pneumatic picks] too, compared with hand hewing.

Nevertheless, as William Ashworth notes in his history of the nationalised coal industry, 'whether it was got by hand or machine', coal 'was cut on only one shift out of three', and this was the major technical issue facing the post-war industry.[13] Coal cut on one shift was loaded and taken away from the face in the second shift, while the third shift prepared the face for the next cutting shift. These arrangements were common until the end of the fifties, when machines were introduced that enabled the cut coal to be loaded simultaneously onto the conveyor system. Until then it was clear that coal production rested heavily upon the physical effort of the miners, and upon their commitment to the industry.

This, the problem of 'manpower', came to be the source of major problems facing the Board. It had inherited a large labour force, but one smaller than it had been and with a significant proportion of men over fifty.[14] Eager to retain as many men as possible, the Board turned to the Labour-controlled local authorities for assistance. In Durham there was widespread recognition of the importance of the coal industry for future county development plans, and the authority approached Sir George Pepler, a major influence behind the 1947 Town and Country Planning Act, for advice on employment planning in north-east England. His report noted that:

> from the national point of view, with coal the most precious and urgently needed of industrial raw materials, to introduce into mining areas, without surplus male labour, male employing industries housed in up-to-date factories and able to offer pleasant work at good wages, would inevitably attract men away from the mines with disastrous consequences for coal production.[15]

In preparing the subsequent plan for County Durham in 1950, the Planning Committee stressed that:

> In view of the importance of the coal mining industry to the nation as a whole it might be considered dangerous to propose any major diversification as this would almost certainly mean the attraction away from the mines of the young recruits so vitally necessary to the industry.[16]

In this way the nationalised industry was protected and its immediate production targets supported. There was an assumption that this arrangement would secure the future of the mining settlements for the long term, although it also created a near total dependency on one industry.

The more immediate problem related to the fact that, in spite of all attempts by union officials to persuade their members to remain in work and allow the new conciliation machinery to operate, they continued to strike. In 1948 alone the 1,528 recorded stoppages and resultant restriction of output were claimed to have reduced overall output by 1.1 million tonnes. In response, the NCB suggested that it would take out legal proceedings against the strikers for breach of contract. Once persuaded away from this course, the Board made clear to the trade union leaders that they needed to act. While there was tension between the Communist Party members and a growing right-wing faction within the NUM's National Executive Committee (NEC), there was complete accord on the need to support the Labour government, and most particularly to defend and achieve the success of nationalisation. In his presidential address to the NUM conference in 1948, Will Lawther emphasised the need for discipline, describing unofficial strikes as 'wrong', and more than this:

> They are criminal; they cannot be tolerated or excused. Those who indulge in them must in their less exuberant moments, realise that in an industry where the utmost facilities and opportunities exist for full and frank discussions and consultation, their actions benefit nobody, except those who, if the opportunity presented itself, would drive you back to the depths from which you have risen.

Will Paynter reacted angrily to attempts by miners to coordinate unofficial action via meetings at the Shakespeare Hotel in Neath. Sam Watson stamped even more severely on all unofficial strikes or attempts to build upon them. What these union leaders feared (and the fear intensified after 1951 and the election of a Tory government) was that 'pit militancy' would wreck the newly constructed architecture of a national industry and national union. In South Wales, Paynter criticised the 'lack of trade union consciousness' in the coalfield. He warned that the NCB was considering reintroducing prosecutions for breaches of contract. Paynter was aware that a major source of dispute lay in the piece-work earning system. At the Area delegate conference in 1953, he criticised men 'who earn money much in excess of that paid to day wage workers' and who had struck 'without consultation with representatives of the union at any level'. These actions, he felt, would lead to the 'disintegration of this organisation [the NUM] at a time when we will need it most'.[17]

In Durham, Watson faced no similarly coordinated rank-and-file organisation, and through the centralised power retained in the Area union he was able to come to an arrangement with the NCB, the details of which he described in a letter to Horner:

> In this Area unconstitutional stoppages and restrictions of output are kept reasonably low, and in the main this is due to the agreement we have entered into with the Coal Board that where unconstitutional stoppages of work take place, proceedings for damages will be taken against the workmen by the Board. If, however, the Miners' Lodge is willing to settle the claim out of court, a nominal sum is accepted by the Board in exchange for an agreement pledging the Lodge to constitutional action in the future and the complete observance of all the Conciliation Machinery.[18]

The effectiveness of this strategy was a major explanation for the remarkable difference in strike action that took place across the two regions in this period, as Table 2 makes clear.

Table 2. Distribution of colliery strikes

	South Wales	North East
1943	128	56
1948	247	36
1953	217	17
1958	275	46
1963	274	5

Source: R. Church and Q. Outram, *Strikes and Solidarity: Coalfield Conflict in Britain 1889–1966*, Cambridge, Cambridge University Press, 1998, p. 228.

Heroic Miners

At this time, and as part of its production drive, a powerful heroic view of the miner and the coal industry was orchestrated by the state corporation. In 1947, the Board had seven film crews who worked to produce regular instalments of *NCB News* that were shown in the local cinemas in and around the coalfields. These newsreels celebrated the achievements of the miners, documented industrial accidents and tragedies and successfully developed a powerful heroic view of the miner and mining life. The publications of the Area boards added regular reports on pits and publicity about miners who best represented the new values. Such propaganda was reinforced by production competitions, well-publicised and tied in with the detailed cooperation afforded by the trade union at all levels.

This was the Stakhanovite period in the British mines. Production bannerettes and medals proclaimed the achievements of men and pits that had – often in the most primitive of conditions – broken records and delivered the nation's coal. The artefacts of the industry, the miner's lamp and pick, became icons; enormous effigies of miners stood centrally in the festivals that were jointly organised by the union and the NCB. In Durham, the oldest and largest of the miners' annual gala meetings adopted the trappings of a state celebration, as the miners and their families paraded their banners past their trade union and political leaders, senior managers of the Coal Board and other dignitaries, including the US ambassador. Together, these activities can be seen as an attempt by the state to appropriate the symbolic world of the miner, turning it to the purpose of increased production.

Reflecting on this situation in the Yorkshire mines in the fifties, the celebrated study *Coal is Our Life* observed:

> Nationalisation, a long-standing aim of the miners, has been achieved. The prestige of the miner and the working class is higher than it ever has been and the miner knows this. Does

all this mean that the miner has experienced a basic change in his status and role in the society, a change which goes with a transformation between the miner and his work? In fact no such basic change has occurred . . . the actual changes have been absorbed into the miners' traditional ideology rather than transformed it.[19]

This absorption, in part, relates to the state's attempt to incorporate elements *from below* into a strategy for increasing productivity.

In post-war Britain, nationalisation sealed the coal mining regime of production, and through heroic imagery amplified the significance of the division of labour between men and women. Ideas of masculinity became entwined with coal mining labour and with the figure of the miner, which was to have far-reaching consequences, not all beneficial to the NCB. This was evident in the resistance to the corporation's attempt to introduce foreign-born labour into the mines.

Migration of course was not new to either coalfield. A part of Easington Colliery village is known as 'Cornwall' and the imprint of Irish migration is reflected in the Catholic population of Seaham. As we have seen, in the time of the great expansion of mining in South Wales, workers from the rural West, from Herefordshire and Somerset and as far as Spain all came together in the pit, while Italian migrants introduced coffee shops and ice-cream parlours to the front streets of the valley towns from the Rhondda to Ebbw Vale.[20] Alf Laws recounted how his father, a West Indian, came to the village of Maerdy with his mates in 1912, having been rejected in Cardiff:

And then my father and some of his friends came up here on the train, came out to work in the mine, and they came to the hall, and they were welcomed here. When they said that they belonged to the Steelman's union, they were welcomed. Union was a strong thing in those days. And each one of them was taken home. My father was brought to a man's home and introduced to his family. The man said who he was and said 'And he's coming to work with me tomorrow'. And that was his introduction.[21]

In 1945, however, things were rather different. After a depression and a long war 'fought alone', and with a programme of national renewal, the mood had changed. Although mining was a reserve occupation (no miner was conscripted), 34,000 young miners had left the mines to fight at the front. Ernest Bevin had found a solution in the regular deployment of conscripts to the mines. These men – 48,000 of them, one in ten of all conscripts – came to be known as Bevin Boys. After six weeks of training, they were sent to work underground, joining volunteers and conscientious objectors, and they stayed until their release in 1948. While accepted as a wartime emergency, the arrangement had its problems and cast a shadow over suggestions for similar schemes which might have diluted the skills and solidarity of the mine labour force. The situation was further complicated by other outcomes of the war. As the Soviet Army moved into Eastern Europe, many of those who fled ended up in camps in the UK, some of them moving to the mines. Voices in the Communist Party and others sympathetic to the Soviet Union considered them to be fascist sympathisers, and this created discord. Resistance to foreign labour increased in 1957, when the Tory government under Anthony Eden suggested bringing over Italian miners. The 'sealing off' of the coalfield communities had various consequences, of which the most recognised was the capacity to stick together and survive.

Solidarity and Endurance

Working in the coal industry had always been hazardous. One of the hopes of nationalisation had been that new administrative structures involving the trade union, along with investment in more modern mining technologies, would improve workplace safety. In the early period, however, when coal shortages produced enormous pressures for increased production and public expenditure restrictions delayed new fixed capital investment, there was little change in the arduous nature of work, particularly in the narrow seams of West Durham and the South Wales valleys. Accident rates remained high. At the large Easington Colliery on the Durham coast there was a major disaster on 29 May 1951, when an intense and violent gas explosion killed eighty-three men. The official inquiry into the disaster considered the ways in which pressures to increase production and to implement some of the recommendations of the Reid Report were placing strains on local pit management, which was revealed as having many defects. The inquiry concluded that:

> The manager appeared to be so fully occupied in day-to-day details of administration that he was unable to exercise effective supervision and direction of the mine as a whole. Still less had he time to think out all the possible consequences of a major change of policy such as the decision to adopt longwall retreating with full caving in a district originally planned to be worked by other methods.[22]

In the days and weeks that followed the explosion, the pattern of the day in the local school was punctuated not by the hooter but by the sound of the dead march and the playing of 'Gresford' – the Miners' Hymn[23] – as more and more men's bodies were found in the ruins of the mine and their funerals processed through the main street. The event left a terrible mark on the village, with many feeling some bitterness over the priorities of the management. As one miner recalls,

> It was only after the Disaster that things altered in the pit. It was only after all those men were killed that we had wider roadways and arched girders and greater ventilation. I think it

was only after the Disaster that the Coal Board really began to think seriously about the problems of safety in the pits. I worked in the pits under both private enterprise and under the NCB. I didn't see a big change underground until after 1951.

There was another terrible, if less dramatic disaster facing coalminers' health and safety which was highlighted in the account of coal mining in the 1950s by Norman Dennis, Fernando Henriques and Clifford Slaughter – the results of 'coal dust':

> although it does not immediately affect the work of the experienced collier, it has devastating effects . . . on the long-term health and fitness of miners . . . The incidence of ill-health and death from pneumoconiosis is of terrible proportions.[24]

By the mid-1950s, recorded deaths from pneumoconiosis outnumbered mining accident deaths by a ratio of four to one.[25] The 1943 Compensation Act had, for the first time, identified pneumoconiosis as an industrial disease. However, the compensation arranged for affected miners was not generous and it was restricted to those who had been working underground in the previous five years. This was particularly unfair as it disbarred men who, after years of heavy work underground, had moved to work on the surface or to another employer. But in spite of these complaints there was resistance to change within the Board and the clause was only amended through the persistence of the South Wales NUM, led by its General Secretary Will Arthur.

These efforts, however, took place against a background of strong support by the NUM for increased production, and in 1951, when the NCB was experiencing severe manpower shortages, it agreed that ex-miners diagnosed with pneumoconiosis and legally excluded from the mines should be allowed to return to work through its re-employment scheme – a policy that Hywel Francis and David Smith considered 'startling' and which subsequent investigations revealed as being deeply deleterious to these miners' health.[26] Reflections like these confirmed a view that the production of coal tended to take priority over concern for the health and welfare of the miner. This, together with the issue of compensation, was to haunt the industry for decades to come; but in the immediate future it was forgotten as the British economy changed and coal mines closed, leading the struggle in Durham and South Wales to focus on the very existence of the industry.

CHAPTER THREE

Power Politics

In the mining industry after a decade of relative prosperity when coal was king in the energy empire, a period when the union was preoccupied with lifting the status of its members when reforms and improvements could be paid for by an increase in the price of coal, the scene changed back again to one we were more accustomed to, a crisis of over-production.

Will Paynter, *My Generation*, 1972

In the 1960s a revolutionary change took place in the UK, as oil – shipped on tankers from the Middle East – replaced coal as a major source of fuel for transportation, industrial and domestic heating and as the basis for the new petrochemical processing industry. Other alternatives (gas and nuclear power) followed. This was a major shift within the structure of the capitalist economy, changing the international division of labour and moving production of its key resource away from Europe. Almost overnight, the focus shifted from mines on the coalfields to tankers in the harbours, and the priorities of the NCB changed accordingly (Table 3). Under the aegis of Tory and then Labour governments, coal mines closed at an accelerating rate: at the end of 1960, 698 pits employed 538,000 people; ten years later, just 292 pits employed 283,000.[1] Following the heavy job losses of the late 1950s, this meant that in a short

period of time almost 400,000 miners left the industry – many
with the early signs of pneumoconiosis. Durham and South Wales,
having a large proportion of smaller mines unsuited to the new
machinery, were particularly badly hit during the 1960s, with
eighty-six mines (61 per cent of the Area total) closing in South
Wales and seventy-five (66 per cent) in Durham. While nationally,
the 319 closures comprised just 43 per cent of the collieries open in
1960.[2] As the official biographer of the industry made clear, the
aim of the programme was 'to leave the industry with a bigger
proportion of its capacity in the more productive and profitable
central coalfield of Yorkshire, East Midland and West Midlands'.[3]

Table 3. The pattern of decline, NCB deep mines, 1949–79

National

Year	Number of collieries	Employment	Output (million tonnes)
1949	912	712,000	204
1959	737	658,000	196
1969	319	336,000	156
1979	223	235,000	106

South Wales

Year	Number of collieries	Employment	Output (million tonnes)
1949	194	106,000	24
1959	141	93,000	21
1969	55	40,000	13
1979	37	29,000	8

Durham

Year	Number of collieries	Employment	Output (million tonnes)
1949	126	108,000	26
1959	113	93,000	23
1969	38	34,000	14
1979	19	24,000	10

For those who stayed in the industry there was the promise of a long-term future, based on a highly mechanised industry with over a hundred years of reserves. But the machinery added to the dust in the mines and in the miners' lungs, and the industry remained haunted by tragedy. Across the two Areas, there were clear signs of the decline of the coal mining production regime, and people were promised a new way of life away from the mines, with men and women working in factories and offices.

Machines, Markets and Men

The post-war policy of the NCB, developed in line with the 1950 Plan for Coal, was based on the retention and possible expansion of the numbers employed underground while securely removing all possible coal reserves from the mines. However, with the onset of competition from oil, government policy changed, and so did the mindset of NCB management. In this new competitive phase, production volume became less important than costs and the monetary price of coal per tonne. Coal mines were to be assessed on financial grounds, men were to retire early, be made redundant or transferred elsewhere, and a new machine system was to be rapidly introduced as traditional methods of winning coal were replaced by power-loading machines on lengthening longwall faces. This emerged as a coherent policy, which, from 1960, was pushed ruthlessly forward by a new chairman, Labour MP Alf Robens (later Baron Robens of Woldingham).

In the USA coal had been in competition with oil from an earlier date, and the power-loading system had been in use there since the 1930s. In the post-war period mechanisation of coal cutting in American pits accelerated, in sharp contrast to the minor schemes attempted in the UK. While these had yielded improvements in productivity and costs, only 11 per cent of total output had been converted to power loading by 1955.[4] In part this reflected the unavailability of suitable machinery. However, by 1955 a dozen different types of power-loading machine had been designed specifically for British pits and produced by private engineering companies such as Anderson Strathclyde and Dowty. Together, the introduction of these machines revolutionised the mining labour process, with face teams working together to operate the new equipment. This system was based on the shearer loader machine that united coal cutting with conveyer haulage, allowing for the possibility of continuous coal production. As the machine was driven along the face its cutting disc ripped off the coal, moving it continuously onto the conveyer system. Behind the shearer other members of the team moved the power chocks across, securing the roof and moving the face forward ready for the next cut. So rapid and extensive was this change that by 1965 power-loaded faces supplied 85 per cent of NCB's output. In a single decade British coal mining had gone from being *under*-mechanised to the *most* mechanised operation in the Western economies.

Clearly the pattern of mechanisation was an uneven one. It was purposely linked to the most productive units and to faces in seams of coal most suited to the new technologies. These 'path-finder faces' contrasted with those in the the narrow-faulted seams found in the West Durham and South Wales. As a consequence the push for increased productivity had an inherent regional bias. As one manager explained, 'the full effect of improved efficiency cannot be realised until the high cost collieries are closed'.[5] In this way a plan emerged that was most favourable to the steam-coal regions of the Midlands and South Yorkshire, and these began to be called 'the central coalfield', while South Wales and Durham (once central) now became defined as 'peripheral'. This produced some disquiet with the NCB's northern director, Sir William Reid, who argued that government policy made many of the pits in the North 'beyond saving', as they 'had conditions in which modern mechanisation could not be applied'.[6] South Wales was similarly affected.

By the end of the decade this emphasis on reducing the cost of winning coal had produced what Robens had planned for: a highly capital-intensive coal industry with production pared back to the minimum necessary and coal stocks on the ground reduced to just one-fifth of the 1959 level.

Labour in Power

The machines had entered the coal mines at a time when the market for coal was collapsing, contrary to the assumptions of the Labour government's 1950 Plan for Coal. In the 1960s the governments of Harold Wilson showed little interest in reviving such a plan. In fact, when it came to closing mines, Sir William Reid remembered that 'the Labour government pushed me harder than the NCB'.

In both South Wales and Durham, the miners' union had looked to Labour to support and save the coal industry in their Areas. Alf Hesler, who had succeeded Watson as the general secretary in Durham, argued that the Labour Party was 'our only chance of getting a government which will listen with a sympathetic ear to the problems of labour in general, of this region in particular and especially of the mining community in the North East.'[7] Sympathy was in short supply, however. Wilson was a powerful advocate for technological change: as leader of the opposition, he spoke at the 1963 Labour Party Conference in Scarborough of the 'white heat' that needed to transform the country as it went forward with a 'scientific revolution', and his appointees at the Ministry of Power operated a policy in full support both of mechanisation *and* reducing production.[8] Redundancy payments were available and the rest was left to the NCB locally, in cooperation with the trade unions. To add salt to the wounds, the new power station planned for Hartlepool, adjacent to the large mines on the east coast, would not be coal-fired but nuclear. When interviewed in 1980, Michael Foot said that he had formed the view that this was 'Harold Wilson's way of telling the Durham miners that the game was up.'

As noted, the man responsible for driving through mechanisation and mine closures was Alf (then Lord) Robens in his ten years as chair of the NCB; his opposite number as general secretary of the NUM was Will Paynter. These two men, despite both being products of the British labour movement, were cut from different cloth. Robens was born in Chorlton-cum-Hardy in Manchester in 1910, and left school at fifteen to work as an errand boy and then as a clerk at the Manchester and Salford Co-operative Society. Active in the trade union, he became a worker director and then an official of the shop workers' union USDAW. In 1945 he was elected as MP for the mining constituency of Wansbeck in Northumberland, moving to the new constituency of Blyth in 1950. He served in several junior ministerial roles and was briefly minister of labour before the Conservatives won the election in 1951, and then shadow foreign secretary under Hugh Gaitskell's leadership. His subsequent appointment as chairman of the NCB by Macmillan was questioned by the NUM; in a fierce debate at its annual conference in 1960, Sam Watson came to his defence, seeing Robens as 'a man who has spent his whole life in the working class movement, has twice been a cabinet minister and is also one of the ablest men we have.'[9]

To Paynter, Robens was 'an unknown quantity' but one which he came to appreciate.[10] They had a reasonable relationship, with the miners' leader reserving his criticisms for the government and for Harold Wilson when he became leader of the Labour Party. Like Horner, Paynter remained a member of the Communist Party while general secretary, and he also shared his predecessor's views on the importance of protecting the NCB, which he regarded as a progressive development. He traced his criticisms of unofficial strikes back to his experiences in the twenties, where he saw 'factionalism' leading to defeat. In the post-1945 period, with the advent of a nationalised industry, he felt that flash strikes over *particular* local issues would not serve the *general* interest of the miners or the industry. It was for this reason that he supported the principle of a national union and ran for election as general secretary of the NUM in 1959. One of his major objectives was to remove the piece-rate payment system from the industry. He saw this to have been divisive, inimical to class solidarity and at the root of many of the historical problems faced by the miners. His aim was for a national day-wage agreement for all workers across the industry. As it turned out, Robens's strategy of rapid mechanisation through power-loading machines facilitated this, and an industry-wide National Power Loading Agreement (NPLA) was signed in 1966. Remarkably, negotiations for this forward-looking agreement took place at a time when the industry was contracting, with mines closing at a reckless pace. Even more remarkable was the fact that, in practice, the NPLA lasted for little more than a decade.[11]

Facing Closure

Mine closures began early in South Wales and Durham. In 1957, the South Wales Divisional Board announced that seven mines would have to close, and this set a pattern for the following decade. Ironically, at the time Paynter was leading a delegation of miners from South Wales through the Soviet Union, visiting pits and new mining towns on the Donbass coalfield in Ukraine. On his enforced return he soon became aware of the magnitude of the problem the union faced in dealing with this issue. The Area union considered a number of options, including a stay-in strike and all-out strike action:

> But when we tested the coalfield on this through a delegate conference the reaction was against it, understandably because there were many uneconomic pits whose miners feared that action of this kind could precipitate their own closure. This was a constant factor throughout the whole period.[12]

On the Durham coalfield the Area union, under Sam Watson's leadership, was more accepting of the inevitability of the changes, often describing them as progress. Kit Robinson, who later became general secretary, remembered in interview that from the union offices at Redhills:

> Sammy would point to the trains going across the viaduct in Durham. 'Who wants to work in dirty coal pits; who wants to use dirty coal.' Sammy saw oil as the fuel of the future. Oil and nuclear power. We used to argue about it.

Watson had developed a deeply cooperative relationship with the Area board, which extended into the procedures for dealing with colliery closures. A system of 'manpower planning' was put in place after the appointment of Sir William Reid – son of the man whose eponymous report had guided the first years of the nationalised corporation. Before moving to the North East, Reid had been in charge of the Scottish Area and he had written a personal letter to Sam Watson at the time of the Easington disaster. He described his relocation to the Tyneside offices as a move 'to Sam Watson'.

> I knew Sam and I knew he was a man of great integrity. He knew the problems we faced and he said to me 'for God's sake, help the Union if you can. Help the Union.' I did. Sometimes he'd come to see me and he'd say 'I know I haven't got a case but I've promised the men something. Can you help?'

They met regularly and 'talked a lot', and through their private meetings built up a bond that came to underpin the formal relationships between the NCB and the Area union.

> I said to him soon after I moved to the North: 'Sam, I'll make you a bargain. I'll never tell you a half-truth. I'll always tell you the truth; even if it hurts. But I'll never do anything

without telling you, and I'll never do anything to reduce your prestige.' 'Will you?' he said, 'then I'll do the same.'

Watson retired from his post as general secretary in 1963, but was immediately appointed to a part-time position within the NCB, which he retained until his death in 1967. Kit Robinson, who succeeded him, explained how the close relationship endured:

Sir William Reid was a good man, a gentleman. He had a job to do and it was a most difficult job. Colliery closures are a terribly difficult thing and he didn't like doing it. You see he was a pit man; Robens was a rogue, but Bill Reid was a pit man.

In South Wales, after Will Paynter's election as national general secretary of the NUM, Will Whitehead became president of the South Wales Area and worked alongside Dai Francis as general secretary for the intense period of colliery closures. Both able men and members of the Communist Party, they took the view that closures should be opposed, but that there was little support on the coalfield for coordinated strike action. They followed the lead established by Paynter in calling for a change in government policy, to emphasise growth and recognise that within the UK and internationally there was a need to view energy as a unique and critical commodity that required careful planning.

It became clear during the sixties that two very different styles of leadership had become established in Durham and South Wales. It can be argued that the outcome was much the same, as pits closed at a similar rate in each Area. However, the *processes* were quite different, and these had lasting consequences. In South Wales the emphasis was on resistance wherever possible and the development of an alternative political approach to the running of the industry and its relationship to the energy markets. In Durham the leadership avoided resistance, and suppressed it where it occurred. Here the emphasis was on cooperation with what seemed to be an inevitable process. Informally, in meeting with MPs and members of the government, the pace of closure and levels of subsidy were questioned but rarely condemned outright.

Labour Politics

Nationally the NUM persisted in its attempts to slow down the pace of closure, but for the Wilson government the decline in coal mining was seen as an economic necessity and one which no amount of pressure and argument could alter. The miners' leaders were seen as swimming against the tide of progress, and this view was encouraged by the election victory in 1966 which strengthened the government's position. There was little thought at that time that the coalfield vote for the Labour Party would be threatened by these policies, still less that seats in Durham and South Wales could be lost. The policy would not change and this was made clear in the White Paper on Fuel Policy presented to the House of Commons by Richard Marsh, the newly appointed secretary of state for energy, on 18 July 1967.[13] Pit closures were to continue and coal output was to be cut. The coalfields were going to have to change with the times.

In his diary, Richard Crossman recorded how, after a long statement from Marsh, the 'Miners' MPs were able to have the whole of the House of Commons to themselves for the protest which they wanted to make before accepting their fate'. It was, however, a 'cosy, pathetic occasion.' Marsh had made matters clear. 'Literally scores of pits would be closed down in a year of high recession and unemployment.' In response, however, all that was conjured up was hot air. 'The protest', thought Crossman 'was purely verbal and little more than breast beating.' It was clear that 'these miners (MPs) felt that they were bound to support the Government in an action which really meant the destruction of the mining industry.' In Crossman's view, the miners' MPs had revealed a 'not very edifying loyalty, because people should not be as loyal as that to a Government which was causing the total ruin of their industry.' Quite shaken at this 'pathetic lack of fight', Crossman anticipated the worst.[14]

He was right to hold these fears. As it turned out it was only the Durham Miners' Gala which exercised any check on the catastrophic course of events. For James Callaghan, Gala day in Durham was 'the greatest occasion and greatest privilege you can offer to any Labour MP'.[15] However, in 1967 he and Wilson 'made their speeches to a solemn, unenthusiastic audience'. That day, the men of Silksworth had lowered their banner in protest as they passed the balcony of the County Hotel. At the luncheon which followed the speeches, both Paynter and Robens had made it clear to the Labour leaders that the scale of the projected rundown would involve at least 15,000 redundancies in Durham. This news had apparently caused Callaghan an 'appalling shock'. On top of this was the deep discontent felt in the coalfield caused by the recent announcement that 'our atomic power station is to be built right in the centre of the coalfield at Seaton Carew'.[16] All this had given Callaghan 'cold feet' (something which Wilson, apparently, found faintly amusing), and he was so shaken that, at the next Cabinet meeting, he and Wilson presented a proposal to 'postpone the pit closures this winter in order to cut the number of unemployed by about 15,000.' Coal was at the centre of a cabinet crisis, with Robens making 'deliberate political capital out of the pit closures' with dramatic predictions on the loss of mining jobs.[17] For the miners' leaders, these figures were the last straw.[18]

In response, the union organised a national demonstration in London, culminating in a rally at Central Hall, Westminster, where Paynter, according to Dennis Skinner, 'gave the speech of his life'. He told the meeting that things had gone too far and warned the Labour government that 'there was a breaking point in the tolerance and loyalty of everybody'.[19] The rally stiffened the resolve of the miners' MPs, and helped put more pressure on the government – but on the issue of strike action the union's NEC was divided. The mine closures were unevenly distributed across the different Areas, and this made it difficult to arrive at a coordinated programme of resistance. The idea of a series of 'guerrilla strikes' in secure mines was considered and rejected, as was the call for a national strike ballot. Faced with a divided executive and, in Sidney Ford, a deeply conservative president, Paynter's chief concern became the need to retain unity within the union in a rapidly changing industry. Meanwhile, Robens continued to play both ends against the middle: closing mines though criticising the government's more extreme plans, while assiduously retaining the loyalty of the NUM, which was essential to the NCB's plans for further mechanisation.

As a consequence, and remarkably, there were no stoppages of work over redundancy in the critical closure years, in Durham, South Wales or nationally. This contrasted dramatically with other industries that were not in such severe difficulties. Strikes over closures, redundancies and layoffs were common throughout manufacturing in the 1960s, although employment decline in those sectors paled into insignificance in comparison with the coal industry. The surprising lack of strike action gave confidence to a view within the state that wholesale economic restructuring could be achieved with a minimum of disruption. In assessing the uniqueness of the British mining experience Robens paid tribute to the NUM, saying that without the cooperation of 'the unions and of the men themselves this task could never have been accomplished'.[20] However, there is no doubt that this cooperation was often given grudgingly, especially after 1966.

Manpower Planning for a New Way of Life

During the decade of contraction most of the job losses were achieved through what was termed 'natural wastage'. This involved men (most of them young) accepting that there was no future for them in the industry, and that they could perhaps do better things than digging coal, often in narrow seams, risking their lives. They simply left the industry. One of the most popular anthems of the sixties came from the North East, Eric Burdon of the Animals singing 'We've Gotta Get Out of This Place' at the Club a'GoGo in Newcastle. The idea of 'a better life for me and you' was something that the NCB picked up on in its dealings with the significant number (90,000 nationally) of mostly older men with families who didn't want to leave the industry. Some were made redundant but the majority were redeployed to local mines or to the expanding Areas of Yorkshire and the East and West Midlands through the Inter-Divisional Transfer Scheme.[21] This scheme was managed by the NCB and strongly supported by central government, particularly through a house-building programme planned to accommodate transferees. It was publicised in personal letters from the chairman of the Board, which attempted to evoke the sense of a holiday adventure alongside the allure of a new and better way of life. In the letter Robens wrote of 'many brand new pits and others that have been completely reconstructed' offering permanent employment to those who were 'prepared to move to a long-life pit'. Calling it his 'pick your pit scheme', he advised miners to study the details and then take up the offer of:

> an expenses paid visit to the coal field of your choice, taking your family with you if you like. There you'll be able to see for yourself the pit, the houses, the shopping centres and the club. And you'll also meet some of the people you'll be working with and living alongside.

Many Durham and Scottish miners moved south to Nottingham, with Welsh miners setting up home in Staffordshire. All this was picked up in the music of Jock Purdon, who had been a miner at the Harraton Colliery, known as the Cotia, in a village just south of Gateshead. His song 'Farewell to Cotia' tells of miners who migrated to 'Robens' promised land'.

As before, the local authorities played a major role. South Wales, while 'losing' some miners to Staffordshire also received miners from Durham, with many families from the North settling in the villages near the newly expanded Cynheidre Colliery in the western anthracite belt. The NCB also had plans for the huge expansion of coal production in the Rhondda Valley around its new super-pit at Maerdy. Here the local authority was urged to make a radical extension to its plans for a new housing estate at Penrhys high on the hillside overlooking Ferndale. The NCB's plans for increasing the number of miners did not materialise on the scale predicted and the local authority was left with a large estate for which it had to find tenants. Over time, a new independent community organisation – the Penrhys Partnership – was established there, and one of its members Wayne Carter explained how a new community had to be built:

> One of the problems facing Penrhys and other places in the valleys is that it was built for the mining industry. It was created to house the miners. So, the miners came in and the houses were built to accommodate them, but they didn't build the infrastructure. So, you've got the houses, but not the infrastructure. That's what happened up here. They let the actual heart of a community fall by the wayside and they just built the skeleton of it. They set up a population on top of a mountain of about two and a half thousand, . . . [with] only one shop, a post office, a hairdresser and a bookmaker.

In County Durham the decline of the coal industry had a distinct spatial pattern, with production moving eastwards. Many of the villages in the west of the county were deemed to have no economic future and left to decay through deliberate neglect.[22] Families were encouraged to move eastwards towards Peterlee New Town in east Durham, proximate to the coastal collieries, or to Washington New Town and Spennymoor in the centre of the county, where new factories were arriving. This was not achieved without disruption and discontent, with many unwilling to leave their existing homes and communities of friends and relations. There was also unhappiness with the increased cost of housing, which in the past had led to rent strikes in Peterlee.[23] This pattern of migration away from the closed mining villages towards areas of higher employment also took place in South Wales, and here, as in Durham, the closure of the mines was accompanied by the closure of a complex structure of branch railway lines. A study of the Afan Valley by Teresa Rees established that, isolated by the closure of the railway, almost half of those who moved away would have preferred to stay if circumstances had been different. The lack of a coordinated response to the impact of redundancy seemed clear, most notably the fact that in 'areas of high male unemployment jobs thought only suitable for women have been created.'

> Special Development Area status has attracted firms to the area. However, apart from a footwear factory which has since closed down and a bookbinding company, which began a redundancy programme 18 months ago, they have mostly been light engineering or manufacturing firms employing small numbers of women . . . certainly the sort of jobs that are available locally such as light engineering, machining or working in the Revlon cosmetics factory in Maesteg, the marshmallow factory in Ebbw Vale, do not appear to have appealed to the ex-miners.[24]

Women, who had historically formed a small proportion of the coalfield labour force in South Wales and Durham, thus became increasingly prominent as factory workers after the closure of the mines. There was a further expansion of employment prospects for women within the welfare state, with jobs in local authority administration and public sector education and health services. The social arrangements that had underpinned the coal production system were disappearing along with the mines, in a way which many found destabilising. Male unemployment re-emerged, challenging the assumption that full long-term employment would result from the nationalisation of the industry, and the passing of the 1967 Special Development Areas Act revived memories of the 1930s. In both coalfields the long-term unemployment rate shifted from a steady state of 2 per cent or below to around 5 per cent.

Men, once hailed as heroes of the mine, came to see themselves as 'industrial gypsies', moving from mine to mine, or to one of the manufacturing branch plants drawn to the mining areas by government regional policy. In Durham, ex-miners moved into the Courtauld and Black and Decker factories in the centre of the county, and to Dunlop in Washington New Town. However, the Engineering Employers' Federation strongly and successfully resisted the Ford Motor Company in its attempt to locate a mass assembly facility in the region.[25] In South Wales the expansion of the Hoover factory in Merthyr was an important source of new employment, as were the component factories of the Ford Motor Company in Swansea, Morris Motors at Llanelli and Metal Box in Neath. Cwmbran expanded and became a focal point for people leaving the eastern valley towns for employment at the armaments factory in Glascoed, or at British Nylon Spinners and Girling Engineering. In these ways the change in the economy and social fabric of the two regions was achieved without significant inward migration. While migrants from the Commonwealth were encouraged to travel to other parts of Britain, South Wales and Durham now had their own labour reserves.

However, life had changed, and reflecting on all this in South Wales, social historians such as Gwyn Williams wrote of how the old industrial areas were being 'degutted' as all life was drained away to the sites of multinational corporations. This seepage, he said, 'sucks life and spirit out of the cordons of working class communities which are being transformed into commuter belts of atomised individuals.'[26] And, in spite of the complacency of the Labour government, these disturbances to the social structure of the areas did have political implications. Mine closures removed the miners and their union from their positions of dominance within the labour force and in civil society. They also brought about the demise of the coal production regime with its strong dependence upon women's domestic labour. Women's wage labour (often part time, often non-union) became a central feature of the new post-mining economy, drawing in new workers for capital at a time when labour markets were tightening. These were jobs that were specifically designed for women – they were badly paid, generally on piece work based on tedious repetitive tasks and they offered flexible part time contracts to accommodate child care. Interviews at the Clix zip factory in Peterlee in 1979 revealed that the women there were aware of the way in which 'women's work' was being defined. While they valued the job some of them, like this thirty year old, felt dissatisfied:

> That's all I have done all my life, flogging in a factory getting a number out. I've never ever done a job where I can just do it and enjoy it. There's always a number at the end of it. You cannot tell me that that's exciting.

Another reflected that: 'women are supposed to be compatible with men as far as wages et cetera goes. I don't believe this at all. It's not true. I don't believe that a man would do this job, It's too tedious.'

These shifts in the social order had implications for party loyalties. Things that were once a given ('we've always voted Labour') became more tenuous. In South Wales, Plaid Cymru re-emerged as a radical alternative to the Labour Party, and Gwynfor Evans was elected as its first MP at a by-election in Carmarthen in July 1966. In 1967 and 1968 Plaid came a close second to Labour in the two formerly impregnable mining seats of Rhondda West and Caerphilly. In both Durham and South Wales there was a significant decline in the number of

NUM-sponsored MPs, and as the general election in 1970 approached there was a decline in the level of active support for the Party. The dramatic closure of so many mines under a Labour government, changing the social structure of these areas and peoples' way of life, would not be forgotten.

'Buried Alive by the NCB'

As some mines closed, others stayed open, and there remained the threat of injury and death underground. This was made clear at the Six Bells Colliery in Abertillery in 1960, when an explosion killed forty-five local men, issuing a stark reminder of the dangers involved in mining coal 'on behalf of the people'. The chairman of the report into the causes of the explosion concluded that it was impossible to say with certainty what had caused it. The mine was encircled by the chapel, the welfare hall and rows of terraced houses where the miners lived with their families, all in close proximity to the pit. In three families both the father and the son were killed in the explosion. One man remembered that his father had worked in Six Bells for twenty-two years but decided to leave:

> he was there when the explosion happened but he was working in a different part of the pit, and after he'd seen what actually happened he wouldn't go back . . . what he saw . . . played on his mind and he never went back underground after that explosion. He was very lucky that he survived and when I told him that me and my brother were going to the pit he wasn't happy about it.

Two years later nine men were killed at the Tower Colliery, and then in 1965 another thirty-one were killed in an explosion that took place at the Cambrian Colliery.

These tragedies – 'disasters', they were called – the drama that surrounded them, and the seemingly endless search for survivors, all had a profound effect on mining communities. Then, on 21 October 1966, the waste tip of the Merthyr Vale Colliery slipped down the mountainside, engulfing the local primary school at Aberfan and killing the children and teachers there: 147 in all. This tragic event, perhaps more than any other, affected the ways in which miners, their families and the wider public understood the nature of the nationalised industry. It was symbolised by the absence of Lord Robens, who kept his engagement at Guildford where he was being installed as chancellor of Surrey University rather than travel to Aberfan (he eventually arrived at the Welsh village the following evening). This contrasted with the image of Will Paynter, wading through slurry and coal waste in borrowed Wellington boots, fearing the worst and worrying that the union had not been more alert to the dangers.

The disaster at Aberfan compounded a growing feeling that the bureaucracy of the Board was detached from the experiences of its workforce. It was most starkly expressed in the words of a grieving father who intervened at the inquest, driven beyond limits by the coroner's talk of 'asphyxia and multiple injuries', to say that the words he wanted on the death certificate of his child were these: 'Buried alive by the NCB'. Others agreed, and there were cries of 'murderers'.

The report of the Aberfan disaster tribunal mentioned 'bungling ineptitude by many men', but there were no prosecutions and it was not seen as a resigning issue for the chairman. He had insisted in his evidence at Mountain Ash that he was 'not a technician'. Subsequently, in his role as chairman, he explained that the NCB could not pay for the removal of the tip. Neither would the Labour government, as the secretary of state for Wales, George Thomas – Lord Tonypandy – made clear. The cost would have to be borne by the disaster fund set up by the local council, and in an act of dubious legality the fund was raided for £150,000.[27]

A Growing Resentment

The combination of widespread colliery closures, chronic ill health and tragic accidents also affected the ways in which miners were coming to see the future, and with it the role of their trade union and their commitment to the Labour Party. In South Wales the general secretary of the NUM Dai Francis formed the view that, in the way the closure programme was carried out, 'there was no difference between the old . . . coal owners and the National Coal Board. They were now turning it into state capitalism.'[28]

Moreover, the coal mines that were still open contained a very different labour force, one that had experienced closure and uncertainty but remained in an industry where, despite a new national day-wage agreement, their wages had been held back while production continued to soar. In the North East, Jim Perry of the Durham Mechanics recalled that

> The mood of the men was beginning to change towards the end of the sixties. Miners had been exhorted to perform for the country's good and for the benefit of the industry; we had acquiesced in the massive contraction of the industry and were persuaded to accept rises that neither equated with increased productivity in the industry nor kept pace with the cost of living. Beyond entreaties for greater effort lay something implicitly more unsavoury, it was that if we did not toe the line the pit would be closed. The threat of closure was sufficient to hold most of the miners in tune with the moderates' refrain.

And the closures continued. In the twelve months up to March 1969, fifty-five pits closed and over 55,000 men left the industry, with more to follow in the year ahead. This was at a time when there were few jobs available outside, and nothing that paid enough to fund a 'new way of life'. The reality of work outside the industry had dawned, and the NCB was finding it more difficult to find volunteers for redundancy from men who were becoming increasingly difficult to manage. These were the issues picked up by Lawrence Daly in his successful campaign to become general secretary of the NUM in opposition to the Lancastrian Joe Gormley. The objection had once been that the miners were being turned into 'industrial gypsies'; now their future, said Daly, was 'the economic scrapheap'.

The closures had also changed the topography of the industry. Over the 1960s the concentration of mine workers in Yorkshire and the East Midlands, the central coalfield, had increased from 32 per cent to 44 per cent of the national total. By 1972 these Areas were producing 52 per cent of the NCB output, mainly for electricity generation.[29] Here there was a growing confidence that the miners' work was essential and that they would no longer be held back in their demands by the threat of closure. The work had changed too: everywhere the new power-loading faces were driving forward remorselessly, pouring out the coal and making collieries, for the first time, bear some resemblance to factories, with far less autonomy for the miners.

Growing unrest in the large coastal collieries in Durham over wages and the conditions of work, combined with dissatisfaction over the compliant approach of trade union leaders, produced a new militancy in that most moderate area. In South Wales, organised elements within the miners' union – 'the unofficial movement' – were building on this same dissatisfaction in a campaign in support of resistance and strike action.[30] But it was in Yorkshire that the changes were most marked. Once renowned for its insular approach under right-wing leadership, two members of the Communist Party, Jock Cane and Sammy Taylor, had been elected as agents with a more militant approach toward the management of the NCB. Young miners, many of them members of the Young Communist League, were organising their own meetings away from the control of lodge officials, and the Barnsley Miners' Forum became a centre of debate and talk of radical action.[31]

In 1969, all of this frustration and anger came together in an unexpected way. In that year the NCB announced the closure of the Afan Ocean Colliery at Abergwynfi, one of the most productive in the South Wales Area. Determined that this had to be fought, the Area executive called for strike action, only to be voted down in the delegate conference. Within two months, however, over half of the coalfield was on strike – not against closures but in support of a longstanding demand aimed at improving the wages and hours worked by the men on the surface of the mine. These were often older men who through injury and disability were no longer fit to work underground at the faces. It was an issue that had been in negotiation for some years, and on which the NCB under Robens had persistently obfuscated and refused to commit. The justice of the case, the procrastination and delays in the official channels, the failure of the union to resolve the issue, all came to a head in Yorkshire when all the pits came out on unofficial strike. Very quickly the strike spread beyond the Yorkshire Area, with pits in South Wales coming out immediately and many in Nottingham responding positively to the Yorkshire pickets. Collieries in Scotland, Kent and Derbyshire followed, to be joined by three of the increasingly militant coastal collieries in Durham. Within two days almost half the collieries in the country were closed. The strike lasted for eleven days and spurred the NCB to settle the issue through a full settlement of the existing NUM wages claim.

Miners had never been disinclined to strike. The opposite, in fact. In the post-war period, strikes among coal miners were common, which so contrasted with other industries that they were recorded in a separate series and excluded from the national statistics. Every year there were many hundreds of strikes in the mines, almost all of them unofficial, most often affecting only one colliery and lasting for a day or two. These strikes were over payment, local working conditions or management and control issues. While disinclined to support strike action over mine closures – the Achilles heel of the NUM – wages and conditions along with matters of injustice were a different matter altogether, and the surface workers' strike revealed how quickly the spark of strike action could be carried across the coalfields. Commenting on the overall situation, William Ashworth saw 'signs . . . that the cooperation of labour was diminishing'.[32] At the time of the election of a Tory government under Edward Heath in 1970 therefore, the miners were a smouldering presence.

CHAPTER FOUR

From Heath to Thatcher

*If I emerged from Oxford University as a confirmed Tory, eight
years working on Tyneside made me a radical one. I wanted to see
the nation's industry and economy properly run. I wanted socialism defeated forever.*

Nicholas Ridley, *My Style of Government*, 1991

In the sixties 'industrial relations' had emerged as a major issue
and scapegoat for British industry, so much so that one of the
first steps of the Labour government of 1964–70 had been to
establish a commission under Lord Donovan to look into the
issue. Significantly, the coal industry did not emerge in these
discussions as a major problem: the nationalised coal industry,
with its industrial union and agreed machinery for conciliation
and consultation, was seen as highly rational. The strike in 1969,
however, was a foretaste of things to come, and in 1972 the
NUM organised a national strike that dramatically changed
perceptions, revealing the miners' capacity (through halting the
supply of coal) to disrupt society and with the support of other
workers to change government policy and make significant gains.
In 1974 Prime Minister Edward Heath, facing another strike,
called an election with the question, 'who rules the country?',
and lost.

The NUM began the 1970s with a large proportion of its membership deeply angry over their wages and conditions of work, and frustrated by the inability of the leadership to negotiate successfully with the NCB. At the annual conference on the Isle of Man these views were made clear, with many looking back at a decade of inaction and cooperation that had delivered little but mine closures. The South Wales Area proposed that the union's wage claim should be put to the Board, and if it was rejected then a national strike should be called. Although the new general secretary from Fife, Lawrence Daly, explained that a national strike would require a national ballot, the resolution was passed, and this was to have enormous consequences. The vote was in favour of strike action but with a majority of only 57 per cent, at a time when the constitution required a two-thirds majority in a national ballot for strike action.[1] Such a majority had been obtained in South Wales, Scotland and Yorkshire, and these Areas went on strike in defiance of the result, rejecting the national decision, feeling that the need for a two-thirds majority was disproportionate and citing the previous conference resolution in support. Eventually everyone returned to work but there was a growing determination that without an improvement in wages there would be a national strike. To this end, and before the next ballot, the rule on strike action was amended with the requirement dropped to 55 per cent.

After the retirement of Sir Sidney Ford, Joe Gormley was elected as president in an acrimonious contest with the veteran Scottish Communist Michael McGahey. Building on the surge of militancy among the miners, many expected a McGahey victory, which would have had major consequences for the union. But, as Vic Allen assessed, the miners were clearly not prepared for such a change at that time.[2]

However, many of them were still prepared to strike for higher wages, and after another national ballot, the NUM announced on Thursday 2 December 1971, the first week of winter, that 59 per cent of miners had voted for strike action. The country was hit by a mass strike, something for which it was unprepared. As Tony Hall commented, 'the predominant attitude in [NCB headquarters at] Hobart House and in the government as well as in the country at large was that the miners no longer counted for anything'.[3] They were in for a shock.

The Battle of Saltley Gate

This was the first national stoppage in the coal industry since 1926 and it was a highly organised affair, coordinated by Lawrence Daly through a national strike committee. The TUC advised all its members not to cross picket lines but drew back from offering coordinated support. The NUM's approach was based on a sophisticated picketing strategy, involving large numbers of miners moving from site to site, effectively stopping the movement of coal. The power stations were identified as key locations and with maps provided by the national committee. Each of the NUM's Areas was given a region to picket: Yorkshire to East Anglia, South Wales to the South West, and so on. Locally the movement of coal to schools, hospitals and other socially necessary locations was approved by local miners' committees, which throughout the strike showed considerable initiative. In South Wales an agreement was made with all transport unions that no coal delivered to docks in the region would be moved. There were other such agreements, and informal ones too, that added up to a remarkably successful strategy.

After one month with winter on the side of the NUM, the Central Electricity Generating Board (CEGB) faced voltage reductions and power cuts. Two events in early February altered the dynamic of the strike. The first involved the death of a miner, Fred Matthews, who was run over by a truck while picketing Keadby Power Station near Scunthorpe. This helped the strikers win public sympathy, and if anything strengthened their resolve. The other event took place, however, not on the coalfields or at a power station but in the West Midlands at a coke depot at Saltley Gate in

Birmingham, where an enormous stockpile of almost a million tonnes of coke had been accumulated to defeat the NUM blockade. Over 600 lorries a day were coming to Saltley, many of them with non-union drivers, all ignoring the pickets who were being strongly marshalled by the police. The call went out for reinforcements, and busloads of miners arrived from Stafford, South Wales and mainly Yorkshire. Even with that strength of support the gates were kept open and lorries continued to arrive. Arthur Scargill was leading the Yorkshire contingent, and he spent many hours in negotiation with the local engineering trade unions to raise support for the miners. It was agreed that the car plants and workshops would strike and their workers would join the miners at Saltley Gate, which resulted in a successful blockade of the entrance and left the police with no option but to admit defeat. Scargill described it as 'the greatest day of my life', for in his view 'the picket line didn't close Saltley, what happened was the working class closed Saltley' and in doing so demonstrated its enormous power.[4]

There is no doubt that Saltley was a decisive moment and it was followed by more power cuts through February, leading the government to declare a state of emergency and impose a three-day week in an attempt to conserve coal supplies. Heath set up a court of inquiry under Lord Wilberforce that sat immediately, and quickly – reporting within a week – arrived at the conclusion that there was much merit in the miners' case: 'Working conditions in the coal mines are certainly amongst the toughest and least attractive and we agree that miners' pay levels should recognise this.' On this basis, and the evidence of increased productivity and relative wage rates, Wilberforce concluded that 'the miners' basic claim for a general and exceptional wage increase should be recognised.'[5] The increase should be backdated and the agreement should last for sixteen months. This was accepted by the government, but (to the alarm of members of the Board) *rejected* by a narrow majority at the miners' executive committee, which bridled at the sixteen-month clause and wanted to take the opportunity to settle other longstanding issues. The negotiators all ended up at 10 Downing Street, where Daly and Gormley continued the talks until 1.20 a.m. on Saturday 19 February, with the NUM having won a number of improvements over the favourable terms suggested by the inquiry. Daly put things succinctly when he said that 'we have won more in the last twenty-four hours than we have won in the last twenty-four years.' The deal was put to a vote of the members and was agreed almost unanimously. It was the miners' greatest victory.

The success and impact of the strike produced a dramatic transformation in the state's view of the miners and the NUM. Brendon Sewill was an adviser to chancellor of the exchequer Anthony Barber:

> Many of those in positions of influence looked into the abyss and saw only a few days away the possibility of the country being plunged into a state of chaos not far removed from that which might prevail after a minor nuclear attack. If that sounds melodramatic . . . it was the analogy that was being used at the time.[6]

During the strike new kinds of union leadership had emerged nationally and locally. Lawrence Daly was centrally involved in coordinating the aggressive strike strategy that was being implemented on the ground under the leadership of men like Arthur Scargill in Yorkshire. Both Daly and Scargill had been extensively involved in New Left politics, and their outlooks reflected the lack of patience with the status quo that was emerging in the coal mines. Scargill was soon to be elected as a full-time official in the Yorkshire Area of the NUM. In his speeches he repeatedly referred to the established industrial relations in coal mining as 'collaboration'. He was particularly critical of Paynter's fears over strike action and argued for a much more aggressive approach. The NCB had changed too, with Robens being replaced by his deputy, Derek Ezra, a man of Liberal politics and sensibilities, less forceful in character than his predecessors. As a civil servant he had joined the

Board at the outset in 1947 and felt a deep commitment to the coal industry.[7] Ezra hoped that things could now be stabilised and the industry run on a professional basis – but the coal mines would never be stable again. The OPEC oil cartel exacerbated this mix of militancy and distrust by further increasing the price of oil, changing energy markets in ways that questioned the capacity of Robens's pared-down coal industry to deliver at a time when, ironically, the Central Electricity Generating Board was keen to replace much of its oil burn with coal. The NCB had already expressed concern about its ability to retain its labour force, adding to the NUM's view that a further substantial wage increase was needed for the miners, something which conflicted with the government's prices and incomes policy. Frustrated over lack of progress, in November 1973 the NUM imposed an overtime ban, a procedure which succeeded in reducing the supply of coal while also revealing the extent to which the industry relied on the miners working excessive hours. So successful was this strategy that it led to another state of emergency being declared. Energetic attempts to broker a settlement resulted in numerous meetings involving the NUM, the NCB and the government, with new president Joe Gormley taking the lead for the trade union, often in private meetings with the prime minister. These proved fruitless and ended with the NUM balloting its membership on strike action.

On this occasion the result was decisive, with 93 per cent of miners in South Wales and 86 per cent of those in Durham voting to strike. The NUM called a strike to start on 9 February 1974; hearing this news, Edward Heath on 7 February dissolved Parliament, and in the general election that followed was narrowly defeated. Harold Wilson formed a Labour government, with Michael Foot as minister of employment eager to settle the situation in the coal industry. The strike ended ten days later. The miners had had another victory, but it was more subdued this time. For the Tory party it was catastrophic. The knives were out for their leader and they would not forget what the miners had done.

A New Plan for Coal

To ensure the cooperation of the NUM, the Wilson government agreed a Plan for Coal that ostensibly placed it at the heart of a strategy for organised industrial development. It proposed increasing output from 110 million tonnes (mt) to 135 mt by 1985, with the prospect of expansion towards 200 mt by the end of the century. The plan assumed that demand for coal would increase as part of the national economy's general growth, along with the movement away from oil as a source of fuel and with the development of coal-based petrochemicals. This increase in coal supply would be achieved by large investments in new technology and the sinking of new mines, most notably at Selby in North Yorkshire. The additional coal would be used in electricity supply and steel production, underpinned by joint understandings made between the NCB and the other two state corporations – the Central Electricity Generating Board (CEGB) and the British Steel Corporation (BSC) – which together would take 80 per cent of coal output. Although these understandings were non-contractual, they established a framework of joint intent as the basis for formulating the annual plans of the three boards and for negotiations over pricing structures. In this way, after the trauma of the sixties, the deep-mining industry was now considered to be on a stable footing. In the hope of sealing support, Wilson addressed the NUM conference in 1975 with the demand that the miners should embrace the slogan 'not a year for self but a year for Britain'.

There were problems, however. Between 1975 and 1978–9, rather than increase, coal production *declined* to a low of 107.5 mt as pits continued to close, further increasing pressure on the highly mechanised faces of Robens' super-pits. Already facing criticisms about supply from both the BSC and the CEGB, the NCB had, in 1974, proposed amending the day-wage agreement with an additional incentive payment. This productivity scheme would reward the teams working on the faces with bonuses related to their weekly output. Other workers in the mine would also benefit, but to a lesser extent. This proposal was rejected by 61 per cent of all miners in a national ballot, with the men in South Wales and Durham strongly opposed to the deal. However, the NCB and the government were persistent. In November 1974 Ezra visited the North East to address the Area consultative committee on the importance of increased production. He had become convinced of the need for some kind of productivity deal which would keep the industry within the framework of the government's Social Contract.[8] Support from Durham would be essential, with South Wales (together with Scotland, Kent and Yorkshire) implacably opposed to the introduction of incentive payments.[9]

In South Wales any erosion of the national wage agreement, negotiated in 1966, was considered inimical to building national unity within the union. In the fifties, when piece rates had dominated in the industry, this view had been shared by Sam Watson. He felt that there was a natural affinity between the miners in South Wales and Durham, who both faced similar problems of dangerous working conditions and poor geology that limited their capacity to increase production and earn higher wages. Following his retirement, and in the wake of mine closures, however, the new leadership seemed overwhelmed and, as a result, the Durham Area was left rudderless.

In October 1975, Lawrence Daly was severely injured in a car crash. This personal tragedy was also disastrous for the NUM. Daly was extremely gifted, and having left the Communist Party in 1965, before the invasion of Czechoslovakia, had developed an independent brand of left-wing politics that had come to the fore in the 1972 strike.[10] The crash left him incapacitated and placed the running of the union in the hands of its president, Joe Gormley. A Labour Party loyalist and a man of the right, not without charm, Gormley had been involved in the negotiations with Heath and he was keen to provide support for the Labour government and the NCB, for whom the incentive scheme remained a vital issue.

The annual conference of the NUM had passed resolutions that were opposed to the very idea of incentive payments, favouring instead a policy that aimed for a weekly wage of £100 for underground workers. Nevertheless, with Gormley's connivance, the scheme continued to be discussed at the NEC and in negotiations with the NCB. In 1977 another document was brought forward, proposing a revised system of incentive payments, which the NEC, on the narrowest of margins and with the support of the Durham officials, agreed was workable and should be taken to a national ballot vote of the membership. Letters of support for the scheme (including one from Tony Benn) were widely circulated, but in spite of this cajoling just over 55 per cent of the members voted to *reject* the new scheme, despite the Durham vote switching to support from a position of opposition two years earlier.

This result provoked a reaction from some of the Areas where there had been a majority in favour, culminating in a revolt led by Ken Toon of South Derbyshire. At a meeting of the NEC it was claimed (and not overruled by Gormley) that Areas with a majority in favour of the scheme had the right to go ahead with their own local incentive schemes. Lancashire, Leicestershire, the Midlands and Nottingham quickly organised local ballots approving the move. The dam was broken. Durham soon followed along with the rest. This was a development of huge consequence. It sowed seeds of distrust within the NUM, and – in the new autonomy granted to Areas – questioned its status as a national union as opposed to a loose federation. It also raised doubts over the significance of its various decision-making bodies and their validity in the law courts.[11] Above all, perhaps, it changed things in the coal mines. With their wages directly linked to output, there was a clear incentive for face teams to increase the pace of work, often competing with each other and pushing up wages but also increasing tension within the mines.[12] To an extent the NUM's control over its members weakened – securing output restriction (an important weapon in the union's armoury) might be more difficult in the future. With the scheme in place in each of the Areas, output and productivity soared. In 1976 output per man-shift for the industry had stabilised at around 7.75 tonnes. It increased to reach 10.1 tonnes in 1982–83.[13] With more production there was also more dust. Tony Hall talked with local union officials and reported the views of one lodge secretary to the effect that 'We're getting cases of men in their forties with a bad dust problem. But it would be a brave man who would end the system.'[14] These were some of the costs incurred in solving the problems of production; but with the planned opening of the new mines in Selby in North Yorkshire and in the Vale of Belvoir, the output requirements of the new Plan for Coal were under control. It seemed – for a while at least – that the industry was back on an even keel. But even then, concerns were emerging over the capacity of the British economy to develop in ways that would support the scale of coal expansion envisaged in the Plan for Coal.

By this time Wilson had been replaced by James Callaghan, and it was he who had to deal with the 1976 budget crisis and subsequent devaluation, and the onerous conditions imposed by the IMF. In spite of strong opposition from the left in Cabinet,[15] Callaghan accepted the need to cut £8 billion of planned public sector expenditure, and to impose tighter controls over the expenditure of the nationalised industries. This effectively ended the modernisation plans for the steel industry agreed three years earlier, with major capacity expansion at the five main production complexes, and was severely to affect the planned agreement between the NCB and BSC, with obvious implications for the coking coal collieries of South Wales and Durham.[16] Just two years after its signing, the Plan for Coal was dangerously weakened. It was further threatened by a general change of government policy.

At the Labour Party conference that year Callaghan had talked of getting 'back to fundamentals', moving away from the Keynesian orthodoxy that you could 'spend your way out of recession'.[17] The squeeze on the public sector that followed produced strikes and led to the Winter of Discontent of 1978–79. It also set in train a rapid process of deindustrialisation, with a change of management at British Leyland leading to a succession of plant closures beginning in 1978 at Speke near Liverpool. Worker resistance, as at the Grunwick factory, saw the re-emergence of mass picketing, with the miners centrally involved. All this had a deep impact on the Tory Party and its plans for a new radical government to control trade union power.

The Tory Plan

After 1974, the defeated Tory Party had elected a new leader and began planning for a return to government, determined to avoid a repetition of the Heath debacle. It convened working parties and study groups to consider the implications of the failure of the 1971 Industrial Relations Act, and of the two national miners' strikes that followed. Among these groups, the one chaired by Nicholas Ridley produced a report that came to have major significance.

Ridley was the second son of the third Viscount Ridley, a Northumberland grandee and chairman of Northumberland County Council. His great-grandfather, the first Viscount, was a minister in the Disraeli government and home secretary in Salisbury's last government. So, Nicholas Ridley had deep family roots in the Tory Party. He was also very rich: his father had made a fortune in shipbuilding, and Ridley began his business career in what had been the family firm in Newcastle. There, he wrote in his autobiography, he learnt to hate socialism in any form, and trade unions in particular.[18] In 1973, he formed the Selsdon Group, described by Margaret Thatcher as 'Thatcherite before Thatcher'.

Unsurprisingly, the main report by Ridley's working group was concerned with the nationalised industries, now classified in relation to their potential threat to a Conservative government and the disruption that strikes could cause. In producing it, the group built on the work of the Civil Contingencies Unit established by Edward Heath, supported by the crisis management facilities of the Cabinet Office Briefing Room (COBRA). The report emphasised the need for strong budgetary accountability and for ministers to take full financial responsibility, while leaving the management to operate within these limits. It emphasised that denationalisation should not be attempted via a 'frontal attack', but that the monopolies should be broken up and fragmented 'by stealth'. The intensely political document was alert to the need for budgetary flexibility that would allow politically strategic settlements, including wage payments, to be made in response to workers' demands at key moments. More generally, its view of the nationalised industries was aggressive: a new Tory government would need to be prepared, because

> The civil service would resist it. The motivation of all concerned – from worker to Board chairman to Permanent Secretary – is to do the opposite. The key to doing it lies with top management . . . We should start now to recruit chairmen who will be sympathetic to our objectives.

A confidential annex outlined the strategy that the new government should take in relation to the trade unions and highlighted redundancies and closures as the likely cause of major conflicts. It considered that there would be such a dispute in the first eighteen months of the government and that in assessing such disputes the government should keep an eye open for an early victory in a vulnerable industry such as steel.

The miners were seen as the most significant group within the working class capable of challenging the government.

The most likely area is coal. Here we should seek to operate with the maximum quantity of coal stocks possible, particularly at the power stations. We should install dual coal/oil firing in all power stations where practicable as quickly as possible.

The report extended this to an overall strategy that focused on challenging 'the full force of communist disrupters', with a plan for battle 'on ground chosen by the Tories'. It included the need to make a range of contingency plans, including support for importing coal. More specifically, it identified the advantage of having 'good non-union lorry drivers' who could be 'recruited to cross picket lines with police protection'. The committee considered carefully the case for outlawing strike action and considered that this wasn't worth the trouble, as putting trade unions outside the law might occasion events (similar to those around the 1971 Act) that would produce solidarity between unions and across the working class. It recommended passing legislation to enable the state to 'cut off the money supply to the strikers and make the union finance them'.[19] This approach, aimed at weakening the resolve of potential strikers, was combined with a recommendation that the next government should establish a 'large mobile squad of police who are equipped and prepared to uphold the law against the likes of the Saltley Coke-works mob'. So prepared, the Tory Party went on to win the general election of 1979.

Thatcher: Act One

One of the first measures taken by the Thatcher government was the removal of capital export controls, which helped companies to 'off-shore', taking advantage of cheaper labour locations outside the UK. At the same time, the Treasury's extreme tightening of monetary policy and the high sterling exchange rate encouraged cheaper imports, causing British-based manufacturing plants to close at a horrific rate. In 1979 just over 7 million people were employed in manufacturing industries in the UK. By 1985, that number had dropped to 5.3 million, a decline associated with the implementation of new technologies and the rise of low-cost production facilities in the newly industrialising countries of the Pacific, affecting branches of manufacturing industry as diverse as clothing, vehicles and chemical manufacture.

There had been factory closures before, but in the post-war decades these usually involved a period of short-time work followed by temporary lay-offs until production started up again. These closures, in contrast, were permanent, reducing productive capacity, and were less a response to fluctuations in the national marketplace and more to do with the geographical reorganisation of production globally. This process of plant closure and the relocation of employment also attracted new plants to the UK, but these came nowhere near to replacing the manufacturing jobs that had been lost.

Both Durham and South Wales were deeply affected by this process, exacerbated by increasing restrictions that were being placed on the activities of the nationalised industries. There were dramatic changes at the British Steel Corporation under the management of American union buster Ian MacGregor. The entire works at Consett was closed in September 1980, followed by the loss of a further 11,300 jobs on Teesside. South Wales was hit even harder: BSC ended steel-making at Ebbw Vale and reorganised the Llanwern complex, leading to 8,500 redundancies, with another 3,300 job losses at the East Moors works in Cardiff and then 10,000 at the main installation at Port Talbot.[20] The west of the coalfield was also badly affected by the closure of DuPont's plant at Llanelli, which had employed over 1,000 workers. In Merthyr the well-established Hoover factory at Pentrebach made 2,200 redundancies, while jobs were shed on a regular basis from old and new installations across the area.

The pattern and scale of this collapse were illustrated most clearly in the North East, where old established companies such

as Vickers and Parsons joined new arrivals such as Plessey and
Courtauld in closing factories in Newcastle, Sunderland and
Spennymoor. GEC closed its plant at Hartlepool, while
Montague Burton shut down its tailoring establishments in
Gateshead and Sunderland. Timex closed in Washington New
Town, where RCA Records was saved by the sales increase that
followed the death of Elvis Presley. In the old mining villages,
such as Annfield Plain and Stanley, the chill wind was felt as
Ransome Hoffman Pollard closed, followed by Ever Ready.[21]
More generally there was also a recorded loss of over 2,000 jobs
across the sites run by English Industrial Estates. It was carnage.

There was irony mixed with the tragedy, most apparent when
Derek Foster, MP for Bishop Auckland, spoke against the closure
of the British Rail wagon works at Shildon in his constituency.
He reminded MPs that 'The Rocket ran from Shildon on its first
trip . . . We are talking about the destruction of the very birth-
place of the railway.'[22] On this day, he said, the discussion was
about the 'devastation of a very important town of over 14,000
people in County Durham. This destruction of a town comes
hard on the heels of the destruction of Consett, not 20 miles
away.' The government, he added, had, in its first three years, lost
more jobs than regional development policy had created in the
last fifteen.

As a consequence, and in contrast to the offensive strikes of
the seventies, workers and trade union organisers had, by 1982,
become preoccupied with *defensive* struggles which often
involved making major concessions. The defeat of the steelworkers' national strike was followed by unsuccessful local
campaigns to save the works at Corby and at Consett, as Derek
Foster had reminded the House of Commons. There were a
number of factory occupations in protest at closures, and others
involving broader campaigns to highlight the public consequences of the job losses, with the TUC organising national
marches in Liverpool, Glasgow and London. Nevertheless, at a
conference organised for trade unionists in Newcastle upon

Tyne, a view was expressed that UK trade unions were completely unprepared and incapable of resisting these plant closures, which differed so remarkably from what had gone before.[23]

As industrial consumption of coal fell by 15 per cent, the major investments to expand capacity in Selby and the Vale of Belvoir appeared as a threat, rather than a support, to the stability of the industry.[24] This trend was exacerbated by changes in the international coal market. In the wake of oil price increases, oil corporations had diversified into coal production, opening up large new export-oriented mines in the USA, Australia, South Africa and Colombia, and extending these operations to other countries, including Venezuela and Indonesia. This coal (of high quality and low price) was predominantly mined through large open-cast strip mines, and the surpluses began to be offered for sale in Europe. The British government loosened restrictions on allowable levels of imports, at a stroke further unravelling the logic of the Plan for Coal. It was in this context that the BSC, under enormous governmental pressure to restructure its operations, switched its ordering policy away from British coking coals to suppliers overseas. At the same time, the new Coal Industry Act introduced even stronger financial controls over the NCB. Taken together, these changes produced a crisis, to which the NCB reacted by announcing the closure of mines throughout 1980.

The NUM pursued its resistance to these decisions through the colliery review procedure, established in 1972 to operate within the consultative machinery established under the Nationalisation Act. The full procedure had rarely been used, with many union officials feeling that the appeal to the national board was often simply a case of 'going through the motions'. These appeals ended up in Room 16 in the NCB headquarters at Hobart House in central London, just behind Buckingham Palace. The large conference room, devoid of natural light, had become notorious as the place where so many colliery closures had been confirmed: it was known as 'the crematorium' in mining circles. There, on 10 February 1981, the whole NEC of the miners' union assembled for a regular meeting of the national joint consultative committee and heard a report from the chairman of the NCB on the crisis it faced, brought about by the new Coal Industry Act. In a confused and highly charged debate, Sir Derek Ezra explained that there needed to be cutbacks in production by as much as 10 mt. He wouldn't be drawn on how this was to be achieved, simply stating that this would become clear in statements in each Area. However, after being persistently pressed, he revealed that twenty-three pits would be closed. Emlyn Williams, president of the South Wales Miners, was almost lost for words and remembers exclaiming, 'We have been here before, Mr Ezra, to discuss a colliery closure, and for our part we have always done our best to be reasonable and constructive. But *twenty-three collieries . . .*'

South Wales was likely to be worst affected. The previous day an Area conference, called in anticipation of the NCB's announcement, had sanctioned strike action in defence of the threatened mines. At that meeting Williams had said: 'I wouldn't call it a strike. I would call it a demonstration for existence.'[25] Such a demonstration took place outside the NUM offices on Euston Road in London, when a large contingent from South Wales joined others in demanding that the NEC supported a similar response. It did so, unanimously passing a resolution that 'If any attempt is made to put these plans into effect either in individual areas or collectively, the National Executive Committee will recommend through a ballot vote that the members take national strike action.'[26] The following day it was announced that five pits would close in South Wales and four in Durham.

The reaction in South Wales was swift. One of the threatened pits, Coegnant, took immediate strike action. An Area conference on 16 February endorsed the NEC resolution and recommended an immediate stoppage of work across the coalfield. In Durham there was strike action in each of the other threatened mines – Bearpark, Sacriston, Houghton and Boldon – with a demonstration outside Redhills before a delegate

Map 4. Working Collieries, 1981

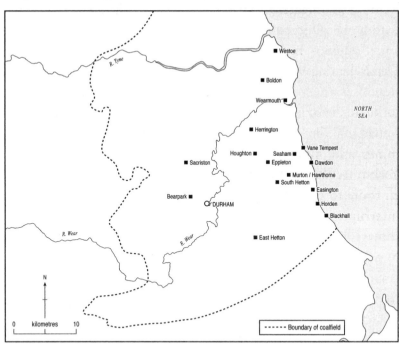

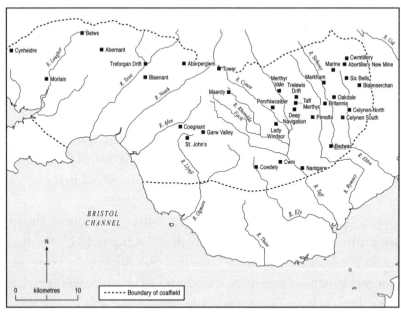

conference on 14 February, which also endorsed the NEC resolution and threatened strike action if the closure list was not
withdrawn. Dissatisfied with this response, the miners at Boldon
and Sacriston picketed the Area offices, demanding further
action in line with that taken in South Wales. This militant
response reflected changes that were taking place within the
Durham Area, most notably in the formation of a rank-and-file
'broad left' group, based on union activists at the large east coast
mines and influenced by the developments taking place in
Yorkshire. When Alan Mardghum was picked up at his home,
en route to one of their meetings, he announced, 'They've just
interrupted *Coronation Street* to say that the strike is off. That
shows how important all this is. They never interrupt *Coronation
Street* . . .' David Howell, minister of energy, had called an
emergency meeting with leaders of the NUM to inform them
that the government had agreed to review the situation while
reducing coal imports from 8 million tonnes to 5.5 million
tonnes over the next year, and to provide more money for the
NCB, which was struggling as a result of the withdrawal of
operating subsidies after the 1980 Act. As a result, the programme
of pit closures, announced a week earlier by the NCB, was
dropped. In this context the NUM president, Joe Gormley,
advised against an indefinite strike by the nation's 240,000
miners.

The NEC agreed. In both Areas there was a feeling of relief
but not elation at having scored a victory. In South Wales there
were many who thought that the strike should carry on, but
only seven lodges supported them. More generally, there was a
feeling that this was merely the calm before the storm, perhaps
a repeat of the pyrrhic victory of Red Friday in 1925. It was a
realistic appraisal of the situation. Behind the scenes, the
Conservative strategy that had been carefully formulated in
opposition remained very real and focused on the longer term.
A cold assessment of the situation within Whitehall had simply
concluded against fighting a strike that could not be won on the

Tories' preferred terms. Their hopes that the closure announcement would divide the NUM had proved groundless, and everything else was in favour of the union.

In spite of her emphasis on the autonomy of markets, Thatcher was very aware of the power of the state and was closely involved in all issues relating to disputes in the coal industry. Michael Portillo remembers that he was in the room when she gave the instruction to 'buy off the National Union of Mineworkers to stop the strike.'[27] When asked to explain the government's climbdown, industry secretary John Biffen famously remarked that he 'hadn't come into politics to be a kamikaze pilot!' He added, thoughtfully, that in his view it was the job of government to dissuade people from using their 'decisive power'. Thatcher, however, had a different view:

> It was the stocks at the power stations that were important, and these simply weren't sufficient . . . It became clear that all we could do was to cut our losses and live to fight another day, when – with adequate preparation – we might be in a position to win.[28]

This apparent climbdown by the government convinced many of the coalminers that the threat of militant strike action would bring results. But there remained a belief that the Plan for Coal, carefully negotiated with the previous government, would remain as a bulwark for the industry against market fluctuations and external instabilities. This proved to be groundless.

Encouraging Redundancy

After the stand-off in 1981, the NCB proceeded with a dual strategy of maintaining output levels while, at the same time, closing mines. This was achieved through the incentive payment scheme, supported by an 'exit strategy' for the miners, implemented through redundancy payments and intimidation.

Redundancy payments were introduced into British industry by the Labour government of Harold Wilson, through the 1965 Redundancy Payments Act. Before that time, highly unionised workforces had resisted redundancy and had been able to impose their own controls through the system known as 'last in, first out' (LIFO). While often presented as offering financial benefits to workers as they changed jobs, the main aim of the Act was to break this area of worker control, which had become known as 'labour market inflexibility'.[29]

In 1980 the Conservative government, through an Act of Parliament, reintroduced the Redundant Mineworkers Payment Scheme (RMPS), which significantly increased the severance payments available to coalminers above the level provided under the 1965 Act. These payments were to be routinely increased at key points throughout the next decade. This became linked to a loosening of the rules of the Mineworkers' Pension Scheme, lowering the age at which men could access their pension funds. Added to this, mine managers were prepared to be extremely flexible in the interpretation of the rules in order to facilitate redundancies and mine closures.[30]

In this way, coalminers were presented with the offer of a large redundancy payment alongside the threat of it being time-limited and possibly withdrawn. This often proved decisive for men who wanted to leave the industry and who thought that there might be other employment for them. For those with personal reasons for leaving, the payment came as an unexpected bonus, with 'taking redundancy' and 'the lumper' (lump sum) becoming part of the local vernacular. For those who wanted to stay in the industry, however, the fear wasn't only the loss of the payment but also that jobs on the coalfaces in the 'receiving pits' to which they would be transferred would soon dry up. This was experienced as a critical pressure and one that was orchestrated by local pit managers, who had become expert in presenting the early closure of a colliery as beneficial to the men who worked there. These tactics proved successful throughout 1982, when UK collieries and especially the coking coal mines of Durham and South Wales continued to close with many men leaving the industry, for the most part into an early retirement. A decade after the victory in 1972 things were beginning to look very different and the future of both Areas was filled with uncertainty.

Trouble Ahead

After a war in the South Atlantic, another general election victory in June 1983 increased Thatcher's majority in Parliament and strengthened her position in the country. In the new government Nicholas Ridley was moved into the Cabinet as minister of transport. There were other changes. The Downing Street Policy Unit enrolled a very different director to take over from Ferdinand Mount: John Redwood was a merchant banker with deeply monetarist views on the economy and on the role of trade unions. He would come to play a critical role.[31] In addition, a number of special advisers were recruited, including David Pascall of British Petroleum, and John Wybrew of the Royal Dutch Shell Group, both joining the unit on secondment. The UK's two major oil producers were thus in key positions of influence. Both were known for their strong opposition both to nationalisation and to active trade unionism within their drilling operations, and both were operating in direct competition with the coal industry. They were joined by Peter Warry, chief executive of British Energy, the company that operated the UK's nuclear power stations and another of coal's competitors. The stage was set for the next act in the unfolding drama.

The government had held back from an earlier confrontation with the miners because it felt coal stocks at the power stations had been insufficient. This was no longer the case, and there were those who were alert to the risks posed by the build-up of power station stocks. One of these was Dennis Skinner. Talking with him in the House of Commons at that time he expressed his concern that:

> They're producing too much coal, too much coal. 'Leave something for tomorrow' is what the old miners used to say. There's too much coal coming out of those mines.

Much of this coal was being stockpiled at the power stations, and there was a savage irony in the miners literally digging the grave of their industry.

CHAPTER FIVE

Conflagration: The State Against the Miners

The dispute was clearly a battle to save the trade union movement against a political decision once and for all to weaken the movement so that it would not hinder a free market economy. Otherwise what was the Ridley Report about? . . . It is my opinion that the political/industrial consequences of the Ridley Report were not fully understood by many of the leadership of the miners, and certainly not by the TUC.

Stephen Kendal, coal industry chaplain, 1985

In 1984 the coalminers began a strike that lasted a year. The strike directly involved over 200,000 workers and their families, including all of those in South Wales and Durham. It was a national strike, but not all of the country's miners participated. A complex affair overlaid with deep political divisions, the strike combined animosity and mutual aid in equal measure, its internal dynamics played out in a bitter conflict with the various apparatuses of the British state. During the strike over 20,000 miners were arrested or hospitalised. Two were charged with murder.[1] Over 200 miners served time in custody, including the president of the Kent Miners, who spent two weeks in jail. A total of 995 miners were victimised and sacked.[2] Two miners were killed on picket lines, two died on their way there and in

Yorkshire three teenage children died foraging for coal. In the coalfield areas convoys of police vans – forty or fifty at a time, with motorcycle outriders – became regular features of the roads and motorways, creating an extremely oppressive atmosphere. Mining villages were cut off by the police. People talked of having their 'backs against the wall' as they stayed on strike to save their pit. At the time of the strike the National Coal Board (NCB) had 174 working collieries, with a labour force of 230,000. Within ten years they would almost all be gone.

Already by 1984, the coalfields of Durham and South Wales had changed remarkably. Their central place in the industry had been diminished by the closures of the sixties, and mines had continued to close even under Labour's new Plan for Coal. The major industrial investment under the Plan had taken place elsewhere, in what had become established as the central coalfield, in the Midlands and Yorkshire, as the NCB increasingly focused on the power station market. In contrast Durham and South Wales, as part of the periphery, received much lower investment and endured continuing colliery closures.[3] In Durham the mines that remained were concentrated along the eastern seaboard, where in Easington Colliery village, for example, over 90 per cent of male employees worked in the mine. Inland small collieries remained, and also a large coke works at Derwenthaugh in the Derwent valley. The general picture, though, was one of eastern concentration, with miners living in the centre and west of the county travelling quite long distances to their new mine, and becoming remote from the activities of the union lodge. This contrasts with South Wales, where, although the coalfield was similarly diminished, the mines (and mining jobs) that remained were spread more evenly from east to west, with clusters of dense employment built up around Abertillery, Mountain Ash, Maesteg and Ystradgynlais. This produced two very different coalfield patterns, with clear implications for trade union organisation.[4]

Prelude

When miners talk about the 'great strike' of 1984 they rarely fail to mention what happened in the preceding years. The national leadership of the NUM was adamant that there was a plan to close a large number of collieries (Scargill referred to it as a 'hit-list') and that without strike action it could not be stopped. Almost all of the Area leadership shared this assessment. In Nottingham the newly elected secretary Henry Richardson was a strong proponent of this view and like his president Ray Chadburn, was clear that while mines in Nottingham were more secure than most, none were completely safe. In South Wales the leadership had been particularly disheartened by the low level of response to an earlier strike call in January 1982, with Emlyn Williams fearing that 'the leadership is ahead of the rank and file and this is not a healthy situation'. His predecessors had had similar worries and they had seen the problem to lie with an 'anti-struggle' movement within the Labour Party.[5] However it was obvious that events were bearing down on them which presented an opportunity for organised resistance.

On 21 February 1983 a sit-down strike took place at the threatened Lewis Merthyr Colliery. Led by the Area's vice president, Des Dutfield, who worked at the mine, it came at a propitious time. For many months the Area leadership had been developing a strategy to secure the continuance of mining in South Wales. It had threatened the NCB with an Area strike in January unless there was agreement to increase investment in threatened mines and recommence recruitment. The Board backed down and agreed to the NUM's demands and the strike was called off in spite of stern opposition from the militant lodges. Their opposition proved justified when those promises were broken, confirming the perfidy of the Board and for some, the gullibility of the leadership. Into this intense and emotional situation was hurled news of the intention to close Lewis Merthyr. Amid considerable anger seven lodges (Britannia,

Coedely, Maerdy, Penrhiwceiber, St Johns, Trelewis Drift and Tower) came out on strike in support of the Lewis Merthyr men and they were joined by the rest when an Area ballot on 24 February confirmed support for industrial action. By the end of a long February, South Wales miners were on strike again. The hope was that by their actions they would ignite support from miners across the country.

In order to achieve this, delegations were sent to speak at meetings in the other coalfields. Dai Davies and Charlie White travelled to Durham to speak to a delegates meeting which responded positively to their account of the situation in South Wales and the need for strike action. They agreed that the executive would move this forward but cautioned that while *their* support was complete it shouldn't be assumed that their members were of the same mind. At that time there was a feeling, especially in the Wearmouth colliery, that the face workers were cutting coal and earning bonuses with a regularity that insulated them from any discussion of the future of the industry. It was a similar story in Nottingham and, in a way, this was to be expected. However, what was not foreseen was the lack of enthusiasm for strike action in the Yorkshire Area, something which St Johns lodge secretary Ian Isaac was to describe as a 'very bitter experience' creating a sense of abandonment.[6]

At this point the Area leadership had two possible courses of action. The official strike could continue with South Wales standing out as a beacon of protest against mine closures, or it could ask the NEC to call a ballot for a national strike on the issue. It chose the latter, although the reports received from the other coalfields could not have inspired confidence in the result.

There would be a national ballot. The NUM President Arthur Scargill spoke to a packed meeting in Sunderland, uproarious in its support of the strike. With miners in South Wales remaining on strike, two thousand of them travelled to all the pits in the country on the day of the ballot, arguing for support. Tony Ciano travelled further than most, from Cynheidre to Easington, where he was well received. He spent the night in the canteen talking with men as they came on and off shift, explaining the situation in South Wales and how this was an issue that would affect them all.

It was to little avail. The ballot result revealed that 61 per cent of the miners had voted against strike action. Only in Kent and South Wales was the required 55 per cent majority exceeded. South Wales, of course, voted strongly in favour – 68 per cent – with some lodges registering huge majorities (94 per cent in Penrhiwceiber). But there was no avoiding the conclusion that they were on their own. In Durham there remained a consistent and large majority voting against strike action, confirming the Area's position on the right wing of the NUM – that deeply ingrained 'moderation' crafted under Sam Watson's leadership – while in Nottingham, the 'Yes' vote fell to a new low of 19 per cent. It was the third consecutive defeat within a year in ballots calling for national strikes (see Table 4) and had a deeply demoralising effect, especially in South Wales but also for the nascent rank and file leadership in Durham where some people talked of 'packing it in'.

At the time, some felt that South Wales had made a strategic mistake in calling for the ballot and that the strike should have been allowed to continue, drawing more miners directly into the dispute as had happened in 1981. With a general election in the offing, it would have been politically a more propitious moment. Also, Norman Siddal was not the kind of Chairman envisaged in the plan outlined by Ridley. He was someone unlikely to risk wrecking the industry, so much so that Ben Curtis has concluded that 'the Lewis Merthyr strike was in itself a turning point where history refused to turn'.[7] What the strike revealed most clearly perhaps was the uneven way in which the mining crisis was playing out across the coalfield, and the corrosive impact of the incentive scheme on the collective national solidarity that had built up in the union between 1969 and 1974. The task for the NUM leadership, nationally and regionally, was to find a way of uniting the membership in opposition to the closures that were to come.

Table 4. NUM national ballots, results by
          Area (percentages), 1982–83

BALLOT	January 1982 wage claim		November 1982 overtime ban		March 1983 closures	
	Yes	No	Yes	No	Yes	No
Durham	46	54	31	69	39	61
Durham Mechanics	32	68	22	78	32	68
South Wales	54	46	59	41	68	32
Yorkshire	66	34	56	44	54	46
Scotland	63	37	69	31	50	50
Nottingham	30	70	21	79	19	81
National	45	55	39	61	39	61

There was anger in South Wales over the lack of support from other regions, the results in Scotland and Yorkshire being seen as particularly hurtful. Many agreed with the conclusion arrived at by Tyrone O'Sullivan, lodge secretary of Tower Colliery: 'In future we don't want another ballot. We must use the mandate that was used in the last ballot. We should say "no more ballots in South Wales"'. Looking northward, however, they took encouragement from some of the changes that were taking place in Durham. The visits in early 1983 had been a positive experience, and led to more formal links between lodges in the two Areas. Tower, for example, 'twinned' with Easington, and a delegation from the east coast village travelled to Aberdare in the autumn of 1983. Similar links were made between St John's and Wearmouth. The weekend schools organised for miners in South Wales were opened up to delegates from Durham, with Welsh miners attending a similar school in the North East. Several groups travelled from South Wales in July 1983 to attend the centenary gala of the Durham Area. Delighted by the festivities, many expressed surprise that this was their first visit to what was an exceptional mining occasion. These contacts encouraged a view that the miners in Durham were increasingly supportive of a more militant approach to the crisis facing the industry. Arthur Scargill had again been elected to speak at the gala and was well received. In the recent election for the miners' representative on the National Executive Committee (which was normally dominated by the full-time officials), Easington Lodge chairman Bill Stobbs had emerged as the successful candidate. Then, remarkably, Bill Etherington, a known militant, was elected to the leadership of the historically moderate Durham Mechanics. The gravity of the crisis and the threat posed to the pits in the North East seemed to be affecting the way people thought about the future.

In the midst of all this, collieries continued to close. Brynlliw, Blaengwrach, Wyndham Western, Lewis Merthyr and Britannia all closed in 1983. In Durham it was a similar story, as the closures of Eden, Houghton, East Hetton and Marley Hill were followed by the rundown of Blackhall, one of its large coastal collieries, the reserves of which became linked to the adjacent Horden mine, resulting in many redundancies. The growing concern over the future of the Northern Area was confirmed in an NCB document that questioned the future of the Herrington and Eppleton collieries as well as the giant Hawthorn-Murton complex. Perhaps these were the shocks needed to make people seriously consider their futures in the industry. It certainly focused minds on the executives of both the Miners' and Mechanics' Unions, with Etherington maintaining a strong vocal presence. In the rank-and-file groups of left activists there was a feeling that the time was coming when Durham would have to make a stand.

But it was going to be difficult. As Emlyn Williams reflected in his presidential address to the South Wales Area in May 1983:

> The most difficult thing in the mining industry is to get coalfield solidarity for action over a single pit, particularly when

the men in that pit can be relocated to other pits or given redundancy payments which act like bait to a fish.

In attempting to build a platform of resistance to closures the NUM and its local lodges had formulated the idea of a *job* as a collective possession, insisting that 'no one has the right to sell his job' and emphasising the impact of job losses upon mining localities highly dependent upon employment in the industry. This was developed more broadly through the Campaign for Coal, a series of information and discussion pamphlets put together by the national office of the NUM as an aid to workshops and local meetings, taking the arguments beyond its own membership. The campaign focused on the general advantages of coal mining to local areas and the wider economy, in addition to the jobs in the mines. There was opposition, however. In Durham, at Labour Party meetings in Peterlee in the east, the chair argued that deep mining couldn't and shouldn't be saved, as 'no man should be expected to work underground in those conditions'. In Stanley in the west of the county, local councillors were vociferous in their criticisms of the NUM leadership, believing that the region needed to move away from coal as part of a broader modernising agenda.

The miners were in a hard place. Across both Durham and South Wales, 1984 dawned with little hope that prospects for coal mining would improve. Nevertheless, there seemed to be a growing resolve to prevent the worst from happening.

Closures, Mining and the NUM

Arthur Scargill had been elected president of the NUM in December 1981. He had fought the election on a platform of resistance, promising an end to what he described as the 'collaborationist approach' of the union. His victory was overwhelming, polling 70 per cent of the vote. Under the rules, each of the Areas and groups within the NUM was able to nominate, and Durham and South Wales, along with ten others, had both gone for the Yorkshire president. The campaign for his election was built upon a pamphlet, *Miners in the Eighties*, that carried a supporting foreword from Will Paynter strongly approving of the pamphlet's opening sentence: 'Britain is in a deeper crisis now than at any time since the Industrial Revolution', wrote Scargill, addressing the problem of rampant deindustrialisation, with

> our steel, engineering, machine tools, car and textile industries . . . being systematically destroyed . . . There is no solution in sight. Tory policies are accelerating the decline and destruction; our whole future is being sacrificed for the sake of monetarist political dogma . . . The coal industry and British miners are at the centre of this political maelstrom and if the decline continues the coal industry could suffer by default if not by design.

Looking back to the events of February, when the government had withdrawn the list of mine closures when faced with strike action, Scargill noted that pits (many of them on that earlier list) continued to close.

> In South Wales collieries are being put back on the list. In the North East and Nottingham pits are being closed in spite of the apparent guarantees at the time when the list was withdrawn. These pit closures will only be stopped if there is a determination on the part of our membership to resist.

He concluded that 'the NUM must demand an undertaking and signed agreement from both the government and the Coal Board guaranteeing that no pit shall close unless on the grounds of exhaustion.'[8]

Scargill had developed these arguments in large meetings around the coalfields, where they had met with considerable support and applause. After the defeat in the February ballot in

1983 he concentrated his attention upon the 'hit-list' of collieries that had been identified by the NCB for closure. He was supported by Michael McGahey, who, unable to stand for president by the age-limiting rule change that Gormley had introduced, had been elected to the position of vice president. The two worked closely together and were joined in 1983 by Peter Heathfield, the left-wing Derbyshire official elected as the replacement for Lawrence Daly as general secretary. For the first time in its history the three key national officials of the NUM were from the left of the union. The balance within the NUM had shifted toward Scargill's view of the threat facing the industry and the union. His sense of a strengthened position was buoyed by the considerable informal support received from contacts with NCB managers at all levels of the organisation, who shared many of his concerns and had deep worries for their own futures. These views of industrial decline seemed to be supported by the findings of a report on the coal industry published in 1983 by the Monopolies and Mergers Commission (MMC). Ordered by the Thatcher government in the previous year, it identified the presence of a long, loss-making tail of high-cost collieries. The likelihood that this would lead to pit closures on a massive scale seemed even more believable after the retirement of Norman Siddall and the appointment of Ian MacGregor as chairman of the Board.

Siddall had taken over from Derek Ezra in 1982 but retired early after fifteen months. He was seen by Martin Adeney to have

> typified much of the best of the old NCB – an encyclopaedic knowledge gained from starting at the coalface, coupled with an understanding of the importance of human relations and pit communities. But he also epitomised the house management style – gruff, blunt-spoken, introspective and impatient at the restrictions imposed by politics.[9]

His view of industrial relations was that 'if someone is looking for a fight the best thing is not to give him one'. MacGregor's view in contrast was to bring on the fight, the sooner to get it over with. A Scottish emigré to the USA, he had cut his managerial teeth fighting strikes in the coal and metal industries there. He had returned to the UK to assist in the restructuring of British Leyland and then BSC, where he earned the sobriquet 'Mac the knife'. To the coalminers his appointment was, in a word, incendiary. Nothing could have done more to convince them of the validity of Scargill's predictions and of the need to prepare for strike action. As one Durham miner put it at the time, 'it was when they appointed MacGregor that I began to think that Scargill was right and that we were in for a bad time.'

MacGregor at Hobart House

On 1 September 1983 Ian MacGregor took up his position as chair of the NCB. Sticking determinedly to his belief in 'management's right to manage' and brooking no interference by trade unions, he had become renowned in American business circles as a skilful and relentless breaker of strikes. Eric Varley, then industry minister in the Callaghan government, remembered that:

> He had a record of industrial efficiency and overall performance . . . He was saddened by the fact that . . . our role in the world was going down. He wanted to contribute and believed he could, based on his US experience. That is how he was encouraged.[10]

Before coming to the NCB, MacGregor had left his mark on two other state-owned companies, locating the 'British disease' in low productivity and uncontrolled trade union activity. He quickly assessed the situation at the NCB. Relying on the MMC report (which he came to refer to as his bible) he decided on a plan of large-scale redundancies and colliery closures that could be used, in part, to fund wage increases for the miners who remained.

Following the announcement of MacGregor's appointment, a miscellaneous Cabinet committee (MIC101) was set up to monitor the coal industry. This was transformed into the Cabinet Ministerial Group on Coal (CMGC) on 14 March 1984, chaired by the prime minister and attended by ministers responsible for each of the key departments of state.[11] Its membership makes clear how centrally concerned the government was with the detailed management of the strike. On 15 September the minister of power, Peter Walker, was able to report to the meeting the view of the new NCB chairman that:

> Closures produce considerably greater economies than the results of practicable pay moderation. Mr MacGregor had it in mind over the three years 1983/85 that a further 75 pits would be closed . . . There would be no closure-list but a pit-by-pit procedure. The manpower at the end of that time in the industry would be down to 138,000 from 202,000.

In this plan, therefore, 60,000 miners would lose their jobs (updates were to increase the rate and pace of closure), a number that was in line with the NUM's estimates and often repeated by Scargill. This would include everyone on the Kent coalfield, two-thirds of Welsh miners and 48 per cent of those working in the North East. Scotland would also be badly affected, and South Yorkshire too, given the previous massive expansion at Selby. The committee understood that this was highly sensitive information that needed to be treated in the strictest confidence. As we shall see, the content of the plan was persistently denied by MacGregor, who would continue to insist that Scargill was exaggerating the threat and misleading his members.[12]

MacGregor was the perfect tool for Thatcher – an 'invader' from another place and culture who had no understanding of or sympathy for the feelings and established culture of the coal industry. What was at stake, in his view, was 'our right to manage and our fundamental responsibility for the bottom line'.[13] For him the NCB resembled a government department rather than a business; he thought of Ezra as 'a committee man *par excellence*', while Siddall 'had learned to be concerned about upsetting the union'. This attitude was anathema to MacGregor, who wrote in near disbelief:

> The traditional school in Hobart House believed that it should not do anything that upset the NUM. At its most extreme this view was expressed in the opinion – held by many of the younger people in the building – that far from upsetting the NUM, we should always seek to make an accommodation.[14]

In building support for his position, the new chairman began to establish links with the regional directors, identifying those who shared his ideas and who could be relied upon in the impending clash. Men like Albert Wheeler in Scotland, Ken Moses in Derbyshire and David Archibald of the North East Area were firm allies, whereas Phil Weekes was too close to the trade union in South Wales. MacGregor altered the Board too, recruiting new independent members. Here, he was offered considerable help and advice: David Young, for example, head of the Manpower Services Commission, suggested that he approach Tim Bell at Saatchi and Saatchi to help with the NCB's public relations during the strike. This appointment produced 'consternation at all levels and hysteria from Geoff Kirk [PR director], who shouted: "You can't use him . . . he works for the Tories"'. More significant, perhaps, was MacGregor's association with the Eton-educated property speculator and former bankrupt David Hart. They met at a meeting of the Institute of Economic Affairs, with MacGregor already familiar with Hart's brother through his position at Lazard's in New York. Much younger than MacGregor and with an exaggerated, flamboyant style – his nickname was Spiv – he became invaluable, building support for, and

confidence in, plans to break the strike that went well beyond the
normal industrial relations practised by the Board. He was
particularly influential in Nottingham where he collaborated
with the miners who opposed the strike, assisting in the removal
of the established NUM leadership.[15]

The Strike Begins

The crisis struck on 1 March 1984, when George Hayes, the
South Yorkshire Area director, announced that the mine at
Cortonwood was to close. The timing of the announcement was
odd, coming as it did ahead of the national consultation committee meeting scheduled for 6 March. The decision had not
followed the accepted procedure and it involved a colliery that
had, in the preceding months, been identified as one with a guaranteed working life, fit to receive men from other closed mines.
MacGregor's account of the decision as being insignificant isn't
convincing, and there is little doubt the response in Yorkshire
had been anticipated. The men at the pit went on strike and the
Yorkshire Area, drawing upon an earlier ballot vote, called for an
official Area strike to begin on 9 March. By the time the national
consultation committee met in Room 16 in Hobart House to
announce plans for a reduction of capacity of 4 million tonnes,
miners' pickets from Yorkshire had travelled into the Midlands
coalfields of Nottingham, Derbyshire and Leicestershire asking
for support in the way they had done in 1969. On 8 March, the
NEC supported the Yorkshire strike – as it was entitled to under
Rule 41 of the union – and Scargill called on other Areas for
support.[16]

In South Wales, the miners' disillusionment over the lack of
support they had received for their own strike the year before had
led to resistance to further industrial action in the pits. At an
Area conference of lodge delegates held on 9 March, everyone
agreed the coalfield was in a new and critical situation, but many
felt that it would be difficult to persuade their members to come

out again and on an indefinite strike. However, in response to an impassioned speech by general secretary George Rees ('strike now or say goodbye to South Wales forever') there was a unanimous vote in favour. A similar conference of delegates was held in Durham on the same day. The executive committee considered the future of the coalfield, with the specific threat to the Herrington Colliery, and recommended strike action to take place from Monday 12 March. After a heated debate, the vote at the Area council was tied and finally passed with the casting vote of the chairman – Area president Harold Mitchell – who was bound by his executive's recommendation. Here too there was concern about the vote in the lodges that would take place at the weekend.

In both coalfields the lodge meetings raised similar questions about the procedure, about the likely outcome and about a future national ballot. In South Wales, remarkably, eighteen of the twenty-eight pits, many of them threatened with closure, voted *against* strike action. Complicated feelings were at work here, but the events of the previous year had a weighty influence. People recalled that deputations to the Yorkshire mines hadn't always been well received, and there was mention of bad experiences at Cortonwood. Everyone remembered that barely half of the Yorkshire miners had voted in support of South Wales in the national ballot, so to ask 'why should we support them now?' was to be expected. However, by the Sunday, with Yorkshire and Scotland on strike and likely to be joined by Durham (and Kent) the strategic implication of these votes was becoming clear. Far from leading the attack against closures, as Rees had planned, there was a possibility that the South Wales Area, renowned for its tradition of militancy and clear thinking, would be isolated. Here the 'unofficial' and decentralised tradition of the Area came into play; this time with the clandestine support of the area officials. A meeting of rank-and-file activists was called in Hirwaun, determined to take forward the case for strike action by picketing all the mines across the coalfield. At the Rose Heyworth

(New Mine) Lodge in Abertillery a tempestuous meeting on the Saturday had ended acrimoniously, with many against strike action. On the Monday, however, the lodge minutes recorded that: 'Lodge officials met the men in the canteen and all went home except 32, after the day shift no other man worked except safety men.'[17] The news that other Areas had joined the strike played an important part in this; so too did the awareness of the Area's status and tradition within the NUM. These were the issues raised by the pickets – 'South Wales couldn't afford to be stood on the side-lines' – and with the support of respected local lodge officials and speakers from the Kent coalfield they proved to be decisive. All of the miners in South Wales joined the strike.

In Durham there was a different dynamic. The Area decision to call a strike was generally accepted, as the east coastal collieries combined with the more threatened inland pits in a near unanimous call for strike action. Here too a great deal rested on the stature and reputation of the lodge officials. At Easington a crowded meeting voiced suspicion of being bounced into a strike without a proper ballot. The officials focused on its youthful labour force, and emphasised the need to look to the long term. They eventually won the day. Easington and Durham would come out on strike until the time of a national ballot. At Murton, a threatened mine, the miners voted against striking. However, the lodge of the mechanics' union had gone the opposite way. As one of them explained, with some pleasure: 'I saw Geordie, he had come from the Special Meeting. He told me that the pit would be working as they had voted against the strike. I had to tell him that it wouldn't be working because we had voted to strike and we would picket them out!'. Seaham was the other anomaly. Both of the Area officials hailed from the Londonderry's stronghold, and here the three major mines – Seaham, Vane Tempest and Dawdon – voted against strike action. Nevertheless, the Area's decision was enforced on the Monday, initially through picketing. Subsequently, all of the Durham lodges observed the Area decision to strike.

In these rather different ways, South Wales and Durham entered a strike that was to last until the following March. Controversially, the NEC avoided the question of a national ballot, and instead referred the issue to a national delegate conference. This was a significant move and followed the one taken in the autumn of 1983 that had led to the imposition of an overtime ban. Many saw this decision by the NEC to be an abrogation of its responsibilities. For others, who had long criticised the NEC as unrepresentative, it was a positive democratic step involving the union's lay activists in a critical decision. The meeting took place in the City Hall at Sheffield on 19 April, six weeks after the strikes had begun, with thousands of striking miners thronging the streets with their banners and chants – 'here we go, here we go'. The meeting made two key decisions: it changed the percentage needed for victory in a ballot from 55 per cent to a simple majority, and decided overwhelmingly against balloting the membership for a national strike, instead allowing the strike to continue officially as a series of Area disputes. This was a permissible interpretation of Rule 41, and was influenced by the experience of South Wales in the previous year. It was also felt that, as the problem of pit closures affected some regions more than others, it was right to see it as an Area issue. The previous imposition of an Area-by-Area route into the incentive scheme also had a bearing. This had weakened the sense of national unity within the union, and it had also dented a belief in the integrity of the rule book.

However, not all of the Areas of the NUM decided to join in, with the Nottingham Area distinctive in its strong resistance to strike action. New pits were sunk there in the twenties and here (in the Dukeries) a deep pattern of paternalistic management was established within which the non-political unionism of Spencer had deep roots. The pits were modern, working high unfaulted seams, very different from those in Durham and South Wales. It was this Area too that had expanded production under mechanisation, recruiting men and families from Durham and

Scotland as the pits there closed. There had been none of the dramatic closure programmes experienced in those Areas, and it was expected that the industry would remain secure into the future. As a consequence of these and other factors, a ballot in Nottingham had seen 73 per cent responding negatively to the question 'Do you support strike action to prevent pit closures and the massive rundown of jobs?'. No lodge in the Area recorded a majority for strike action. However, many men were on strike there, and some stayed on strike after the ballot vote. This created a major division that the NUM could not resolve, and it became a central dynamic in the dispute and a central pillar in the strategy developed by the NCB and the government.

Strategic Routes

The strike placed both the NCB and the NUM on a war footing. Ian MacGregor talked of his 'field commanders' in the areas and of building 'second fronts' in the battle with Scargill's troops. To this end he established two committees, one of 'strategic warfare' and the other of 'economic warfare', which in combination would attempt to outmanoeuvre and financially wreck the NUM.

The NUM had no comparable command structure, and from the beginning Scargill had made it clear that in his view the miners could not win the strike alone.

> The forces opposing us, though wobbling, are strong. To defeat them it will take people and cash on a massive scale. Every sinew in every factory, office, dole queue, docks, railway, plant and mill will need to be strained to the maximum. Not tomorrow or the next day but now . . . What is urgently needed is a rapid and total mobilisation of the labour and trade union movement to take positive advantage of a unique opportunity to defend our class.[18]

Here, we see an echo of the experience at Saltley Gate and the need for the miners to receive the mobilised support of other organised workers. By this time, of course, the situation had altered dramatically (and the reference to the dole queue made this clear), particularly in the engineering industry that had provided the support twelve years earlier. In practice Scargill would now be looking to the old solidarities of the triple alliance (coal, steel and rail) with broader support from the transport unions, while also hoping for particular issues or events that would trigger wider support. The government and the NCB had changed too, and were united in the aim of *preventing* any of this happening by containing the dispute within the coalfields – isolating the NUM. MacGregor put it plainly when he described 'the tightrope we had to walk all the time to keep the miners' strike from becoming a national trade union issue'.[19] Here, the government had prepared the ground by facilitating an expensive wage settlement in the electricity supply sector. In the vexed area of transport, it had secured a settlement with the rail unions and Ridley himself, as minister of transport, intervened to assure the dockers that the National Dock Labour Scheme guaranteeing continuity of employment would be honoured by the government. This was in effect a lie: the scheme was abolished in 1989. More generally, the government, in order to be able to endure a long strike at a time of its choosing, had invested heavily in additional land to provide stocking sites for coal around power stations. Many of the coal-fired stations had also been adjusted to allow them to burn oil. All of this to ensure one thing – unlike in 1972, the lights would remain on during the strike.

The failure of the Nottingham Area to join the strike was a major bonus for the NCB, something that was appreciated by MacGregor: 'The key to the whole strike was Nottingham and its 31,000 miners. If we could keep this vast and prosperous coalfield going, then I was convinced, however long it took, we could succeed.'[20] In the first week of the strike, before Nottingham miners had voted in the Area ballot and while their pits were working, pickets had arrived from Wales, Kent and, mostly, from South Yorkshire. At this time the situation in the coalfield was uncertain, with the Area officials and their executive fully supportive of strike action, seeing it as the only way to prevent colliery closures in the Area. Brian Evangelista was deputy manager at Moorgreen Colliery, and he remembers that

> You had a lot of managers very sympathetic to the miners. *Very* sympathetic. The problem is that at a very senior level you had a lot of people vying to be the next Chairman. They wanted to be the biggest macho-man in the coalfields.[21]

MacGregor, incensed by news of Yorkshire miners picketing, met with the prime minister, telling her that he wished he 'had a bunch of good untidy American cops out there'.[22] At a meeting of the Cabinet committee that followed on 14 March, Thatcher made it clear that 'helping those who volunteered to go to work was not sufficient; intimidation had to be ended and people had to be free to go about their business without fear. It was essential to stiffen the resolve of Chief Constables.'[23]

This set the tone of the dispute, with the miners divided into honest men who wanted to work and the bully boys who wanted to stop them.[24] The distinction, once established in Nottingham, was linked to a policing policy that had deep effects across the coalfields. In a handwritten note on the minutes of the meeting of 27 March, Thatcher observed that 'it is important to distinguish between endurance with Notts and without. Endurance is significantly higher indicating the value of the police operation'.[25] The scale of the police power used in 1984 was enormous, and it had a major, even decisive, influence upon the outcome of the dispute, for undoubtedly MacGregor got what he asked for and more. The state was much better prepared for a national strike than it had been in 1972, and a national reporting centre (NRC) had been set up in the Home Office to coordinate help and provide assistance between chief officers of police in England

and Wales. On 5 April 1984, Douglas Hurd, the home secretary, was able to tell Parliament that since 14 March the NRC 'had co-ordinated the responses to requests from chief officers for assistance from their colleagues in policing related to the miners' dispute'. The controller of the NCR, David Hall, chief constable of Humberside, described this as 'the most mobile and sophisticated police reserve yet assembled in Britain'. Through its offices,

> Roadblocks monitored entry to the county, approaches to collieries and other NCB installations, as well as the NUM's own offices . . . to the annoyance and embarrassment of the Area leadership as it then stood. Helicopter and light aircraft patrols scanned the main road arteries. Large detachments of police blockaded each pit with, on one infamous occasion, as many as three thousand uniformed men mobilized at Harworth Colliery to control thirty pickets. It was a massive and effective response.[26]

In this way, the full resources of policing were made available to stop miners as they travelled together in cars or buses to picket in Nottingham, or to attend meetings or (even) appointments at law courts.[27] Half of all those arrested for picketing in the first three months of the strike related to incidents in Nottingham.[28] All this was exacerbated by the NCB's draconian dismissal policy. These linked processes of police restrictions, arrest and the actions of the courts, allied with common law actions, sequestration and receivership, began to exert a slow stranglehold upon the ability of the NUM to operate.

Meanwhile, David Hart continued to travel from his base at Claridge's hotel in London to the East Midlands in a chauffeur-driven Mercedes, talking with working miners. Hart was pushing for the establishment of a Working Miners' Committee in opposition to the NUM, and helped to provide the encouragement and financial support that enabled individual miners and small firms to take common law actions against the NUM.

Breaking Resistance

The summer of 1984 marked a turning point in the strike, beginning at Orgreave, a coking plant in South Yorkshire, on 18 June.
Orgreave produced coke for the steelworks at Scunthorpe and
the workers there were sympathetic to the miners but concerned
to protect their jobs and those in the steel plant. The situation at
the plant escalated as the NUM organised its first (and only)
nationally coordinated picket. The police were well aware of the
NUM's plan, and miners immediately noticed a new approach,
as their coaches were not being stopped but rather directed into
the throat of the valley in which the coke works was sited. Here
the miners were confronted by a battle line of police in riot gear.
Behind the line, police mounted on horses were visible, while
over to the right stood teams of dogs with their handlers. One
man from Bettws reflected that:

> We sat down in the field for over an hour, until about a quar-
> ter to eight, laying down in the sun, marvellous. There was a
> hell of a lot of pickets gathering. Well, by the time we realised
> it, it was too late. We were blocked in completely.[29]

This became clear when the police decided to clear the field with
the use of horses. At that point, one of the pickets described how
'it was set out like a military campaign', and one in which the
normal rules no longer seemed to apply. One man from
Abertillery explained that:

> A man came out with a loud hailer and said 'if you don't shift
> I'm going to charge you all with the Riot Act'. We were all
> going boo and shouting at him when all of a sudden, they
> opened up and the horses came. I tell you it frightened you to
> death.[30]

A reporter from Radio Sheffield remembered

looking up and suddenly seeing two lots of horse sweeping in from the left and right simultaneously on the pickets. It was like a scene of war, a battle. They swept, the police went forward. The miners obviously didn't realise what had hit them.[31]

After the horses came four aggressive advances by the riot police, with the customary banging of their shields with truncheons. One man from Maerdy explained how they were

a fearsome sight. I've never faced police like that before – never since the strike started . . . they came into us and there was no differentiating. They were catching a few older chaps who couldn't run . . . they were catching them, whacking them on the kidneys to put them down.[32]

Brave men admitted to being seriously scared by what was happening. Encouraged by the union president to turn back, one miner from Durham responded, 'I'm not going back down there Arthur – it's murder down there.' Ron Stoate, lodge secretary of the Penallta Colliery, remembers that the scale of the force and organisation that had been brought against them left him with the thought that: 'if they want it this bad they could have it!'

At Orgreave the NUM organised a mass picket on a par with the one they had formed at Saltley Gate in 1972. On this occasion, however, the closures of factories and steel plants meant that they were not joined by thousands of workers from other industries. And, in contrast to 1972, the police were well prepared. There can be no doubt that the intention was to give the miners a good beating and to make a number of exemplary arrests under the Riot Act.[33]

Tom Callan, the moderate, quietly spoken general secretary of the Durham Area, reflected later that:

Everyone concerned with mining communities had their eyes opened by the repressive power of the state as police rampaged

through our villages. Many young men are now languishing in
jail because of their fight for jobs and dignity. The Thatcher
government went to war against us – the working class – and
these courageous young men are prisoners of that war . . . We
owe these men a great debt.

Negotiations and Lies

Negotiations were recommenced with the NCB in July and the
talks involved a long semantic discussion during which it was
agreed that pits would be closed if they were exhausted or unsafe
but no agreement could be found on the definition of a third
category that the NCB wanted, or on the strengthening of the
review procedure.[34] Talking on the telephone at the time, Peter
Heathfield was clear that 'we've been on strike for six bloody
months, we're not going to be going back with nothing to show
for it. It would be 1981 all over again.' This view was supported
by MacGregor, who explained that, while he would have agreed
to withdraw the names of the five listed pits, this would not have
affected his commitment to exercising his right to manage the
industry as he felt necessary in the future.

This hard approach was combined with the subtleties of the
NCB's new propaganda machine that had begun with a large
advertisement on 'How the Miners on Strike have been Misled'.
A letter signed by the chairman was delivered to all miners'
homes. It explained that 'If these things were true I would not
blame miners for getting angry or for being deeply worried. But
these things are absolutely untrue. I can state categorically and
solemnly that you have been deliberately misled.' This, of course,
was another lie, framed by Tim Bell and part of the planned
'back to work movement'. Miners were being encouraged to
return to work with promises of wages, support and protection.

In Durham the strike held firm until the last week of August,
when one man who lived in Bowburn in the Durham City area
and had worked at the East Hetton Colliery at Kelloe before

transferring to Easington approached the pit yard in the bus provided by the NCB.[35] His access to the mine was resisted by hundreds of miners from the village, who barricaded the entrance. The lodge officials' request to speak with him was refused. He was surrounded by police and (breaking an agreement made by the local manager) was eventually secreted into the mine on the following day. He was a symbol, and for MacGregor another case of the honest man prevented from going to work by the 'bully boys'. Police from London flooded into the village, which was effectively sealed off, with all cars and buses turned back. One bus contained Tom Callan, who approached the police blockade to explain that he was the general secretary of the NUM. He was told, 'I don't care who the fuck you are – get back on the bus.'

At Wearmouth, the large mine in Sunderland, another crack opened in the miners' solidarity, with men beginning to return to work – encouraged by the NCB – through the massed ranks of police. Bill Etherington was particularly angered by the fact that the first of the Mechanics' members to break the strike there were men who were only in a job through the strong support and advocacy of the union. Two had been bad timekeepers and dismissed, the other had been disabled in an accident and 'the management, the same management that had wooed him back to work, said there was no job for him.' The active engagement of the Area management with striking miners continued and focused on those who were isolated from the lodges, living in the west of the county, with Wearmouth being particularly badly affected by the influx of men from the west.

In South Wales, and in contrast to Durham, the Area director continued to cooperate and share information with the NUM, in spite of continuing pressure for more to be done to break the strike. Overcoming their initial reluctance, the miners remained firm, revealing something of the spontaneous rationality that had come into play: *being on strike* created a dynamic of its own that was very difficult to break, when everyone was together and united. The only significant break in the resistance came at the

Cynheidre Colliery, located on the far western edge of the coal-field in the Gwendraeth Valley, drawing in miners from two villages. In early November a 'back to work' group became active there, making contact with David Hart. As a result, sixteen miners broke the strike, a number that was to increase to ninety, creating bitter feelings of anger and distrust.

In the autumn, therefore, the miners' union was pinned back, its funds frozen, its picketing strength weakened by court orders and demoralised by the police violence. Martha Gellhorn was living in Chepstow at the time and, after seeing TV images of the miners in dispute, the war correspondent decided to visit the scene. She journeyed to Newbridge in the eastern valleys and as a result of what she saw there, came to refer to the police as 'storm troopers'. In her considered view the source of violence was being 'systematically misrepresented in the media', because 'it was exactly like a war. They were fighting for their territory, their community. They said "if the mine closes the village dies." Mrs Thatcher had all the money and the power of the State against these people.'[36] This view was shared by one young man at the Nantgarw Colliery. Of his most powerful memory of the strike – recorded thirty years later – he said, 'the violence that was inflicted upon me and the violence I witnessed fellow miners receive will stay with me for the rest of my days.'[37]

Mining Communities

The logic that underpinned the government's approach to the mining industry and to the trade union contrasted with the views and experiences of NUM members and their families in what they called 'mining communities'. Here, there was a logic of support that challenged the logic of money and argued that the sustainability of these places as homes for children and old people was linked irrevocably to the durability of the coal indus-try. Here, the view of the strike, of what was happening and the meaning of it all, was very different. In mining communities it was recognised that work in the mine was hard and that there were better jobs; but in these places mining jobs were the best that could be had – and without them, the places would die. Viewed in this way, the strike was in an honourable cause, and one made all the more so by the treatment of the pickets and the cruelty of legislation which removed social benefits from strikers' families. It was this idea of a *just strike*, contrasting so sharply with the viewpoint of Thatcher and MacGregor, that helps to explain how opinion polling into the summer found consistent optimism among strikers and their families, and the belief that Scargill would deliver victory.

In this context, across both coalfields, various forms of support groups had emerged to give assistance to the strikers and their cause. These arrangements were seen by the *Financial Times* to involve something akin to an 'informal welfare state'. They lasted for a year, motivated by a determination that 'they won't be starved back to the pit'.[38] In South Wales, the men who worked at the Celynen Collieries in Newbridge were supported by a miners' wives group that helped maintain the strike until its end. These women remember the strike for the way it changed them and opened up new experiences. Dorothy Phillips saw herself as an 'ordinary housewife', yet she spoke at a large meeting at Exeter University as part of their fundraising activities. She was able to overcome her nerves with the anger she felt over the injustice of it all, especially the state withholding welfare payments in lieu of supposed (but nonexistent) strike pay.

> What the government did was to take away benefits from people on strike [they] would normally have been entitled to and this made some of them feel guilty, almost that if they were eating something, they were taking food off the tables of their wives and children. We set up a soup kitchen . . . and we started making meals so the men could eat and their families could eat.[39]

In Durham, in Easington District a community group called SEAM – Save Easington Area Mines – was set up before the strike had begun, influenced in part by the Campaign for Coal. Chaired by a district councillor, Heather Wood, the group organised meetings, lobbies and discussions and, once the strike was underway, became the main focus for coordinating the daily support for miners' families, organising regular meals in communal kitchens (500 meals a day, 800 in school holidays), distributing thousands of food parcels, speaking at meetings and involving people across the communities. A number of other support groups were established across the county, with the one in Durham City working through the local Labour Party. Vin McIntyre recalls:

> We supplied eight hundred parcels a week. We thought that there was maybe forty or fifty miners living in the Durham constituency, since all the mines had disappeared. But it turned out that there were close to a thousand miners living in Durham City, working on the coast . . . in the coastal pits. And because of the difficulty – they couldn't travel to the pits to get relief during the strike – it was agreed by all groups around the County meeting together, that support would be provided on the basis of where the miners lived rather than where they worked.[40]

In South Wales, while some miners also travelled to work there, the distribution of the pits meant that most of them still lived close to a working colliery. Siân James, for example, lived in the upper Swansea valleys, while her husband worked a good distance away at Abernant:

> So we chose to become involved with the Neath, Dulais and Swansea Valleys Miners' Support Group . . . a truly amazing group of people . . . organised around nine support centres, three located in each of the three valleys we were responsible

for, offering full support and welfare for just under a thousand individuals.[41]

It is clear that women were centrally (but not exclusively) involved in these activities and that for many of them it was a life-changing experience. Pat McIntyre was right to warn against exaggeration, stressing that the activists made up only a small minority of the women affected by the strike (perhaps 5 per cent), with many more staying at home or bringing in a wage.[42] But it was a significant minority. In Durham, and with the assistance of Bill Etherington and Ann Suddick from the office of the Durham Mechanics, the Durham Miners' Support Groups organisation was set up as a loose coordinating structure with regular meetings held at the miners' hall at Redhills. Mary Stratford remembers:

> I used to love going to those meetings . . . People used to do anything to get to those meetings. Because people could turn up and everybody had a voice. You had your voice and you could vote . . . I think that that was the best thing that ever happened because it stopped the trade union leaders . . . overtaking us.[43]

In all these ways, considerable support was provided in both areas to the families of the strikers. It was funded by ongoing collections and donations from individuals and groups, often far away from the coalfields, providing a new emotional and political dimension of the struggle. In South Wales, links through the Communist Party led to the Neath, Dulais and Swansea Valley Support Group linking with the London-based Lesbian and Gays Support the Miners (LGSM). In Durham, a strong link was made with the women at Greenham Common. More generally, union branches, community groups and university campuses across the UK linked up with NUM lodges and support groups. This support became critically important during the autumn as the NCB ratcheted up its campaign to encourage miners to break with the strike and the numbers of those returning to work slowly increased.[44]

In Durham, Bala Nair remembers the 'community spirit, the coming together of human beings . . . the number of people who came and just filled the trolley up' when standing outside Asda collecting for the miners' families. But in Stanley he also remembers:

> The quarrels that we had with the constituency Labour Party. A lot of us, including me, had the most, not bitter, but definitely very heated arguments because our constituency had to follow Neil Kinnock's dictates . . . that the miners should have gone back to work.[45]

Pat McIntyre's detailed account of these times reveals a Party organisation that was essentially moribund, with meetings dominated by elderly male local councillors who were, at best, lukewarm in their support for the miners on strike. Across the west of the county negativity dominated, with some meetings rejecting even the possibility of a 50 pence-per-week collection. Few Party members would agree to take part in street collections, while some (including several councillors) were hostile both to Scargill and the strike, wanting the men to return to work. When some did, much of the support for the strikers stopped.[46] Labour had inherited many of the centralised features of the DMA, with the rigid adherence to Party lines and the dominance of powerful men in key positions. On occasion this worked to the benefit of the support groups, because of the influence it gave to sympathetic individuals. Mick Terrens, an ex-miner, was leader of the Labour group on the County Council. On his own authority, he overruled the 'official' line to ensure that the school kitchens were kept open through the summer months, giving access to the support groups without insisting on a financial contribution.

The End

In the New Year, as confidence in a victory began to ebb and the viability of the NUM seemed to be threatened, yet another round of negotiations (this time involving the TUC) foundered on the same rock. Rumour spread that as the strike approached its anniversary men would automatically be dismissed under the 'twelve-month rule'. In both Areas, visitors to miners' homes were reporting severe distress, with threats of house dispossessions. South Wales general secretary George Rees was moved by a meeting of the Cynheidre Lodge in which one man pleaded, 'I have lost my wife, my family, my house, don't turn me into a scab.'[47]

The NEC met in February and, after considerable discussion, agreed that there was no alternative but for the men to 'stand firm' and for the strike to continue. But in South Wales, the union leadership and executive committee had come to regard this as untenable. It proposed a resolution recommending a national return to work without a settlement. The Area had been made aware of the possibility of large-scale breaks in the unity of the strike and the resolution was passed unanimously at an Area conference on 1 March. In Durham there were similar debates in the lodges and in the support groups. At Lumley, Mary Stratford remembers them asking:

> How much longer could people go on . . . they couldn't have gone on any longer and that was the only time that I disagreed with my brother and my husband throughout the strike . . . the vote had to be to go back. Because the only other option was to decimate the whole thing . . . because my family would have split . . . because nobody could go on any longer.

The strike at the Eppleton Colliery, that had formerly held out strongly, was in a state of collapse, to the anguish of the lodge officials. At Easington, where the majority of the men had stayed on strike for a year, there was a strong feeling that the men in the village could decide to return en masse. In these circumstances the lodge committee met to discuss the options and, overcoming the opposition of its chairman and NEC representative Bill Stobbs, decided to call a special meeting in which it would propose that the strike should end without an agreement and that this proposal should be taken to the Area executive. The proposal was supported, although many of the younger miners wanted to carry on. In Durham, concern was expressed about ending the strike without sacked men being reinstated, but the executive supported the resolution, with only Tom Callan, the general secretary, and Dave Hopper of Wearmouth Colliery, voting against.

A special delegates conference was called for 3 March at the headquarters of the TUC in London to discuss the future of the strike. It was a more sombre and acrimonious affair than the earlier one at Sheffield. On the South Wales resolution to end the strike without an agreement, the National Executive Committee had met the day before and the vote was split, with eleven on each side and the president refusing to use his casting vote. So there was no recommendation from the NEC. But the resolution was supported by Durham and it passed by the narrowest of majorities: ninety-eight votes to ninety-one.

The amazing strike was over. It had changed many people's lives and had a decisive impact on UK industrial relations. It was the last moment when trade union power was exercised as a coherent force in Britain. In its longevity and in the scale of local organising and support it stands as a landmark in post-war industrial history. If the 1972 strike could be compared with a 'minor nuclear attack', this one was more akin to trench warfare. It was held together with determination and endurance on both sides, and with the NCB radically changing the rules of the game that had previously been applied to strikes and industrial relations. The South Wales miners, after a reluctant beginning, remained the most comitted in their support of the strike and the NUM, with 95 per cent of them remaining on strike until the end. In

Durham the strike was weakened by the return to work of large numbers of men, many of whom lived in the west of the county far away from their lodges.

Epilogue

The strike would live on in people's memories and its consequences would be experienced in many different ways. Dave Parry, a young activist during the strike in South Yorkshire, was asked by a German visitor on its thirtieth anniversary what he considered to be the main significance of that year of struggle. He replied: 'that it could be done'. This fact, easily overlooked, is perhaps the most profound of all: that 200,000 workers and their families could embark on what most of them considered to be a just strike and stay together for up to a year, with little or no official financial support, under the permanent bombardment of the media, the coal employer and the Thatcher government. Finally driven back to work under threat of redundancy and eviction, many were still convinced of the virtue of their cause and continued to argue that 'Scargill was right, you know. They did shut the pits. We were right all along. Maggie Thatcher stole our jobs.' One young miner in Durham expressed the view, quite forcibly, that 'we could do with one of these every two years and then people would really see what this system is like'.

There were many issues at stake in the strike. The presence of oil and nuclear power executives seconded to the Downing Street Policy Unit for the duration made clear that the future of the UK's energy supply was in question. After the strike there would be no place for British coal in the domestic energy mix. Not that this was an environmental shift; the future was to be with gas, oil and coal imports. There was also something very authoritarian about the government response – an insistence on management's right to manage writ large. As we have seen, MacGregor understood the action of the miners as insubordination, and when ministers talked of 'law and order' the emphasis was on *order*.

But as Raymond Williams argued, 'Listening to some ministers, it is easy to pick up their real sense of order. Which is command; obedience to lawful authority; indeed when combined with the "right to manage", obedience to all authority.'[48] This was written as the strike ended and attention turned to the tactics and strategy of the miners' union and its leadership. Many of the activist miners would have agreed with one in Durham who said, 'the government learned from 1972 and planned for this better than we did'. Nevertheless, there are few who could think of an easy way out of the situation – something that would have saved the union and the industry. As time has passed, people have looked back, sometimes with regrets. One of the militants in Penrhiwceiber who had urged the picketing of mines in March came to think that 'with hindsight that may have been the biggest blunder ever made':

> Arthur wouldn't have gone without South Wales, historically the most militant Area in the British coalfield. If we had held back then everything would have been so different. There would have been a ballot and Nottingham would have voted in the ballot to come out on strike and everything would have been different. We wouldn't have lost the coalfield. But 'strike fever' is like 'war fever' once that flag is up and you are charging in.

Strikes and industrial conflicts are not played out on chess boards; they are things of the moment, when people do the best (and sometimes the worst) they can, making decisions in the circumstances that face them. The NUM would obviously have been in a much stronger position if it could have maintained the overtime ban and reduced coal stocks in preparation for a strike in the autumn. But since 1981 all the campaigning and arguing within the union had been about one thing – pit closures and the need to fight. This was the 'strike fever' that couldn't be calmed.

Here lies the strength of Raymond Williams' assertion in 1985: the key question was not what was done wrongly – not to second-guess the past – but what it had all *meant*. For him, the actions of the government, taken together, amounted to 'the dislocation of our habitual social order and the destruction of specific communities'. Ralph Miliband had put it another way five years earlier, at the end of the first year of the Thatcher government. He called it 'class war', a war that was to reach its climax in 1984.[49] The conditions were being established for the dominance of what Williams described as the 'alien order of paper and money', backed up by 'abstract accounting' and quite detached from 'any settled working and productive activity'. The strike was finally to open up the coalfields to 'the logic of a new nomad capitalism which exploits actual places and people and then (as it suits them) moves on'. For Williams, the deep meaning of the strike for *human society* lay in the fact that 'in a period of very powerful multinational capital, . . . virtually everyone is exposed or will be exposed to what the miners have suffered'.[50] In this, he did have the hope that the form of activism developed during the miners' strike, one that linked trade union action with community organisation and involvement, could pave the way for a new and different kind of labour movement.

Chapter Six

Of Managers and Markets

People are now discovering the price of insubordination and insurrection. And boy are we going to make it stick.
Ian MacGregor, *Daily Telegraph*, 10 March 1985

In the wake of the strike, the National Coal Board adopted a radically different approach to the trade unions, removing facilities for lodge officials, ending many local agreements and foreclosing on national negotiations with the NUM. At the same time many collieries were being closed, and managers began to talk the language of markets and costs, and especially 'cost per gigajoule', a change in terminology that emphasised the fact that the coal industry was firmly located in the energy market, and that its future would be determined there.

During the strike, significant amounts of coal were imported, especially through small ports along the east coast, and electricity supplies were maintained by running the Magnox nuclear reactors at full capacity and by the significant replacement of coal with imported oil.[1] The vulnerability of coal in its major (and previously secure) energy market was to foretell a worrying future. In 1988, two energy economists considered that 'a constant theme of CEGB policy, amounting almost to an obsession, has been the desire to reduce its dependence on British coal.'[2]

This new approach was outlined in a document entitled New Strategy for Coal. Dated 11 October 1985, it was drafted by Ken Moses, who along with Albert Wheeler from Scotland had been incorporated into a new management team at Hobart House. Both these men had been at the hard core of MacGregor's resistance to the strike. Moses was made the chief of mining operations, and Wheeler became operations director and later joint deputy chairman of the NCB. Their elevation into these key roles signified the extent of the victory of the anti-union 'market strategy' outlined by MacGregor.

The planning document outlined a future built around the need to 'phase out the industry's dependence on subsidy' by 'abandoning fixed production targets and adopting a more flexible approach' based around costs and 'market requirements'. It emphasised the need to 'maximise output in our low-cost collieries and opencast sites as a means of reducing average costs'. Consequently, a large number of coal mines would have to be closed. The most productive ones that remained would need to be dramatically reorganised through the intense use of heavy-duty faces and retreat longwall mining and with a greater reliance upon subcontracting. The so-called Wheeler Plan embodied the practical application of the new strategy to the routines of the mines with its emphasis on 'robust management rules'.

The NCB was deaf to warnings that the international coal trade (increasingly dominated by the international oil and major mining corporations) was capable of destabilising domestic producers. Rather, it informed the House of Commons Energy Committee that it took the optimistic view that 'notwithstanding the external uncertainties' it was 'very unlikely that collieries which might have a viable long-term future would be closed prematurely'.[3] The committee was not completely convinced – with good reason, for within a decade this approach had effectively terminated deep-mine coal production in the UK. The process began first in South Wales and Durham.

Return to the Mines

The return to the mines was scheduled for Tuesday 5 March. Gareth Rees remembered how the occasion was marked at Maerdy with a demonstration organised by the lodge and the Council of Wales. As dawn broke,

> the miners of Maerdy marched the mile or so from their impos-
> ing Workmen's Hall back to work at the pit. They marched
> behind their lodge banner and the colliery band and at the head
> of a column of over 1,000 supporters: women's groups, support
> groups from Mid and North Wales and elsewhere, trades
> unions, the Labour Party, Plaid Cymru, the Communist Party,
> the churches, and many others were there. Being Maerdy – the
> 'little Moscow' of the 1920s and 1930s, and now the last pit in
> the Rhondda valleys – it was a unique event: the forest of
> clenched-fist salutes as the miners entered the colliery, the mass
> of media crews, the very size of the demonstration.[4]

Elsewhere the return was of a different order. At Tower several thought the demonstration at Maerdy to be overly triumphal, especially following what one man called 'the biggest defeat in our history'. At Celynen North the men met outside the Sloop, the local pub where they had gathered every day for their picket-ing duties, and then marched with their banners through Newbridge under the tunnel and to the pit. As Gavin Rogers remembers,

> There was a big island outside the managers' offices and I can
> always remember the firemen and the overmen and the
> management clapping and saying 'well done boys'. Well in
> this island there were stones and everybody got hold of those
> stones and we just belted the officials with them. We came
> back around, went into the canteen, put our banners in and
> went back to work.

In Durham the miners of the Easington Lodge following their earlier vote returned to work a day earlier, on the Monday, 4 March. There was disagreement over how this should be organised. The idea of a march back through the village behind the banner and the band was considered, but some thought it to be too celebratory. In the end, the men just returned to work with the women and supporters of SEAM clapping and cheering them through the gates. The following weekend, though, the lodge marched through the village with the banner, stopping to make a presentation to the owner of the fish and chip shop for all his help during the strike, and to generally thank the village and the wider community for staying together throughout the struggle.

The Yorkshire, Scotland and Kent Areas had voted against returning to work without an amnesty for the miners who had been sacked during the dispute. Here, the return to work was desultory and delayed across the week. In these separate and different ways, the strike ended as it had started, at different times and in different ways in different places.

The hope for the NUM had been that the return to work would be accompanied by an extension of the conflict, with the maintenance of the overtime ban coupled with other forms of output restriction. This drew a caustic response from MacGregor: 'If they thought they were marching back to where they had left off, they had a rude shock coming to them.' For him this was the occasion when the NCB would break free from the constraints imposed by nationalisation and exert 'management's right to manage', most clearly through the colliery closures, which Moses and Wheeler would enact. Capacity would be reduced not by 4 million tonnes, the figure given in March 1984, but by over 25 million tonnes. For South Wales this meant immediate large-scale closures. Durham was to suffer less badly in the first instance, with fewer initial closures, but the outcome for both Areas was to be the same – the total closure of the industry. Colliery closures – that most intractable of problems, the focus of the strike and the problem that had riven the NUM for decades – had returned to centre stage.

In Durham the NUM had changed its leadership. Dave Hopper from Wearmouth, a leading member of the rank-and-file left group that had effectively organised the Area during the strike, was elected as the new general secretary He had been the only member of the executive committee to vote against the Easington resolution to end the strike. He was joined by David Guy from Dawdon as Area president. With the support of the executive committee they were determined to resist mine closures. In South Wales too there had been changes, with Des Dutfield replacing Emlyn Williams as president. Dutfield had defeated the vice-president Terry Thomas in the election, with Ian Isaac, the lodge secretary of St John's, in third place. Isaac had been a prominent member of the rank-and-file left group set up in the coalfield after the 1981 strike; his presence on the ballot, with significant support, was indicative of the tension that existed in the coalfield after the ending of the strike.

The Modified Colliery Review Procedure in Practice

During the strike, the deputies' (supervisors') union NACODS had balloted its members, with 82 per cent voting in favour of strike action in support of the miners. Rather than strike, the union's leadership negotiated behind the backs of the national officials of the NUM to produce a modified colliery review procedure (MCRP) containing a new independent element. The agreement was said to be 'sacrosanct'. However, in practice the NCB used various means and devices to evade it. These centred on a new redundancy payment settlement, which was announced by the government with a clear message that it was only available until midnight on 9 October 1985. It was publicised extensively in the collieries and around the coalfields in an aggressive attempt to encourage men to leave the industry 'voluntarily', and to vote in any meeting to accept the premature closure of their collieries.

The NCB, in offering considerable sums of money to men in debt after the strike, successfully subverted the new procedure. As men pressed to leave the industry, the Board took the opportunity to extend the closure programme, further draining the NUM of support. These activities led Peter McNestry, general secretary of NACODS, to describe the NCB as 'totally dishonourable'. They also led to bitter disagreements and conflict among the miners in their lodges.

In South Wales, Penrhiwceiber was one of the first to face closure. A local leader remembers that

> there were three meetings for Penrhiwceiber whether to fight on, or whether to accept and not fight the closure, and there comes a point you know – and I believed in fighting – but there comes a point when you realise the writing is on the wall and you've got to . . . you can run away from it and keep on voting against closure, or you just as well stand up and be counted and accept that's that. It's not defeatism, it's accepting the reality of the thing . . . because we knew the Coal Board were absolutely determined to close Penrhiwceiber anyway . . . because they hated us.

After a year-long strike, with the resultant burden of debt, and a managerial bombardment of (dis)information as to the uncertain future, it is not hard to see how after four meetings men might be predisposed towards accepting the 'inevitable'. However, the decision caused divisions, some of which never healed. In addition, the fact that this had happened at Penrhiwceiber, a pit renowned for its militancy, came as a shock. Tyrone O'Sullivan of Tower Colliery and another leading member of the rank-and file-group, remembered that:

> I used to say 'think of a snowball running down a hill, it starts off small but as it gathers speed you can't stop it', and that is what happened with pit closures. They allowed the snowball

to start running. We should have resisted, we should have gone through the colliery review procedure. Knowing full well at the end of it you still would have been judged by the same people who judged it in the beginning, but you would have slowed it down, you know, stopped the rush. But you had leaders actually recommending pit closures, and you had a leadership structure of older people who were reaching out for their redundancy, dragging young men with them because these were the accepted leaders and they had influence . . . and we let the snowball get out of hand.

The brake that could be put on the 'snowball' lay in the MCRP, and by the autumn of 1985 three pits had voted to resist closure and enter the new procedure: Bates in Northumberland, Horden in Durham and St John's in South Wales.

In St John's, a young lodge leadership determined to save the mine, had involved Neil Kinnock in setting up an independent inquiry into the closure, recruiting expert advice to produce a document in support of the campaign to 'Keep Mining In Maesteg'. The aim was to take the pit into the modified review procedure and lodge chairman Charlie White (who tragically died before the final lodge vote) spoke at meetings around the coalfields, arguing for the need to resist closures. At the fourth mass meeting of the lodge membership, held at the Nantyffyllon Miners' Institute, the recommendation to resist closure was again put to the vote. Lodge secretary Ian Isaac remembers:

> I presented the lodge recommendation to the meeting. I mustered every argument I could. There was a minimum of ten years and more work left in the mine; a new mine at Margam that could be linked [underground] to St John's . . . the industry was being sacrificed on the political altar of the Tory Party . . . The vote was taken: 109 for 153 against . . . We undertook therefore to abide by the democratic decision of the members.[5]

In this way St John's dropped out of the new MCRP, leaving Bates and Horden to test the new arrangements. Here, by contrast, the men repeatedly voted *against* accepting closure in spite of being persistently threatened with the loss of enhanced redundancy payments. At Horden, after many years of accepting assurances from the NCB and local managers as to the future viability of the colliery, there was an acute sense of betrayal in the miners' and mechanics' lodges. This found expression through a new lodge leadership, and a sense that while the MCRP might come to nothing, the Board must, at the very least, be made to go through it. Men who had stood up in meetings quoting the assurances of the management and questioning the 'doom merchants' felt that they had been taken for granted and lied to. They were not going to make it easy for the NCB. This feeling of distrust was amplified by the management's reluctance to announce the closure of the mine. Instead, the labour force at Horden was to become a reservoir to be drawn upon and deployed to mines elsewhere in the county. In these circumstances, one man described how he and his family were

> living in uncertainty, waiting to hear what's going to happen to you, not being able to do anything that'll have any influence. Kites without wind, that's what we are. You know there's nothing you can do and that's not a nice feeling.[6]

What many of the miners were sure of, however, was that they didn't want to go to another mine:

> The Coal Board says that there'll be jobs for everyone that wants them. Well so there might be, but I don't want one of them jobs in another pit thanks very much, not after what they've done to us. You can't rely on them.[7]

Eventually the NCB accepted that the closure of the Horden mine would be dealt with through the agreed procedure. In facing the prospect of the new independent review stage, the Horden lodges were encouraged by the commitment of the newly elected officials of the DMA – David Hopper and David Guy – who, together with Bill Etherington of the Mechanics, stressed the importance of continuing to resist the NCB's plans. To assist the case for retaining the mine, Durham University was asked to produce a report that documented the existing reserves and past commitments made by the NCB. It also attempted to itemise the *costs* that would be involved in the closure of the mine and the attendant social and economic *consequences*. The report calculated the direct costs incurred under the redundancy payment scheme, to which could be added the state funds that would be necessary to regenerate the locality after the mine closed. In addition, there were indirect costs that came with the loss of a major employer, with downward multiplier effects upon demand impacting on local shops and other sectors of the local economy. Taken together, the analysis suggested a pattern of decline that would have a deep effect upon future generations living in the area.[8]

These issues were raised at the review meetings in Room 16 at Hobart House. The corporation's representatives made it clear, however, that while they recognised the existence of these costs and the human consequences of closure, these were not their concern. Nor were they responsible for mitigating them. In fact, the only costs that concerned them were costs of production. Malcolm Edwards, the director of marketing, spelled out the logic of the Wheeler Plan to the tribunal. The chairman was forced to agree, stating in his decision letter, 'Serious consequences will result in the local community if (the colliery) is closed, not only on adult employment and youth employment but on the economy generally.' Nevertheless, 'Where the social consequences of a decline in coal mining in a region would be particularly acute, it is for the government to decide what action to take.'[9]

This result, while not unexpected, had a deflating effect upon the workforce. However, for those members of the lodge delegations that attended the review, the approach and behaviour of the NCB representatives long remained in the memory. Details of their 'arrogance', underhand approach and aggressive treatment of witnesses were often repeated in the years that followed.

Horden's review was followed by that of Bates. In this case the tribunal supported the trade unions and recommended that the pit remained open; a recommendation that the NCB simply ignored. It had made its decision to close the mine and when challenged again had it upheld in the courts. As MacGregor was to explain:

> I believe that some of them thought that they had won a form of independent arbitration on our actions on pit closures, only clothed in other words. However, this was not the case. We were not, nor could we be, bound by the findings of the body . . . The NCB had retained the power to decide which pits are to be operated and which are to be closed.[10]

In the light of this decision, which revealed the reality of the review process in practice, confirming Arthur Scargill's opinion that it was 'worthless', the new procedure was effectively abandoned, at least for the time being.

Colliery Closures, Hardship and Bitterness

In Durham the small Sacriston mine was the first to close, and men there decided that it was probably time to give up on digging coal out of its very narrow seams, ending deep mining in the west of the county. This was followed by Herrington, which had been the Durham mine identified for closure in 1984, triggering strikes and talk of solidarity in the Area. There was every expectation from the new leadership in Durham that the Herrington men would follow Horden into the MCRP: it was widely felt that they owed the Area their support.

The decision went the other way, however, and the Herrington miners voted for closure in 1985, bringing forth anger and condemnation within Durham. In making their decision, the Herrington men had one ear for the union and another for senior management, who well understood their vulnerabilities. In addition to control of redundancy payments, the NCB management also had control over the destination of Herrington transferees. This had huge significance in Durham. A former deputy at the mine explains how this was used to influence the vote:

> Mr Day came to our pit and he said, 'this is the position, Horden was going into the review procedure, so you're behind Horden. If you don't vote to go through the review procedure, I can put all of you anywhere you want to go. I'll give you transfers to any pit you want to go. If you want to go to Wearmouth, you can go to Wearmouth. If you want Tempest, you've got Tempest. I will struggle to put you all at Wearmouth. But if it goes into review procedure you follow Horden. Horden goes to Wearmouth, Tempest or anywhere they want. You get what's left.'

With Herrington's high percentage of men who had returned to work before the strike ended, the key factor was Westoe. Nobody wanted to go there. Westoe was a militant pit where very few had returned to work and where scabs were being treated harshly. They would be more at home in Wearmouth – and this was the offer and the threat laid out by Mr Day: 'the only way you can avoid this [being transferred to Westoe] is for you to go to the union and tell them you want the pit shutting.'[11]

Having achieved the closure of Herrington, the NCB announced plans to close Eppleton and then Seaham. Active local campaigns fought against these closures, attempting to use local political pressure, rather than the discredited MCRP. Both were ultimately unsuccessful, leaving deep mining in Durham reduced to a small string of highly mechanised mines operating along the eastern coast.

South Wales, with its large number of small collieries cramped by underinvestment, was particularly vulnerable to the new approach of the NCB; after a rash of early closures, mines closed annually throughout the eighties. In 1985 the *South Wales Miner*, the newsletter of the Area NUM, carried the graphic headline 'Closure Plague Killing Valleys', with a list of the closed collieries and a prediction that the 'life blood will drain away and our communities will die'. It was a plague that couldn't be checked. By the time of the Blaenant closure in 1990, *twenty-two* collieries had stopped working, with four closing in 1989, including Oakdale, one of the area's proverbial big hitters, leaving just six working mines.

In the space of eight years, both Areas had experienced social trauma as families dealt with mine closures while still digesting the full consequences of the strike and how it had ended. The women who so solidly and bravely supported the strike would, at other times, have told you that they didn't want their sons to go underground; that they hoped that there would be 'something better' for them. But, failing that, 'there's always the pit'. In this and in other ways, the pit – and the jobs it provided – had become understood as part of the *collective property* of many mining villages: it was 'our pit'. These places, these holes in the ground, had become part of villagers' lives in detailed, deep and complex ways that were ruptured both during the strike and in its aftermath.

The issue of strike-breakers, or scabs, mobilised many of these emotions. There was very little strike-breaking in South Wales, although we have seen that the Cynheidre Colliery in the anthracite belt had suffered badly. There, the memories of the strike were bitter ones that lasted long after it ended and the pit closed. As one man explained in 2014, 'there are people I'll cross the road to avoid looking at their faces'.[12] By the end of February, just 478 men had returned to work across the coalfield, very few of them in the ten central valleys, making them a distinct minority in each mine. In Durham things were different, with twice that number returning to the large Wearmouth Colliery in Sunderland, and no mine free from a significant contingent of men who had broken the strike. Here the issue of 'working with scabs' became a highly contentious one. At the Easington Colliery the presence of the man who had first broken the strike was so inflammatory that the management isolated him in remote workplaces on the surface until he left the industry. In other mines, managers required known union activists to work alongside men who had returned to work during the strike. This happened at the Murton Colliery, where David Temple was put to work side by side with one of the scabs. He talked of the enormous self-discipline it took for him to prevent himself from speaking to this man for over a year – shift after shift, month after month – and of the stress that caused him.[13]

The strike – and with it, absence from the arduous work of the mine – had also had a monumental effect upon the miners. One man reflected that before the strike, throughout his life, he had 'needed the pit; I needed to work in it, I've been there most days since I left school. But what I learned in the strike was that I didn't need it. That I could manage without it.' This idea was strengthened after returning to work under the very different arrangements in the mine. Many men, like this one, decided to leave. Although the NUM held to the view that miners should not 'sell their jobs', there was sympathy for those who had accepted the redundancy payment under these conditions because they wanted to get away from the mine and had the bottle to say, 'Enough for me in the coal industry, I want to see pastures green'. This was the view of one militant miner in South Wales who, on the basis of painful experience, retained his ire for 'the people that hung out for the best deal . . . and mass together as weak people if you like . . . *and voted to close the mine*'. In South Wales the voting process continued year on year, extending the agony and testing people's emotions. The men who worked at Oakdale still remember the emergency meeting called at the Pontllanfraith Leisure Centre on a Sunday morning. One man who 'will never forget it' recalled how 'the union man got up on the stage and said, "we've got some bad news for you – the pit is going to close. We can either fight it and lose redundancy or accept it and we would all have good redundancy."' There was a show of hands.

> As soon as the count was taken, they said that by the look of it we had voted to close Oakdale Colliery, and a number of men cheered. I couldn't get over it. Cheering because their pit was going to close. I was absolutely gutted.

Oakdale was known as a moderate colliery, but had surprisingly voted for strike action in 1984. However, five years later it seemed that the lodge officials had taken the view that the closure could not be prevented and that resistance involved too many risks. Others across the coalfields had taken the same view. This development was a reflection, in part, of a change in mood under the new punishment-centred mode of mine management that came into operation through the Wheeler Plan.[14] Almost a thousand men had been dismissed during the strike, and the return to work without them heightened the sense of broken solidarity. New production systems and work contracts were introduced, as local agreements were abrogated by a management operating with a radically different style and a dramatically different set of priorities. In the mines that survived, working life changed for the worse.[15] In the large coastal collieries of Durham, new face machinery was introduced; subcontracting arrangements developed which broke up the organised solidarity of the underground miners, fragmenting them into contract workers and mobile workers, all operating under new payment rules orchestrated through a new rhetoric of accounting and cost per gigajoule. There was persistent talk of a bad atmosphere in the mines, and in 1988 the secretary of the mechanics' lodge at Westoe Colliery felt that his members were so disheartened that it was 'a question of let's shut the bastard pit, so that we can all be away'.

Men talked of the job being completely transformed, by technological changes and also by the fact that 'they have taken away the camaraderie of the pit. It's all gone. And without laughing and joking down the pit it's a rotten dirty, filthy job. The only good thing about the pit was your marras and that's gone.' Feelings like these, coupled with a sense of defeat and compounded by family debt built up over the year of the strike, left many men judging that they would be better off leaving the industry and accepting the closure of the mines.

These were intense and difficult times, and the promised future of a stable, productive and profitable industry outlined by MacGregor was receding daily.

From Management Rules to the Rule of Markets

By 1991 mining employment in South Wales had been virtually wiped out. Following the closure of Deep Navigation and Penallta, only three pits remained in operation: Tower and Taff Merthyr, together with Cynheidre in the west. In Durham it was a similar story. Two large mines (Dawdon and Murton) had closed there in 1991, leaving just four super-pits strung out along the coast – from Westoe in the north to Wearmouth, Vane Tempest and Easington in the south. But even at this reduced level, things didn't stabilise.

By this time, the NCB had become the British Coal Corporation (BCC), usually referred to simply as British Coal. The name change was one of Ian MacGregor's last acts as chairman, 'to indicate amongst other things that we are living in a different age'.[16] The situation had become critical. The NCB had defeated Scargill and pushed through draconian reforms. Yet in its new guise, the BCC organisation was still up against it and ironically began to complain about the rules. It felt particularly bitter about the competition from the oil companies, which it regarded as unfair. Malcolm Edwards complained of how the oil companies would 'rely on their great cash flows to push down hard to drive out the competition'.[17]

In Britain, the market for steam-raising coal (never previously threatened by internationally traded coal) was drawing in more and more imports. In 1988, Shell, Exxon and BP sold over 100 mt of steam coal on the international market. As a consequence, the downward pressure on steam coal prices continued, and with it greater problems for BCC. In the new Plan for Coal, net *exports* of steam coal had been predicted, with imports as low as 1.4 mt. The new reality was far different, and damaging. Steam coal imports had risen to almost 10 mt by 1987, outstripping imports of coking coal, pushing the deep mines out of the market. In contrast, open-cast production remained buoyant, and throughout the 1980s took a greater and greater share.[18] These changes were unlike anything that had happened in any other raw material or commodity market; yet they were welcomed and encouraged by the government as it pushed forward with its plans to privatise the industry.

The sale of the Central Electricity Generating Board was a central objective of the third Thatcher administration, and the CEGB had been preparing for privatisation since the end of the miners' strike. In 1985 it had entered the international spot market, paying £30 a tonne for 120,000 tonnes of Colombian coal to be delivered to Fiddlers Ferry Power Station on the Mersey, and it continued with this policy of international purchases in subsequent years, supplying Fiddlers Ferry and its power stations on the Thames.[19] This prepared the ground for the new private duopoly, PowerGen and National Power, which took over the industry in 1991. When faced with the EU's new sulphur dioxide (SO_2) and nitrogen dioxide (NO_2) emission targets, the new owners (unprepared for the heavy investment needed to adapt the coal-fired stations) looked to new import facilities to procure cheaper low-sulphur coal in increasing volume. More importantly, a liberalisation of the market allowed smaller producers access through the National Grid Corporation, building new generating capacity, using the expanding supply of gas from North Sea developments – the so called dash for gas.[20]

This uncoupling of the state-owned electricity-generating sector from national coal production unleashed forces that worked like a pincer on BCC. Consequently the coal company continued almost manically to press for further cost-cutting and productivity gains. Energy sector analysts, and even some members of BCC management, viewed this as a disaster waiting to happen, and certainly the coalminers were in no doubt about what lay ahead. Despite its crucial role in enabling the NCB and government to defeat the strike, the Nottingham Area was not immune: twelve collieries had already closed there by 1992 and another seven were set to shut down, including Cotgrave, Silverwood, Bevercotes, Bolsover and Ollerton.

Striking Back

In 1992, with Thatcher gone, the market-driven strategy for energy supply continued under John Major, his deputy Michael Heseltine in the front line. By this time the impact of CEGB privatisation was being felt. With increasing government pressure on the corporation to balance its books, BCC announced that, given 'the urgent need to bring supply and demand back in balance', a further thirty-one collieries needed to close. Some of these closures would be temporary, but ten that were set for immediate closure – including Vane Tempest in Durham and Betws and Taff Merthyr in South Wales – were mines considered to have no future under any circumstances. This 'group of ten' was subsequently enlarged to include the remaining Durham pits and, ultimately, Tower in South Wales. The first phase of closures had eliminated the 'loss-making tail' identified by the Monopolies and Mergers Commission; this second phase, set to denude the industry of many of its major producers, was being determined by market criteria established in an ongoing review by the John T. Boyd Company of Pittsburgh, Pennsylvania.[21] In its inquiry into this process, however, the House of Commons Employment Committee found that 'One of the most striking aspects of the decision to close such a large part of the mining industry was the difficulty we found in identifying what planning, if any, had gone into the reshaping of the industry.'[22]

In fact, there was little concern for 'reshaping' other than through reducing the industry down to highly cost-effective units to be made available for its planned privatisation. As a consequence, miners in Durham and South Wales, many of them aged under forty, and having survived previous closures and being moved to another pit, now faced final closures and their exit from the industry. There was no future for them in the UK as miners. It would be the end. The planned closures were met by widespread organised resistance, with the NUM in Durham following the South Wales example of campaigning across the whole area, beyond the mining villages, holding meetings in towns such as Barnard Castle and drawing the support of a wide spectrum of people concerned about the future of the region. There was unanimous support for a one-day national strike called by the NEC, and for a demonstration at Parliament. In Durham, George Robson, the NUM finance officer, recalled:

> We fought a campaign lasting 11 months and we had the general public behind us. We were quite amazed by the response. We organised the biggest mass exodus of trade unionists in history from this area to demonstrate in London on two occasions in four days. I remember chartering trains at £10,000 a go and sending six out of Newcastle Central station absolutely filled with trade unionists and I also chartered about 40 buses.[23]

The week of the NUM demonstration, another took place, on the Sunday, this time organised by the TUC, with a quarter of a million people marching through London to Hyde Park. As

the rain poured down, local radio stations featured the march
and encouraged Londoners to attend. People waved from buildings and cheered from the pavements. George Melly – the jazz
and blues singer, critic and writer – received applause as he
doffed his fedora in support of the marchers. The areas and
lodge banners were much in evidence, the Tower banner among
them; many of the miners from the closed pit at Horden were
there too, now marching under the banner of Easington Lodge.
Their mood was one of grim resignation. 'We knew it would
come to this didn't we? The men have had enough you know.'
Conversations reached back to 1984–85: it seemed that 'Arthur
was right; they've done it just as he said they would.' As George
Robson remembers,

> We took our bands and banners with us and we witnessed
> absolute sympathy from the people of London because they
> realised that Arthur Scargill had been right all along . . . when
> he warned that the government had a hidden agenda of pit
> closures.[24]

Two women from Cheltenham, who had come down on the bus,
declared that 'there are no mines near us but we are near to South
Wales and what they have done there – closing down the mines
– is terrible. We've always thought a lot of the miners.' It seems
that a lot of people on that march felt some connection with the
mines: through kin, proximity and a remembered past, coal
mining had played a highly significant role in the national
culture. In 1992, many people imagined that they were witness-
ing the end of something important in British social as well as
economic life.

By then, announcements of job losses and closures had become
commonplace. In Sunderland, the future of Coles Cranes, saved
from liquidation in 1984 by another takeover, once again seemed
insecure. In South Wales there was drama at the ICI Nylon
factory near Pontypool. Established as British Nylon Spinners

(BNS) after the war as a joint venture with Courtauld, it was at that time the factory with the largest floor space in Western Europe, employing over 6,000 workers. BNS collapsed in 1964 and ICI continued alone. The plant's capacity slowly declined and in 1992 the sale of the site to DuPont seemed to signal the end. The future of Hoover, another long-established factory at nearby Merthyr Tydfil, seemed in doubt after a major financial fiasco that cost the company £20 million,[25] foreshadowing its sale to the Italian washing machine manufacturer Candy. In the context of uncertainties such as these the miners had the exceptional capacity to call on national sentiment. It was to no avail, however.

In spite of a one-day strike, the two national demonstrations in London, meetings of two parliamentary select committees and the court judgment supporting the rights of miners to access the new modified review procedure, the closures went ahead.[26] They were not achieved, however, without the government having to ramp up the level of redundancy payments further. Nevertheless, here again, a combination of legislative power at Westminster and direct power by management in the mines produced a *fait accompli*, convincing all but the most diehard that 'resistance is futile'. Such was the success of this strategy that ministers felt able to divert criticism with the suggestion that the closures were *welcomed* by the miners. In the House of Commons, the shadow trade and industry secretary Robin Cook responded:

> I fully understand why those miners voted for extra redundancy money. The only thing about which they were being consulted was whether their pit would close this year or next. It is a grotesque travesty of the language to say that any of them have taken voluntary redundancy. Let us at least give them the dignity of recognising what the government forced on them – compulsory redundancy in all but name.

More Dirty Tricks

With the closure of Easington, Vane Tempest and Westoe, the great reserves of coal under the North Sea were abandoned. The Wearmouth Colliery, with the easiest access to considerable reserves, was mothballed and kept available for a potential buyer – who never arrived. In South Wales, Betws and Tower remained open for a time, but then they too faced the axe. Betws closed and then reopened under a management buy-out scheme, leaving only Tower.[27]

In the Boyd review, Tower had been identified as one of the long-life pits, nineteenth on the list. However, as the days passed, other mines on that list, assumed safe, were being closed. The lodge secretary Tyrone O'Sullivan remembers that

> half way through the year [1993] my manager started meeting privately down in a hotel in Brecon. There was nine of them and they were meeting there . . . and they were planning to buy Tower Colliery.

By exploiting the front of the pit and then switching to opencast mining,

> they were going to become millionaires in four years . . . What they didn't know was that every Monday morning, after they met, somebody would slip an envelope under my door, telling me everything they had said. So I knew exactly why they wanted to close the pit, and I knew why now, because they wanted to buy it and it had to be before April 1994, because I did believe that that was the last redundancy scheme, because eight months before privatisation they needed to clean the decks.

And so it proved – but it would be difficult: 80 per cent of the Tower miners had previously worked in collieries that had closed. For them, Tower was the end of a long road. One man who had started in the industry in 1957 had worked in *eight* other pits, each of them closed. Another, David Compton, had famously moved to Lancashire when the Six Bells Colliery closed in 1986, and then worked in Bickershaw and Parsonage until they closed. He was then transferred to Hem Heath and Silverdale in Staffordshire, finally moving back to South Wales and to Tower. So here, there was a strong commitment to coal mining and considerable experience of British Coal's employment practices. When the closure was announced it was accompanied by an addition of £9,000 to the agreed redundancy payments all men would receive.

> We took the vote and we voted very close, something like 65 per cent to 35 per cent, to fight to keep the pit open, and we then became the first pit ever to turn down the offer of redundancy with the £9,000 on the table. We turned it down ... They wanted to close the pit quietly, and there is no way they can buy the pit if it is a noisy closure, so they had to close it quietly and this £9,000 was to buy us off, so that didn't work.

Irritated by the determination of the men to resist the closure, and spurred on by the thought of riches, the management attempted to get the men to change their minds in ways that reveal the spirit of the times.

> They then started phoning underground at 1 o'clock and asking the men, 'Do you think you will get enough people to sign redundancy which will go over the 50 per cent?' That would have done them. They would have claimed that as a ballot, although they would never have allowed us to get away with that ... Then they said, 'Do you know that you people underground are down there and the men on the surface are now signing the redundancy up here?' Really dirty tactics.

Things got worse. After the local MP, Anne Clwyd, had her own sit-down strike for twenty-seven hours at the bottom of the shaft, the management agreed to keep the pit open. However, this was to be on the most punitive of terms for the miners. This became clear when O'Sullivan met with the manager.

> He throws this document at me, our wages have been reduced by 33 per cent and we have got to increase our tonnage by 100,000 tonne. All of a sudden, this wasn't a victory, this was punishment now: 'you accept them now, you can't get away scot free, it is punishment now'.

In spite of this, the lodge committee voted unanimously to recommend that the miners reject closure. It was a step too far. Threatened with the loss of redundancy payments *and* more pain and poverty at work, the men voted to accept closure and take redundancy. They had done enough, however, to scupper the possibility of an underhand buy-out by the managers. Instead it gave them the idea of doing the very same thing for themselves.[28]

A Privatised Industry

The coal industry, when privatised in 1993, comprised only sixteen of the 219 mines operating in 1980. All the mines in South Wales and Durham had closed, with a total loss of 40,000 jobs (see Table 5). The market-driven policy had reduced the industry to a rump of mines in South Yorkshire and the East Midlands. Many of the Nottingham mines that had worked through the strike of 1984–85 had been closed. Cecil Parkinson, the new secretary of state for energy, made it clear that the government's successful handling of the coal industry was to be the 'jewel in the crown', 'the ultimate privatisation'. Such grand promises by the Conservative Party were a far cry from the messy, even tawdry, affair that took place.[29] The transfer of ownership on 1 January 1993 carried none of the symbolic richness that had typified vesting day in 1947. It was a market transaction, nothing more. Even at the time, claims of optimism had a distinctly hollow ring. In spite of some early good

fortune, the trend in coal consumption continued on a downward
path, bringing more casualties in its wake.

Table 5. Decline in Mining Employment, 1971–91

	1971	1981	1991
South Wales	38,000	25,000	1,200
Durham	22,000	15,000	4,900

Table 6. Colliery closures, 1985–94

	Phase one	Phase two
South Wales	Bedwas Colliery 1985 Blaenserchan Colliery 1985 Celynen South Colliery 1985 Treforgan Drift 1985 Abertillery New Mine 1985 Celynen North Colliery 1985 Penrhiwceiber Colliery 1985 Aberpergwm Colliery 1985 St Johns Colliery 1985 Garw Valley Colliery 1985 Maerdy Colliery 1986 Cwm Colliery 1986 Markham Colliery 1986 Nantgarw Colliery 1986 Six Bells Colliery 1987 Abernant Colliery 1988 Lady Windsor Colliery 1988 Cynheidre Colliery 1989 Marine Colliery 1989 Merthyr Vale Colliery 1989 Oakdale Colliery 1989 Trelewis Drift 1989	Blaenant Colliery 1990 Deep Navigation 1991 Penalta Colliery 1991 Taff Merthyr Colliery 1992 Betws 1993 Tower Colliery 1994
Durham	Herrington Colliery 1985 Sacriston Colliery 1985 Horden/Blackhall Colliery 1986 Eppleton Colliery 1986	Dawdon Colliery 1991 Murton/Hawthorn Combine 1991 Seaham/Vane Tempest Colliery 1992 Easington Colliery 1993 Westoe Colliery 1993 Wearmouth Colliery 1993

RJB Mining, the main purchaser of BCC's assets, had never made a secret of the fact that it would probably close Point of Ayr and Bilsthorpe collieries. However, the closure in 1997 of the new super-mine at Asfordby in Leicestershire (allegedly for geological and safety reasons) was a strong signal that the industry was once again in crisis. The most spectacular collapse, however, was associated with Coal Investments plc, a company established by Malcolm Edwards, former marketing director of BCC, for the purpose of reopening five of the collieries that had been closed or mothballed after the crisis of 1992. It also purchased the Cymgwili anthracite drift mine in South Wales. Edwards's sense of his own destiny as a major coal entrepreneur was misplaced, however, and the company was forced into administration at the beginning of 1996. This process of attrition continued. Year on year the privatised mines closed, including the giant collection of super-pits that made up the Selby complex in North Yorkshire. By 2013, just four large deep mines remained in operation, three of them owned by UK Coal, a company with extensive open-cast mining operations. These included Daw Mill in Warwickshire, listed by Boyd as the best colliery in the country. But a number of severe and fatal accidents had caused concern over the way it was being managed, and this was exacerbated in May 2013 when an underground fire virtually destroyed the mine.

Consequences

The privatisation of BCC was conducted with considerable haste and there were many administrative loose ends, creating considerable problems and concerns for the local authorities on the coalfields. This was particularly true in the sensitive area of environmental control and pollution. For some years there had been concern over the rising water table in the old coal districts as routine pumping came to an end, and this worry was to continue with occasional flash floods and other problems. These increased in the twenty-first century and were particularly acute in the valleys of South Wales. On 21 January 2021, eight people were evacuated from their homes in Skewen as outpourings from old mine workings flooded their houses. Skewen was part of a collection of collieries that had stretched from Neath to Llanelli, and water had filled the workings, bursting out after the heavy rain. Local people remember the 'big wheels' that the NCB had used to operate the pumps that controlled the water level. Flooding was one problem; the instability of the coal tips perched high on the valley sides was another. The disaster at Aberfan was a constant reminder of this danger and it was brought home to the people of Tylorstown in the Rhondda when Storm Dennis hit in 2020, causing a dramatic slippage down the valley side. Fortunately, there were no casualties, but the shock was enough for Lisa Pinney of the Coal Authority (that had taken over the NCB's responsibilities) to admit that 'old coal material on a hillside could cause a risk'. A subsequent joint investigation with the Welsh government established that there were 294 old coal tips that should be classified as 'high risk' and in need of regular attention and inspection. It concluded that current legislation was 'neither sufficiently robust or [*sic*] fit for purpose in relation to inspection and maintenance'. Chris Bryant, Labour MP for the Rhondda, found the situation 'shocking' and was 'astonished that no proper register of disused coal tips was made when the mines closed'. The emissions of gasses from the abandoned mines were also an issue. Along with the risks of flooding, they gave rise to a significant financial burden for the local authorities and the devolved administration.[30]

For the local authorities, whose economic development strategies and employment planning had been inextricably linked with the coal industry, privatisation was a nightmare. This was the case across South Wales, but was experienced most acutely in Durham by Easington District Council, where over 70 per cent of male manual jobs in the area had been in mining. With the onset of the strike in 1984, the realisation dawned that all the

pledges made by the NCB as to the future of mining employment might be worthless. In these circumstances, we were asked
to carry out an analysis of the likely scale of mining job losses in
the District, and their economic and social implications, locally
and more widely. Our report, 'Undermining Easington', examined a range of possibilities regarding the loss of coalmining jobs,
and its implications, attracting some criticism for undue pessi-
mism.[31] In the event, even our most pessimistic scenarios turned
out to be over-optimistic.

Reflecting on these changes, and to get some European comparisons and perspectives, we visited the offices of the European Coal
and Steel Community in Brussels, where we met with its senior
executive Walter Weber. He confirmed that the British policy of
dealing with colliery closures had been very different from that
followed in France and Germany, where redundancies were
planned more carefully and linked to training for alternative
employment into other sectors such as civil engineering. In his
view the UK government had looked no further than 'the pension-
ing off of the miner', and the logic of individualism had dominated. The NCB and the government had used redundancy
payments and the mineworkers' pension scheme to force agreement to mine closures, while simultaneously absolving themselves
from any further obligation, and with little concern for the effects
of any loss of community on the coalfields. The consequences of
this became clear in the decade that followed, when questions of
work and social cohesion emerged as central issues for the people
and local authorities of the two areas.

CHAPTER SEVEN

Thatcher's Redundant Entrepreneurs

The people who left the mines didn't leave it on their own accord, they left the pit because there was no pit. They didn't have no choice, did they? The pits closed and they had to leave. When in the factory, if you talk to them, a majority of them would say that they would rather go back in the pits.

Worker in the Crumlin Pot Noodle factory, South Wales

The House of Commons Employment Committee commented of the 1992 colliery closures that 'there was insufficient thought given to or account taken of the major employment consequences of the decision to close the pits'.[1] From the earliest days of the Thatcher government it had been clear that Conservative strategy for the coal industry and the energy sector more generally was framed in response to the power of the coalminers' trade union. This consideration had been outlined with some care, in contrast with the absence of any real interest in the impact of government policy upon regional economies and local communities. At most there was the thought that freed-up labour markets would reallocate redundant mine workers into more productive and profitable employment, and that *enterprise* would play a critical role in this. But nothing was worked out in any more detail. Looked at in this way, the experiences of redundant miners in Durham and South Wales can be seen as a major example of market failure.[2]

In stark contrast to the massive mine closures of the 1960s, the redundancies of the 1980s were not accompanied by major state intervention aimed at attracting new industries. In fact, the funding made available was minimal, and devoted to perfunctory retraining of the redundant men for jobs in new industry and the encouragement of enterprise and entrepreneurship. Two government-funded schemes were launched by the NCB. The first was a three-year retraining agreement with the Manpower Services Commission, in which £10 million was allocated to retrain up to 10,000 redundant miners. The second was the British Coal Enterprise (BCE) scheme, announced by the energy secretary Peter Walker at the height of the conflict in 1985.[3] It was the only specific government measure set up to address the effects of the pit closures. The BCE was to act as a specialist agency, providing support funds for new businesses in the places hit hardest by mine closures. It pledged that 'all of the jobs lost in mining during the present restructuring will be replaced by alternative opportunities over a reasonable period of time. This may be judged to be five or six years.'[4] Existing enterprise agencies would be provided with business premises; they would offer retraining programmes for redundant miners and provide financial assistance for new businesses opening in the coalfields. Taken together, these initiatives fuelled talk of creating 180,000 jobs.

It became immediately clear that, given the scale of the problem, the finance allocated was a drop in the ocean; it was far less than the funding that had been made available to facilitate the closure of the industry through the Redundant Mineworkers Payments Scheme (RMPS). Moreover, there were numerous complaints about the quality of the training and whether what was being offered was appropriate. BCE's funding was increased from £10 million to £40 million, after which it was to claim in 1987 that it had created 20,000 jobs in areas where pits had closed.[5] Its funding was increased again, and in the following year it maintained that £43 million had been committed, bringing government support to a total of £326 million in over 2,000 projects, with the creation of 26,000 jobs. In 1987, Merrick Spanton, as chairman of BCE, was able to assert that:

> Our achievements show that Arthur Scargill's talk about the death and destruction of mining communities is nonsense. We have a caring image and within five years we should have helped through loans in creating as many jobs as have been lost in the coalfields.[6]

There were many problems with all this. Mostly they had to do with BCE's seeming lack of accountability and the consequent difficulty in establishing an evidential basis for its claims. There was a suspicion that jobs were counted twice as they were moved from one part of the area to another, collecting grants along the way. The figures were very likely inflated, because it proved difficult to reconcile the reality of jobs on the ground with BCE's public claims. Such was the distrust that when in March 1988 BCE claimed to have created 2,800 jobs in the mining districts of the North East, the figure was openly disputed. One Durham MP commented, 'The BCE will not give me details for firms helped in my constituency and until they do, I suspect the figures they give.'[7]

As the debate hardened the terms were altered, with BCE *not* claiming a figure for jobs created but rather emphasising how it was 'helping to create jobs'. In 1988 it clearly saw itself as pioneering the spirit of enterprise, claiming that nowhere had this 'fructified more dramatically in the last twelve months than the coalfield regions of Great Britain'. Yet none of these statements were supported by evidence of successful indigenous entrepreneurial activity or of coalminers successfully transforming themselves into owners or managers of SMEs. In South Wales, a study of those who had received funding to set up their own companies found that none had been coalminers; all had some previous experience in their field of enterprise and many had drawn upon strong family support.[8] The professionals working in the enterprise agencies in Durham had come to a similar conclusion, finding success in helping people who were 'already in jobs who've got the spark, who want to do their own thing, who've got a bit of management training and experience behind them, who've got a bit of capital behind them'.[9]

These environmental or social-class factors were absent from the background of almost all of the redundant coalminers. As a consequence, it seemed that the flagship intervention aimed at promoting employment growth offered help to those who needed it least. Rather than subsidise the retraining of ex-miners, it gave a leg-up into starting a small business to individuals whose qualifications, previous experience and family backgrounds had already equipped them for such a career.[10]

In 1993 Phil Andrew, chief executive of BCE, was forced to admit that only 10 per cent of miners had used their redundancy payments to invest in new companies. He described this, once again, not as a failure of the organisation (in developing training and support structures, for example), but rather in the characteristics of the coalminers themselves. It was they who were failing, as 'the majority of men want to work for other people, not set up their own business'. This, like 'dependency', became seen as another part of the traditional culture of these areas, at odds with modern developments.

The problems and pitfalls facing redundant workers were recognised by the other enterprise agencies operating within local authorities on the coalfields. These had had considerable experience of offering support to small businesses through a variety of schemes, and were aware that the most sought-after kind of self-employment involved one man working alone, as a joiner, electrician or taxi driver. As one agency official pointed out, however, BCE expected further employment to be created: 'If you've got one man starting up as a joiner, unless he's going to employ a joiner as well, it's outside their terms of reference. So the bulk of our clients . . . wouldn't be suitable for British Coal funding.'[11]

Furthermore, as we have been told many times, not everybody can be self-employed. Expansion can lead to a self-defeating spiral of competition. This was well understood by the redundant miners. One explained:

> I was thinking about it. But there's a lot of overheads to start your own business, and you've got to have plenty of work on. And with the people that's around here doing roofing – there's loads . . . There's so many people roofing in the Valleys . . . Obviously the ones that have been going for a while are going to get the business before the ones that are new.[12]

Many enterprise agencies that pre-dated BCE had learned that the best advice to give to unemployed people with a redundancy cheque was to put it in the bank, 'as you're just going to lose it'. Most people took that advice, or had come to the same conclusion through their own reasoning; they used the money to pay off mortgages and other debts they had incurred during the strike.

In its efforts to justify its existence, BCE began to emphasise that its investments were not solely targeted at miners, but provided jobs for anyone in any and every traditional coal-mining area.[13] This shift allowed BCE to claim that in the previous ten years it had helped to create 130,000 jobs in the British coalfields, through a total expenditure of £101 million on over 5,000 projects. When criticised for this broader focus, it highlighted the Job and Career Change Scheme designed to help redundant British Coal employees into new jobs, which had been successful in 57,000 cases – a quarter of all the men involved. Even this claim lacked credibility, though, and was not supported by any of the detailed local studies covering the search for work made by specific groups of redundant miners. Many of these men felt that they had been cut adrift without support.

Redundancy

As we have seen, in the first wave of closures in the eighties, men who had decided to stay in the industry were transferred to surviving collieries. In the North East, miners from Horden were able to move to Easington, Dawdon and Wearmouth. Similarly, in South Wales, men from Penrhiwceiber had the option of moving to Tower or Deep Navigation. Many then left the industry with their redundancy money, however, and this was sometimes a source of bitterness. A good number of these men gave up and simply retired. Others – younger ones for the most part – looked for work in local factories and often found that the jobs there paid considerably less than those in the mines. Many of them experienced periods of unemployment.

Markham Colliery in South Wales closed in 1986. The mine had been the centre of the small and rather isolated village situated in the Sirhowy Valley, midway between Blackwood and Tredegar in the eastern coking-coal belt of the coalfield. The colliery's 506 miners were given the news of the closure in September 1985, along with their neighbours in Abertillery, at the New Mine, and in Newbridge, where both of the Celynen mines were also to shut. In this area, coal mining was still at this point the dominant industry, providing employment for over a quarter of all men, a fact which the economist Vickie Wass sees as having a critical effect upon the outcome of the closure. She established that 179 of the men elected to transfer to one of the local collieries – down the valley to Oakdale or across to Marine in Ebbw Vale or Six Bells – while the remaining 326 accepted redundancy.

The latter group became the main focus of Wass's study. After the pit closed, 70 per cent of the redundant men did not return to employment at all. Some (36 per cent) had decided to retire and did not look for work, but the others were committed and assiduous in their efforts to find another job, often more so than found in other industries. Despite this, their outcomes were worse. Over half of those actively seeking work had found nothing after two years, and those who were successful had, most commonly, found themselves in a number of different temporary appointments. Those who had become self-employed were single-man operations in the service sector, not innovating new companies with employees. Moreover, few of the redundant workers took up the option of retraining, something which Wass relates to the quality of the training on offer and its perceived lack of relevance. Wass is critical of the NCB and the Department of Employment for offering the redundant miners very little advice on job searches. In her view the training schemes were limited, and biased in favour of able young workers. She paraphrases the Job and Career Change Scheme as admitting 'we expect the courses to be undertaken by men under 50' and points out that 67 per cent of miners made redundant in Britain in 1985–86 were over fifty years old.[14]

Age was critical in all of this. At Markham it was men between the ages of thirty and fifty who were most likely to find work. Ironically, the terms of the RMPS (the lump-sum payment increasing with service and the presence of additional weekly payments for those over fifty) ensured that it would be the older men who participated and would perhaps be prematurely and unintentionally retired. This bias against the over fifties in the labour market was seen to be more acute on the coalfields than in other industrial or urban settings.

As Wass pointed out, however, the capacity of employers to discriminate on grounds of age was connected to the fact that too many redundant men were chasing too few jobs. Beneath all the flannelling of BCE lay one critical fact: insufficient jobs were being created in the post-mining economy. For the 326 Markham men who left the industry (and the other 179 who had moved to another mine, only to be made redundant within a few years), this situation was difficult to navigate. To demonstrate how outcomes varied, Wass provides three case studies. One ex-miner, a lodge official, accepted his retirement from work, but through his union activities was able to keep in touch with his old workmates and lead an agreeable and relatively active life. This contrasted with another who, made bitter and disillusioned by the strike and the closure, accepted that he had retired but struggled without a job, and failed to develop new interests. He became isolated, and sat reading the paper, or watching the world go by through his window. He had stopped going to the club but didn't know why.

The third – a younger man, aged forty-eight – was unemployed. He missed the mine, he still woke up early and made tea and tried to keep himself busy, but mostly he described himself as 'fed up'. Wass explains:

> His social life outside the family deteriorated to virtually nil following the colliery closure. This is something that he and his wife regretted, particularly because during the strike they had seen the village come together to share and thereby lessen their difficulties. But 'now everyone goes back to their own patches, does up the houses which they have bought and we never see them'. His wife explained that since the redundancies many of the wives, who had been responsible for the close social networks in the community, had to go out to work full-time and without them contact had disappeared because the men didn't get involved.[15]

In Durham, three of the four mines that closed were inland, with Sacriston the last of the collieries working the thin coking-coal seams to the west of the county. What remained were the large mines along the eastern coastal strip, and one of these – Horden – was listed for closure. By 1985 the workforce in the mine had been reduced to 800 men, who were unilaterally placed by the mine's manager into a 'labour reservoir' of men to be transferred to other collieries, thereby avoiding established procedures relating to rundown and closure. For many who still lived in the village, the memory of Horden as a major long-life colliery where coal was mined from faces miles offshore, remained compelling. But, as the lodge secretary explained in frustration, they had

> been pinned, back and back and back. It's like a vice they've put us in. We were a big pit, now we're down to two faces. Every way the Board has pushed us back. It wasn't so long ago you know, only about eight years or so, they were recruiting men in a big drive for labour . . . The Board was saying there was a secure job here for life . . . they were misleading people and playing about with people's lives . . . I think there's been a lot of mismanagement and there's still a lot of good coal to be mined . . . But they shouldn't have one time told a man to come then only a few years later told him he wasn't wanted any more when they'd been promising a future like they did. That's criminal.[16]

An almost identical situation was experienced by the miners at Cwm Colliery in the village of Beddau in Glamorgan, producing high-grade coking coal. At its peak it employed 1,500 men, and in 1977 the NCB had estimated its productive life at 100 years. Like Horden, Cwm was seen as a long-life colliery and as such had received many transferees from closing mines. It's clear that this cumulative experience of closure had a deadening effect upon the workforce. It also had an effect on their decisions after the closure. As one Cwm miner explained:

> I thought a long time about transferring. I really did. I sat down and thought about it and thought about it. I really did . . . and I kept coming back to the same sort of answer all the time: if they can shut Cwm they can shut any pit in South Wales.[17]

This echoes language used by a miner from Horden: 'If it can happen here it can happen to the next one. I'm not going to gan [go] like; if Horden closes I'll take my redundancy here and to hell with the pits.'[18] At Horden, those who decided to leave and take the redundancy payment faced a difficult task, as unemployment rates in the area were comparable to those identified by Wass at Markham. We managed to contact fifteen of these men in 1999 – eight were over fifty and none under thirty at the time of the closure.[19] Five of the over-fifties, as well as three of the others, were on some form of invalidity benefit, and had been for some time. Three mentioned this as a source of anxiety. One man who helped as a volunteer for meals on wheels worried that this might be used against him in any investigation into his disability. Another man's wife deliberately curtailed the hours she worked, in order to maintain his disability benefit. The various conditions described spoke of the severity of work in the mine: arthritis, spondylosis, bronchitis, vibration white finger, spinal injuries. All the others who had found work had also experienced some period of unemployment, and most of them worked in unskilled jobs for lower wages than they had received in the mine.

The End of the Road

By the early nineties, the option of transfer to another colliery was almost non-existent and a younger workforce knew that, down the line, it faced mass redundancy. Drawing on the experience of others who had gone before, these miners knew that finding work outside of mining was going to be difficult, would result in a loss of wages and could well involve moving away from home. While the agencies responsible for economic regeneration maintained an air of confidence, they were aware that the new wave posed a far greater and more intractable problem than had the earlier closures: here was a much younger group of men, less easily pensioned off.

The Coalfield Communities Campaign organised a survey of redundant workers at selected mines, which included Taff Merthyr in South Wales and Vane Tempest in Durham, where the average age of each workforce was thirty-seven and forty respectively.[20] Conducted a year after the mines had closed, unemployment figured heavily. Half of the men were out of work at the time of the survey and the majority had experienced some period of unemployment since being made redundant; 2 per cent were self-employed, and the remainder had found a job or were in a training scheme or educational programme. More of the Taff Merthyr men (46 per cent) were employed than their counterparts in Vane Tempest (26 per cent). In both cases factory employment was by far the most common kind of work and represented a drop in payment: 90 per cent of both groups had experienced a significant reduction compared with their wages in the mine. Of those without employment, 55 per cent of the Taff Merthyr men and 32 per cent of those at Vane Tempest were claiming sickness benefit rather than unemployment benefit.

These findings were reinforced by a careful study of the impact upon miners of the closure of the Westoe Colliery, the most northerly of the coastal Durham mines, located in South Shields at the mouth of the Tyne. Here, Nerys Jones established that while 1,200 men had been laid off, only 860 registered with BCE and of these just 10 per cent had found work eight months after the closure.[21] Her own survey, one year following the closure, mirrors the situation at Vane Tempest, with almost half having found work and a third unemployed. She talked with the men about the day the pit closed. One man remembered:

The last day at the pit really got to me, some of the men had tears in their eyes; men who were never ever soft. They were hugging each other when we were taking our lamps off. Some of them had been there all their lives; they'd never see each other again. It was a funny feeling; some were actually crying.[22]

Most of the men who eventually found work had been unemployed for a considerable time, on average eight and a half months. They all refused BCE's offer to train as security workers, 'regarded as the lowest status and lowest-paid employment available', yet 'their expectations of finding well-paid secure work in their trade (if they had one) lowered the longer they were unemployed'.[23] As one man explained:

In the *Gazette* every night there were adverts for security guards: £1.60 an hour rising to £1.80 after three months. When I used to pop into the Job Shop, I used to cringe at the jobs advertised. I thought 'Christ, you can't expect anyone to work for that; you'd be better off turning to crime.'[24]

The study revealed a considerable amount of anger among the men, along with suspicion of the authorities and those involved in the job creation business. They were particularly uncomplimentary about BCE and the claims made about helping redundant miners find employment. There was a persistent theme – that counsellors were mostly concerned with *their* 'outcomes':

All they wanted was to get you off their books, to get numbers off their books. As long as they could say they'd got you work you were off their books, even if it was only two or three weeks' work, you were off their books and that was it, they were quite happy.[25]

In 2000 we carried out a similar investigation into the consequences of the closure of the large Easington mine adjacent to Horden at the southern end of the coalfield. All of the fifty one men had in different ways tried to find work, and generally they shared the view of the Westoe miners about the inadequacy of the support and help that was available to them. Most notably, they expressed antagonism towards British Coal and BCE for what they felt was an uncaring attitude and inept provision of advice. Many men took short courses to obtain an HGV licence, or a certificate of competence in fork-lift truck driving, joinery or plastering, but these rarely assisted them in finding employment. More common was the experience of a series of short-term contracts in unrelated occupations. This man described how he began by

> delivering sandwiches for Eat Well but I had to take the employer to court in order to get the wages he owed me. Then I worked a sewage treatment plant, a job I got through ABC Employment Agency, and Northumbrian Water encouraged me to train for an HGV licence. Then I worked as a driver on South Shields dock on the car transporter ships. I got that job through another agency and was guaranteed a three-day week with the promise of a permanent job.

He was 'paid off abruptly' after three weeks, however, and then reluctantly registered with a security employment agency, well aware that he had reached the bottom of the pile. Another man, forty at the time of the closure, 'found work hard to get because of my age'. He became a machine cleaner on the night shift at the Sweet and Savory factory in Hartlepool, before taking a three-day HGV course. But he lacked the necessary experience to get a job driving, and in 2000 was employed as an industrial 'bag folder' at Structure Flex in Billingham, where he was paid on piece rates.

From 1990 onwards, with the possibility of the mine closing and redundancy seemingly ever present, the miners and their union at Easington concentrated on producing coal and extracting the highest possible bonus from the British Coal incentive scheme. The ex-power loaders we talked with estimated that their average wage in this period was around £24,000 a year, and as much as £600 a week on occasions. Other miners, working away from the faces, were paid proportionately less but still significantly more than the wages they received outside the industry when the mine closed. One man, who had found work at a plastic-moulding firm as a load checker, explained that his wife (who worked as a presser at the Courtauld's clothing factory in Peterlee) had extended her hours and 'took a full-time job because I was made redundant. But between us, we don't earn what I used to earn at the pit.'

The impact of the closures extended well beyond the individual miner, therefore, and into family life and household decision-making. This is most apparent in the employment trajectories of the ex-miners' wives. While only twenty-two of our ex-miners were employed six years after the mine closed, at least twenty-six of their wives were, several having taken additional training courses, and three having graduated with degrees from Sunderland University. In one sense, the year-long strike had prepared the ground for households facing hardship. During that period, many women had extended their hours of work, while others brought forward their decision to return to employment. As one of these women explained, 'I went back to work due to the miners' strike and I never got back home.' Instead, she extended her IT qualification to assist in her office career and studied for two A levels. Generally, however, women found employment in the local retail sector in corner shops and supermarkets, in the clothing factories that were located along the A19 and in health care. Mostly they worked part time and for low wages.

By contrast, twenty-three of the men – all but two of them over forty – were supported by disability benefits, and another six were receiving their occupational pension. As with the Horden men, the disabilities related to the arduous nature of their work in the mine and the conditions underground, with arthritis, spondylosis, vibration white finger and asthma again cropping up regularly. The process whereby these men moved from being active miners to being invalids is an important one. The physical nature of work underground was well understood and one man (who had lost half a finger in an accident) explained that 'injuries in the mine were commonplace'. Men learned to accept the pain of bumps, sprains and cuts, and to carry on. Where these were debilitating, arrangements were in place to move men to less physically stressful work. The familiarity of the mine and its social arrangements kept them going. Now all this had been swept away. This perhaps accounts for the cohort of men who said that when the mine closed, they looked for work and found jobs, but as time passed their injuries became worse. The associated onset of depression, the absence of good advice and the attraction of not having to 'sign on' also helped to create a highly invalided workforce. Like the Horden men, however, invalid status – and the threat of having to be regularly assessed, with the attendant danger of losing benefits – was a source of real anxiety. It was to become a critical issue later, as subsequent governments developed policies to tighten their grip on state welfare expenditure.

Work Without the Mine

The redundant miners worked hard to find a job. Few of them felt that they had much help from British Coal Enterprise. They all tried the job centres without much luck, and some found support in local job clubs. Where work was found, it was mostly through personal contacts and local networks.[26] Secure, well-paid employment was very thin on the ground, with temporary contracts dominating; and wage rates varied, as did the number of work hours available. One man, an electrician, dealt with this by moving from job to job, accumulating *eight* different employers in one year.

In both areas there was a universal understanding that age was a major factor in getting a job, and our own interviews confirmed that this perception persisted through to the end of the nineties.

One man who worked in the Unemployed Centre in Aberdare was convinced that age bias had got worse rather than better.

> The greater part of the miners didn't find jobs, and we used to say over the last ten years if you were over forty years of age and you went for a job in this valley, no employer would admit it publicly, and no one of managerial position in the benefit agency would admit it publicly, and I don't blame them. But it was understood in this community that if you were over forty you were just going through the bloody motions applying for a job, that was the score.

Phil, an electrician made redundant at the Six Bells Colliery in 1987, remembered 'when we went from Cwmtillery to Six Bells they promised us fifteen years work, I think I was there two, maybe three years. They promised us lots.' On top of the broken promises, he reflects on the support and advice he was given by the company when Six Bells closed. He was told to 'go to the local job centre and look . . . look for jobs.' No offer of training, no information on career advice or support – just 'look for a job'. He was willing to do anything and thought that he could find work in one of the (mainly Japanese) firms based in the valleys, manufacturing electronic goods:

> I had one interview to go to Aiwa . . . I was twenty-nine, and was told I was too old to go on the production line, although it was to do with electronics, I was too old, they told me I was too old at twenty-nine. I was a qualified electrician and I was willing to go on the production line to do with electrics, safety boards or whatever they do up there. I got to the interview and they offered a storeman's job – I thought stores was for old men and I'm twenty-nine, I don't want it, so that was it.

As well as age, skill was an important issue: these men – the ex-miners – were clear that they had skills, but that they were

mining skills and not easily transferable to the world of manufacturing. Even men like Phil would say this – that as electricians or
fitters their training was tailored to a world away from a contemporary factory environment. They thought a lot about the kinds
of skills they had as miners and how they related to this new world
of work. One talked of being good for 'donkey work':

> If they'd wanted us to be labourers, carrying and pushing, yes,
> but in factories we didn't fit in. We stuck out like sore thumbs.
> I'm a physical, big man, I was 15 stone and . . . then I was as fit
> as a fiddle. I could lift anybody, I could lift anything, I could
> shovel for eight hours a day!

In the absence of a massive civil engineering programme, the days
of shovelling were gone – but the alternative training or advice
offered proved to be of limited usefulness in obtaining employment. Men talked of being helped to acquire the skill of writing
letters, and then of writing 'hundreds of letters', often with no
reply. What they learned in the process, and through the experience of others living close by, was that men in their forties would
find it hard to find employment, and that the best local job they
could hope for would be as a security guard or school caretaker.
Those who got jobs did so through their own determination,
discovering through personal contacts which companies were
hiring, learning about strategies for the interview and what to
expect.

In the absence of coherent support, these ex-miners needed to
find ways to deal with the corporate recruitment practices that
dominated the local labour market. Younger people were more
employable because they could be moulded more easily to the
expectations of local management. In addition, the widespread
practice of using temporary contracts, sometimes directly or
through an employment agency, was a way of assessing performance, reliability and compliance before offering a permanent
position. In contrast to the regime in the mine, these men

encountered a new world of unpredictability and uncertainty. In this they were not alone, however, and they were able to learn from each other, often bringing a critical eye upon these new arrangements.

The factory, of course was different from the mine, and working for multinational employers brought the redundant miners into contact with new shopfloor cultures. Unilever Bestfoods, which had opened its factory near Crumlin in 1975 to produce its new product, Pot Noodle, employed a large proportion of female workers. As the product gained in popularity the labour force was expanded to include increasing numbers of men, some of them ex-miners, on the assembly lines, where managers emphasised the importance of teamwork. But the definition of teamwork operated very differently to that at the mine.[27] As one man explained:

> In the pit I think it was more comradely, whereas in the factory where you are supposed to work as a team and help each other, you will find that some will and some won't . . . They said there is no helping each other, it is 'help yourself – you don't help the other team', you know and that is a big difference. Because when they were in the pit you would all help each other and look out for each other.

This issue of mutual support and solidarity was often mentioned. One man who returned to Tower reflected on this, saying that in the mine

> you stood together. But if you go outside and what have you, you'll see men struggling on their own. Underground you wouldn't see a man struggle, you wouldn't have to ask anybody to give you hand, they should automatically see you struggling and they come and give you a hand.

It is this sense of solidarity in work that was missed the most. One man in Durham who had managed to get a 'good job' in local government was shocked by 'the back-stabbing' and the absence of the social solidarity he had experienced in the pit and had come to rely upon.

In conversations, it became clear that the comparisons with working in the mine were ever present. This extended from responsibilities and wages right through to the social nature of work in the different industries. In the Pot Noodle factory, time passed slowly:

> Underground you didn't have watches, you didn't know what time it was, eight hours used to go like that. Up the noodle factory you had that clock staring at you for eight hours, until I got into it. It took me at least three months to get the hang of it, I just didn't think I would be able to do it. I didn't think I would be able to stick it, it was so hot, it was so frustrating.

Overwhelmed by the production numbers and by any sense of purpose he reflected on the nature of his new work:

> What a boring, boring job! Every time when I've looked at a job, I've always thought about what Max Boyce said about the pit-head baths being supermarkets now. We're working in a factory counting buttons and I felt like one of them persons. The pit had closed down and I'm working in a factory putting soups into pots, sachets of tomato ketchup in a flaming box. I couldn't believe it. It was so degrading it was hard to believe, I couldn't put it into words.

A man from Easington obtained temporary employment through an employment agency at the crisp factory in Peterlee. His job, he explained, was 'adding novelties to crisp packs as they passed by me on the line – thousands of them'. He wasn't disappointed when his contract came to an end. However, for younger men with children it was a different matter. As one man put it: 'I found it hard starting off, because going from working in the pit . . . it was boring, I had the kids, I had to stick it out, you had to do it for the money, that's all it was.'

In Durham, the north–south route of the A19 provided the link between the business parks and trading estates that ran up from Hartlepool, through Peterlee and on to Sunderland, Washington and Gateshead. Many of the men who had worked in Horden and Easington collieries ended up in one or other of the new factory units that extended along this thoroughfare. It was commonly agreed that the best places were the branch plants of Caterpillar or the Japanese transnational NSK Ltd, based in Peterlee. It was also agreed that 'you needed to know someone' to get in there. In South Wales too, multinational companies had established branch plants in the valley towns and along the A459 – the Heads of the Valleys road that linked Ebbw Vale, Merthyr and Neath. It was around these places – places they knew and those they learned about from friends and family – that people most often looked for work.

Generally, though, it was agreed that to get work that paid a wage similar to that of the mine, you had to travel, you had to go away. For the Durham miners their options were to go west, nearer to Durham City, or north, up to Newcastle; while in South Wales the M4 corridor from Newport to Swansea offered equivalent opportunities, along with the daily commute. These options were often taken by the younger family men. Some moved further still. In the eighties the construction of the Channel tunnel and the Jubilee line in London were the major civil engineering projects in the country. Had there been similar projects in Wales and in the North, many of the redundant men would have found work there. As it was, many ex-miners travelled to London, returning home at weekends.

An Employment Crisis

The campaigning activities of the Coalfield Communities Campaign and the NUM alerted the world beyond the coalfields to the fact that things were not working as they were supposed to. In South Wales, only 45 per cent of men who had worked in the mines in 1981 had found employment ten years later – the lowest proportion across all of the NCB Areas.[28]

In the 1980s government strategy for the coal industry aimed at reducing *both* the number of collieries *and* the number of miners on the list of unemployed. To achieve this, the RMPS incentivised miners to leave the industry, while job centre staff were primed to persuade unemployed miners to register as disabled. As a result, unemployment figures – as measured by the number of people signing on at job centres and claiming Jobseeker's Allowance – came to be seen as an unreliable measure of the state of coalfield labour markets.

In 1996 a report by Christina Beatty and Steve Fothergill pointed out that, after the loss of over 200,000 jobs in the coal mines, the unemployment rates in the coal districts were lower than in 1985 and the difference between them and the national rates had narrowed.[29] This, together with the public statements of BCE, seemed to confirm the Thatcherite programme of closure and enterprise as a considerable success. Revealing the flaw in this argument, the report indicated that two main processes were at work which together countered the narrative of a vibrant economy. First, in the search for work, miners had moved away from home, with net out-migration from the coal districts standing at 50,000. Second, and more importantly, the true unemployment figure was masked because it excluded those who (in the new parlance) were 'economically inactive' – mainly the permanently sick or retired – and described in the report as the 'hidden unemployed'. According to the report, the real level of male unemployment in the coalfields in 1996 was nearer 25 per cent, and 30 per cent in the pit villages themselves. By 1991, new employment had 'offset only just over a quarter of the jobs lost in coal' and was mainly to be found in retail, hotels and catering.

By the mid-nineties, all the evidence confirmed that Durham and South Wales were suffering an employment crisis. Although the scale of funds available for regeneration had increased incrementally, it was unlikely that this would be adequate in the face of the growing structural problems associated with the collapse of the core of the coal-based economy and the general trend of deindustrialisation.

CHAPTER EIGHT

Sticking Together and Falling Apart

Hall, chapel, club:
a society's essentials once,
are now shells, museums without visitors:
like old people whose children have left them.
The community no longer needs them enough
to look after them.
            Grahame Davies, 'DIY', 2003

The tenth anniversary of the strike was commemorated in 1994 with parties and meetings across both coalfields, as people recalled and discussed the events of the strike and their part in them. At the same time, they were adjusting to the fact that in their areas, for so long synonymous with coal and public owner- ship, deep mining of coal had all but finished and their future was in the lap of the market. The Labour Party under the leader- ship of Bedwellty MP Neil Kinnock had lost two general elec- tions to the Conservatives, the second to John Major, whose victory in 1992 achieved one of the biggest margins in the popu- lar vote since Clement Attlee's 1945 landslide. All this created a sense that, in dealing with all the changes that had affected their lives, people there were very much on their own.

The Social Life of the Mine

Although mining took place underground, it had significant impacts on the surface, most obviously in the presence of the distinctive pithead winding gears that carried the men in cages down into the earth and brought out the coal – the 'black gold' that had transformed the British economy. Mining had come to overlay the wider landscape, and so intense and enduring was this intrusion that, for many, the distinction between the naturally occurring environment and the one that was man-made became blurred and indistinct.

In discussions about mining, memories of the local environment, and particularly how the mines affected play in childhood, always emerged. What predominated though was the question of mine labour and the nature of mining as an occupation – of what it meant to be a miner. There was a general recognition that the work was hard. While miners of an older generation might argue that 'modern mining' with mechanised faces bears no comparison to the days when coal was cut with hand tools, realistically no one denied that work underground was harder and more dangerous than most activities on the surface. When pressed, and after more than ten years away from the mine, few of the men we talked with wanted to put themselves through the physical training necessary to go back, even if there were jobs available in the mines. Nevertheless, they said that they missed it – they missed being miners.

In reflecting on this and remembering the time in their lives when they *were* miners, the men used a unique vocabulary to express a strongly held view that their departure from mining was more than just the loss of a job. One man in South Wales explained:

People say about how the mining jobs have gone. It wasn't jobs, it was our way of life. It wasn't a job to me, it was my way of life, it was my whole being. Coal is in my blood.

Another man, who as a boy had resisted going into the mine, until he recognised that there was nothing else, recalled that 'once you're down there, it becomes you, and you become it':

> I miss it now, that's what you don't understand. When you go, once that cage drops and you stop seeing daylight, men lived differently. Down there is a different way of life, it's not a job, it's a way of life and I mean literally *life*. Somebody makes a mistake and puts a post up wrong, the next bloke behind him is going to get the clout, he's going to be in a wheelchair or dead, you know, it's that type of thing. If you hear a rumble and you hear a bang you think 'oh shit,' you know, 'is that just a crash in the goaf or what's going to come next?'[1] I know it might sound dramatic but it did happen. When a guy does have a bump everybody rallies round. Never mind who it is. People say that the mining jobs have gone, it wasn't a job, it was like a policeman – a policeman becomes a policeman because it's a vocation, it's like a doctor, it's the same as us.

These are feelings of great intensity, and they help explain the shock that was inflicted by the abrupt and enforced manner of the closures. When these men said 'Maggie Thatcher stole my job', they really meant it and they were not simply (or even) referring to the wage: they were saying that a whole way of life had been taken away. They talked of missing the mine – its 'comradeship' and 'way of life'. The status of mining as a vocation, built around a distinctive code of conduct, was highly valued, and shed an unfavourable light upon other forms of employment that were merely jobs. In discussing this 'code of honour', men described standing together, supporting each other, never letting anyone struggle on their own, giving people a hand. They talked of discussing the work in the club or on the bus. In Durham, being 'marras' (friends), in South Wales 'butties'. In the absence of all this there was a deep and lasting sense of loss.

Historically, coalminers had established themselves as men of some substance. Although formally unskilled, mining work involved great ingenuity and the capacity to deal with the unusual and unexpected. These tacit skills, allied with comradeship, were essential to the success of mining and, as we have seen, went mostly unrecognised once the mines had closed. Moreover, the miners had revealed skills and capabilities in social and political organisation which were equally important. On the surface of the mine, through their collective action, miners and their families had built local communities out of institutions of their own creation. All this, taken together, had, over the course of generations, injected pride and dignity into their craft.

The miners' welfare halls built between the two world wars were pivotal institutions, alongside the chapels and cooperative stores. The trade union too played a crucial role, and had in those years persistently petitioned for public ownership of the mines. These structures provided an umbrella of support, a space in which people could develop their individual talents and personalities in civil society.

Glyn Owen, reflecting on times in Penrhiwceiber when the mines were working, remembered,

> If you went to pubs or clubs you would always have a group of these people there, and there would always be miners who would tend to be leaders in all the discussions that went on, whether it be about the church or the school, you name it, miners' tongues would be at the clacking. And the lodge committee and especially in Ceiber, they would actually lead in everything. People would automatically look to tradition and to the lodge committee . . . that is what the lodge done: any problem we had, whether somebody had a problem like with the council or whatever, they tended to go to somebody on the lodge.

A woman in that village described the day the vote was taken to close the pit, evoking some elements of that past life:

> On a Monday night I always go out, I go to . . . the chapel. I would come out at about half past eight and they would be coming out of the meeting in the hall so the first person that I saw, who I knew, I asked, 'How did the meeting go?' and he said, 'They are closing it. We have accepted the redundancy.' That finished me then . . .

This memory frames the drama of the occasion (the vote to accept closure) in the context of the institutions that the workers had made themselves: the meeting hall and the chapel. For every club in the South Wales valleys, there was also a chapel. In the 1850s one new chapel was opened every week.[2] They closed at the same rate in the 1980s and 90s, along with the mines. One woman recalled the changes in this way:

> We used to have three services: morning, afternoon and night, children in the afternoon. We had two services then, in the morning and the afternoon, because you couldn't get the ministers for the nights, and over the past year now it has been either morning or afternoon according to when you can have a minister.

A similar pattern, although with a later start date, affected the co-ops and the miners' welfare organisations, the miners' institutes and welfare halls. In Wales and Durham the Miners' Welfare Halls are remembered with affection. These were the places where people met as strangers and became best friends, husbands and wives. They were at the heart of social life. The buildings survived into the 1990s and sometimes continued to serve a social function within the community. Mostly, however, they were transformed into furniture showrooms, bingo halls, strip clubs and squash courts – removed from the social realm, commodified and incorporated into the shoddy end of commerce.

It was sad to see this callous treatment of things that were once precious to people, and difficult to escape a feeling of loss. By the nineties, in many mining towns and villages, the broad area of the *social*, once regulated by committees and common owner-ship, had withered. This also extended to the ways in which privately owned establishments operated. In the village of Murton in County Durham, for example, miners used to meet in a local pub situated across the road from the pit. Known collo-quially as the Back of the Shaft, it was full most evenings and, containing a meeting room and social facilities, was a place where people would go to meet. John Cummings, when secretary of the mechanics' lodge at the mine and leader of the local council, could be found there with his Jack Russell ('the picket dog'), ready for a drink or an argument, and to be questioned. This ritual continued at the weekends after his election to Westminster as MP for Easington. By then, however, the audience was consid-erably reduced, with fewer and fewer miners calling in as people talked of 'not going out much anymore'.

The closures of the mines had far-reaching social consequences, threatening the coherence and density of the social relationships and institutions that had built up around the industry over the last century. In the seventies these were managed in ways that allowed older miners to leave the industry early, before retire-ment age, and for others to be transported in buses by the NCB to another local pit. Commenting on this, one lodge official in South Wales felt that 'the demise of the coal industry you could say had taken place gradual down here . . . more gradual down here than up in the North. It was more gradual down here in a sense, so it was easier.'

The sense of gradualism in South Wales came from the settle-ment pattern, which reflected the local geology. As we have seen, in Durham mines closed from west to east, with the industry finally located in a string of mining towns and villages along the seaboard. In South Wales, by contrast, selected mines closed within valleys and around central points, so there was no local experience of the *erasure* of mining, as had happened in towns such as Crook and Bishop Auckland. Consequently, when the final closures came to the North East, they had a profound but spatially limited impact, confined to villages and towns such as Horden, Easington, Murton, Seaham, and even Sunderland and South Shields, the place once known as Three Collieries after the Harton, St Hilda and Westoe pits.[3] In these places miners still lived in large enclaves – often in houses that had been built or owned by the coal companies – and the closures had an immediate effect upon the senses: the absence of large groups of men and fleets of buses coming and going as the shifts changed. There were similar changes in South Wales, but the impact was far more dispersed. Mines closed across the whole of the old coalfield, from Six Bells and Marine in the east to Cynheidre in the west. In towns such as Abertillery, Oakdale, Mountain Ash and Aberdare, miners had come to live side by side with other workers, so the closure had a broader and perhaps more symbolic impact, affecting not only miners but also their neighbours and younger generations that had never experienced coal mining. Everywhere, though, there was a sense of an ending: no more the sound of the hooter and the voices of men as they surrounded the mine, coming and going. No more the sound of coal emptying into the trucks that would take it to the power stations and steelworks.

In all of these places, the decline and disappearance of the coal-mining industry was experienced with a sense of loss, expressed sincerely and with deep emotional conviction. Once the pit closed and the men had been paid off, the mine itself disappeared, the winding gears that once dominated the landscape taken down with great speed and the pithead levelled. One man, after reflecting on the salvaging practices of the 1950s and 60s, which often extended over a number of years, said:

> After the '84–'85 strike they couldn't wait to get rid of the evidence, they was guilty as hell and they knew it and now

there's not a sign of where we used to work. It's like as if we weren't valued. All what we done for all those years, all for what our forefathers had done for all those years – and don't forget the First World War was won on bloody coal in them ships – but all of a sudden, we didn't count for naught.

This process of dismantling and clearing the surface of the mine was a critical part of state-led regeneration policies for the mining districts organised by English Heritage in England and by the Welsh Development Agency in Wales. For the people in the villages, however, the clearing of physical space came to be understood as the enforced removal of the past. The Ocean Deep Navigation Colliery, commonly known as 'the Ocean' when under the private ownership of the Ocean Coal Company, became 'Deep Nav' after nationalisation. It was renowned for being the deepest colliery on the South Wales coalfield, with two shafts reaching depths of 593 metres and 696 metres. Located in Treharris, south of Merthyr Tydfil, it was part of the second wave of closures that ended production there in 1991. Subsequently, with the speed that had become customary, the buildings were demolished, the site cleared and landscaped.

At that time, Tony Armstrong worked as an engineer at the hydraulic machine company Hymac – a subsidiary of Powell Duffryn – making excavation machinery in nearby Rhymney. He visited the Deep Navigation site with a colleague to observe the dismantling of the colliery. They were intrigued to see the size of the wheel drum and the way that it had been constructed – tapered at both ends – to adjust the speed of the cage as it was lowered through the deep shaft. They marvelled at this engineering innovation and were dismayed when the salvage team

took an acetylene torch to it and just cut it up: an amazing thing like that; perhaps unique. You would think that they would have found some way of keeping it – as a monument or something. But to just cut it up. We thought it was awful.

This account of two engineers, observing the dismantling of one of Britain's industrial achievements, resonates with the ways in which men and woman from the colliery villages talked of grieving for the closure of the mines. People felt at a loss, overtaken by the *scale* of the closures in a way that had a severe psychological effect, very much akin to grief.[4] In reflecting on this grief, community members reacted angrily to the forces from outside that had defeated the strike and then physically removed the last material evidence of mining: 'I think that they are trying to tell us something – I think they're telling us that this is the end. There's going to be no more mines and no more miners.'

Gender at Work

Most of the miners we talked to were influenced by their parents in their choice of employment. Almost all of them had followed their fathers or brothers into the pit – so much so that mining was remembered as a *family* industry. Irvin Lyons, the lodge secretary at Horden, always insisted that the colliery was a family pit. Here and in South Wales, for the men who joined the industry as boys, their first day remained with them in memory and with great precision.

> I remember the first day walking in there, it was on a Monday and I had to walk over to Aberavon, and get the red and white bus down to the pit. Pitch black, January 15th it was, and I was walking in there. Walk off the bus, and as you walk through the gate it is like a whole different world altogether, there is a buzz.

The most important features of this 'whole different world' were that it was underground, and that it was made up of men alone. These two facts – so obvious and self-evident that they were rarely mentioned explicitly – underpinned the organisation and culture of mining labour in Britain. Hidden from view,

mining was not easily subjected to surveillance or detailed super-
vision, and it had a high degree of autonomy. It differed funda-
mentally from most manual labour, where by the 1990s single-
sex workplaces were a rarity, and tasks were increasingly regulated,
monitored, subject to audit and (in the service sectors) open to
the public gaze.[5] Being underground, mining was unseen and in
some ways mysterious – an easy topic for storytelling and the
craic for which miners in both regions were famous. The heroic
aspect to miners' lives that Richard Burton recalls in the epigraph
to this book gave the miners a means of establishing their masculinity, something that was made clear in times of strife when they
would be urged to stand together 'like men'. A sense of this
comes through in accounts of daily life in the 1960s:

> I would hear the Celenyn North hooter going which meant
> my father was at the end of his shift. I can remember my father
> and about five or six of his mates walking up the street . . . he
> used to say 'all right boys', go in our house, have his dinner put
> on his lap. Within 10 minutes of him having his dinner he
> would be in bed . . . I thought how amazing, he would come
> straight from work, have his dinner and straight to bed. He
> would get up, have his tea put on his lap, within an hour he
> would be up the club.

The man thought of his father as lazy until he started working in
the pit with him, when, seeing his strength and enormous capacity for hard work, he understood why he went straight to bed,
and never thought of him as lazy again.

This ex-wife of a miner in Durham, however, took a different
view:

> A pit man to me has an easy life . . . At least my man did and
> lots of them did. He went out to work, bait made up and
> everything done for him; come home meal on the table; sit
> and relax while you were doing the jobs. Never lifted a hand

to do anything. Never washed up, never made a bed, just rolled into bed and rolled out. I used to always say, 'I'm last into bed and first out'. And that was the life.

What both accounts make clear is just how complete the division was between work in the home and work in the mine. The club – exclusive to men at this time – became an extension of the workplace, while in the house, men did very little indeed, for the domestic realm was women's work.[6] As one man in South Wales put it:

> Prior to the demise of the coal industry . . . for generation after generation, the man went out to work, the woman stayed in the house, the system remained the same. Then all of sudden what has happened? I know it is an evolutionary process, but it was a bang-bump change.

Of course, the changes were more gradual than this and had begun on the sixties, but the rapid closure of the mines in the eighties did have a 'bang-bump' effect. By this point, however, the domestic labour of women that had played such a critical part in the establishment of the coal industry had somewhat eased. Shower faculties were established in the sixties (even as mines closed). A decade later, overalls were provided and laundered. Furthermore, in many if not all homes, the acquisition of consumer durables such as washing machines, tumble driers and hoovers as household incomes rose helped to ease the burden – although investment in the home also reinforced the significance of the domestic sphere, 'the house' looming larger in local culture as the communal life of 'the chapel' and 'the club' waned.

Strong patriarchal structures persisted, linked to the idea of men as breadwinners – something that retained a deep meaning in these places. Many men found it morally unacceptable to be financially dependent upon their wives. However, as these

women factory workers in Durham explained in 1979, sometimes things had to be seen as they were in reality:

> He wasn't very happy but we needed the money, so he just got
> used to it. He thought he was the breadwinner but the wage
> he was getting was no good.

And as another explained, in difficult times, circumstances
demanded change:

> He's had an accident and was put permanently on the sick.
> Things deteriorated at home so I decided to go out aside earn
> money to replenish the home – you know, carpets and what
> not.

Following the mine closures of the sixties and eighties, the
proportion of women in the labour force increased from 20 per
cent until it reached parity with men. Women came to hold a
regular presence across workplaces in both regions, moving from
the margins to a central position as waged workers within the
working class. There was more than money involved in this
development:

> Women at that time were relying on a husband. They relied
> upon him to be the breadwinner, But they had no identity. I
> never had any identity at all. I used to be quite a character
> before I got married and then when I got married it just
> seemed as though all I had was the kids . . . As a person I don't
> think I really existed.

Factory work was repetitive and attracted low wages, often paid
on piece rates. But in spite of the tedium of the job, women
found enjoyment in the company of others who, like them, had
spent years at home bringing up a family, and with whom they
could share their problems. As one explained, 'You work because

you want the money rather than want a job. But I like being amongst the girls here. I enjoy the company.' For many, waged work was embraced as a desperate measure to maintain households, and involved considerable sacrifice. But in the way these women talked, it is easy to discern the influence of the wider women's movement and a desire for more independence. The social consequences were enormous, many of them positive, in that they provided a growing number of women with their own income and greater freedom.

The expansion of the welfare state meant that other kinds of jobs and careers were becoming available, especially in education and healthcare, and we have noted the number of women who took up these opportunities after the last pits closed. One could say that as the nationalised coal industry disappeared, a different part of the public sector was expanding, offering more rewarding and less dangerous employment. By the nineties, however, this too had changed, as the privatisation process extended into public services, particularly social care, where private, non-union, low-wage providers came to dominate. Care-home staff found this more than irksome. One 24-year-old care assistant in Derwentside in West Durham, interviewed in 1990, put it in this way:

> We have a diabolical wage here. It's terrible. That is the trouble with the private sector, because they can charge what they like. And I don't really see it's fair, like all the Council homes, I mean, their wages are fantastic compared to what ours are, and we do the same job, basically.

But she, like several others, had moved to a private sector home because it was within walking distance of her house, enabling her to cope more easily with her, still onerous, domestic commitments. A minority of these women had partners working full time on a 'good wage' and were less concerned about wage levels. For them, including some with young children, they needed the job to get them out of the house, seeing it as better than sitting at home getting bored. The common view, however, was that the wages were 'not very good, not at all, but it is a job and I enjoy doing it'. Often, for single women it meant long hours and sometimes more than one contract. One care assistant worked 35 hours in a residential home and 15 hours of one-to-one care for a disabled person, bringing in a weekly income of £122 before tax.

Meanwhile, pit closures left many men, especially those over the age of fifty, without paid work and reliant on various forms of pension and state benefit. This also affected social relations and the distribution of power within the family. Strong feelings were expressed at a meeting we organised in Mountain Ash made up of ex-coalminers, union activists and members of community action groups associated with the new social economy. During a conversation about the impact of deindustrialisation upon people's sense of worth, one of the men explained:

> The point you said about self-esteem, self-confidence and everything else is perfectly correct, but added to that, the grief of them losing the pits and everything is one thing, but the fact that women have taken over is also another thing, because we were the breadwinners, now we're the bloody housewives, so we resent the fact of women taking over. They may be the activists, but we don't want them to be, it's just that we have been so down in the dumps now that we don't give a monkey's who takes over, we're going into another system now, but the men don't count for naught.

This man had been a deputy in the pit, and as he explained, 'I told men what to do; now everybody tells me what to bloody do'. For him and many others, the ending of the coal industry had brought about a significant change of status. A common view emerged during the meeting that women had been quicker to adapt to new and difficult circumstances for the preservation of the household, driven by a conviction that 'if they didn't do something, nobody would'. There was also a sense that women 'will turn their hand to anything, unlike men who won't do women's work'. According to one keen observer of social life in County Durham:

> You go into Murton, go to Easington and you see a lot of forty-five-year-old men walking around with carrier bags, that have left the pit. Fifty-five-year-old men that have left the pit, and when the collieries closed the decision was made – not their decision, but the decision was also made in their own minds – that they will never get another job. Now, that's the stark reality of the situation . . . they feel they're sitting around, you know, all day long, they feel embarrassed that they're sitting around all day long. They've got their own pride, they try to make the dinner, they're bloody awful cooks! You know, they make a crap job of tidying up! You know, it's those sort of things . . . They can pick a hoover up and hoover, but they don't make a good job of it, because that's not where they're from, really, as people. And there's a sort of sense of despair there and worry and the wives know that as well . . . It's this sort of thing, you know, they've lost a lot of their dignity to be honest, as people.

A woman in the Cynon Valley, reflecting on the effects of the mine closures, had similar thoughts: 'I think that they're taking away men's dignity as well'.

Many ex-miners, though, learned to live with the new arrangements. One man in Durham recalled that when he was in the pit, 'you were working, and bed and working and bed, that was all you were doing. But now my wife works and I don't. Everything's changed round. I do all the cooking, all the cleaning.' In one study, Meg Allen found that these arrangements, if not the new norm, were common enough among older ex-miners in families where the women were employed full time. Here, husbands who were no longer working 'carried out all the household tasks, including cooking, cleaning and washing'. Allen noted that the women still took on the major responsibility for the care of children and old relatives, but the new routines nevertheless involved 'a very significant change for these couples'.[7]

Families Living through Decline

The social and economic fabric of the old coal districts revolved around the family unit with its characteristic sexual division of labour. For many decades, Durham was known as the most married county in England, and in South Wales the literature and biography of the coalfield had the 'Welsh mam' centrally placed in the life of mining villages. Women worked in the home and their accounts of their lives often dwell on the significance of family:

> Well I really enjoyed looking after them all, it was hard, there's no doubt about it, but they always had plenty to eat . . . they never starved, we tried our best to keep them neat and tidy. My sister used to make their dresses for Sunday School and all that. So, like I said, it was a happy time for me really. We managed anyway. We weren't well off but we managed.

But not all marriages were as happy. One woman in Peterlee explained how she was very close to her aunt, and

> I knew my uncle always used to come in and hit her . . . When I got my divorce she said 'I wish I was having my time again and I was young again like you. I would have gone for a divorce but in those days it was not heard of. You stuck by him no matter what he did.'

Times had changed. As one of her workmates in the factory explained:

Most women *have* to go out to work, but I think women need
to be independent now . . . Most women want something that
they can call their own. They don't want to be kept down
anymore. I think that is what it used to be.

In contemplating this, people used the language of 'role reversal', and dwelled on the problems that the men had with their
changed status. There is no doubting the enormous differences
in social life that have been brought about by industrial decline
and the social legislation introduced in the sixties. The contrast
between traditional and present-day family life on the coalfields
is remarkable. Cohabitation outside marriage has become prevalent and vies with marriage as the most common household
structure. In 2000 the vicar in Penrhiwceiber commented on
how weddings had changed: once people had married in their
early twenties, but couples were increasingly in their thirties, and
accompanied by their children. In these old coal districts, the
percentage of births outside marriage is well above the national
average, as is the number of births to women under the age of
twenty, and there is a higher likelihood that parents will be living
apart at the time of the birth. These arrangements have been
assimilated into a world where kinship has traditionally had a
deep and a profound significance. In talking of her grandchil-
dren, one woman said that the parents 'aren't married but they
love each other'. Younger women now have greater freedom to
choose whether to stay with a partner or not. One explained, 'I
was with him for about seven or eight years, but I had to get rid
of him.'

Helen Blakeley's study of single mothers in Merthyr points to
the difficulties young women face in building relationships in
the context of poor employment choices and young men who
were 'feckless' and 'unable or unwilling to support their families'.
She notes that 'tussles with the Child Support Agency over maintenance payments and conflicts over visitation rights were not
uncommon, and these troubled relationships were often a source

of huge anxiety.' The women in her study were enrolled in a course aimed at equipping them for examinations that could lead to a career in nursing. This was a 'second chance' but others were not so lucky, and talked of 'taking it day by day'. A woman who had been 'caught pregnant with my son' when she was sixteen regretted that she had been unable to complete her schooling. She had worked in a fruit shop and had stayed there for four years as she liked it, and then worked at the Co-op in Penrhiwceiber. Unsatisfied, she took a night class in computing, which she enjoyed:

> I just feel I want something, but where I haven't got to find care for the children during school hours. You can't do a lot, but I do enjoy computers . . . So if I could . . . get a job on what I've done already it would be good . . . but there's always new stuff coming along all the time. I really enjoy it.

She remembered that she had 'wanted a career myself, when I was younger there was loads of things I wanted to do', and expressed determination that her children should be able to make something of themselves: 'I want them to do something, well I want them to be completely different to what I am, to have something.'

This concern for the next generation, and for children to have a better life, is a recurring theme on the coalfields. It reflects a deep tension between the values of a life linked to kinship and community and the paucity of economic opportunities in these rapidly deindustrialising areas. In the nineties people were becoming acutely aware of these issues. For many, the closure of the mines marked an ending – an ending that had far deeper meaning than the loss of coal production. In some ways it was a loss of hope, and reflected a realisation that the world had changed, and not for the better. One woman in the Cynon Valley told us:

I think it's the same everywhere, it's going to be very hard. I remember my mother . . . would say, 'Oh well never mind times are hard now, but it's going to be better when you leave school.' Everyone kept saying 'oh its going to get better', but it's always got worse. So, I think for everybody, it's not just in the deprived areas anymore, because even if you've got all the qualifications going, it's hard and it's going to get harder.

A man in South Wales described some of the problems of living through decline. He had been a miner, as had his father, and he remembered a time when work was plentiful, but:

For the last twenty years we've lived in a declining area, with declining social structure, declining employment, and then we wonder why young people are demotivated. If young people live in a house where there's conflict between mother and father, there's no jobs, it's a declining area and people are leaving and then we wonder why young people feel so down on themselves.

A sense of decline permeated the coalfields in the nineties, feeding a scepticism over the kinds of jobs that would come to these areas and the possibility of a brighter future. People talked of things going on 'over their heads', of various schemes and consultations that ended in nothing. This was the general mood on both coalfields as the country prepared for another general election on May Day 1997. This time the Labour Party was led by an MP with a Durham constituency. There was a hope that a Blair government might change things. Certainly, things couldn't go on as they were.

Map 5. New Development

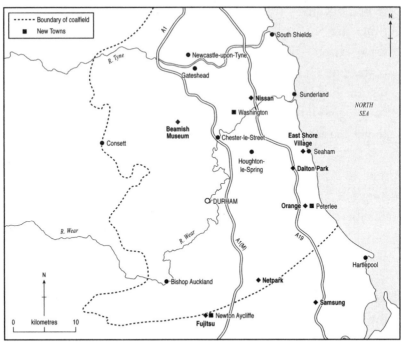

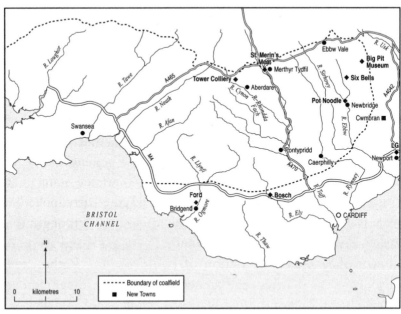

CHAPTER NINE

Regeneration?

What my constituents need is work, but in the eight years I have represented them we have lost the ship yards, the pit and a large slice of our engineering capacity, and I cannot think of a single job that has been created or saved as a result of my efforts. To paraphrase John Garrett, 'Britain has been in decline for the last hundred years. The role of Parliament has been to provide a running commentary.'
Chris Mullin, *A Walk-On Part*, 2011

In opposition, the Labour Party had not strongly contested the closures of the mines but argued instead for the modernisation of mining areas, with better kinds of employment achieved through a more energetic policy of regeneration. New Labour had turned its back on nationalisation with the abolition of Clause IV of its constitution, and also on any idea of the national state as an engaged actor within the economy. Instead, the Party looked to what it regarded as the combined and positive impacts of globalisation, high technology and international markets, and accepted insecurity as a basic condition of economic life. Rather than break with the policies of Thatcher, the new government would provide a radical continuity. Blair was 'Thatcher's most devoted follower, progenitor of what deserves to be termed "Blatcherism"', observed former *Times* editor Simon Jenkins.[1]

Under the Blair governments, 'regeneration' became part of everyday speech among policy makers, local councillors, trade union and social activists and almost everyone else. It filled the pages of local newspapers such as the *Western Mail* and *Northern Echo*. Once it had referred only to improvements and changes to the physical landscape, but now it went beyond this to denote a broad programme of social and economic development. Such matters had been the purview of the local authorities, which had accumulated considerable experience in dealing with the closure of collieries. Under New Labour, however, there was a shift towards policies determined at the UK national level, strongly influenced by the agendas and perspectives of international organisations such as the OECD as to the appropriate content and form of economic development policies. In the Durham and South Wales coalfields the challenge involved the virtual *rebuilding* of a post-coal economy. In both areas it was agreed that this had to be done in a diversified way, with a mixture of manufacturing and service sector jobs, moving away from overdependence upon a single industry. This was in line with the thinking of the Coalfields Task Force (CFTF) established by the Blair government in 1998 to examine the situation on the English coalfields.

The CFTF was chaired by Paula Hay-Plumb, the managing director (operations) of English Partnerships, the government-sponsored agency responsible for regenerating derelict land. She had been directly involved in the transfer of British Coal's redundant property portfolio to the agency. The vice chairman was Stephen Fothergill, director of the Coalfields Communities Campaign and professor at the Centre for Regional Economic and Social Research at Sheffield Hallam University. The final report and its recommendations bear the stamp of their joint interests and expertise. CFTF commissioners were drawn from senior administrators in local government and Whitehall; they expressed shock at the 'dreadful conditions' they had encountered on their field visits, seeing the situation in Easington as especially grim.[2] They became convinced that the coalfields had 'distinctive and unique' problems emanating from their history and the dramatic and hasty closure of so many mines, and they were 'left in no doubt about the scale of deprivation and decline' to be found there. For the CFTF what stood out was the 'unique combination of concentrated joblessness, physical isolation, poor infrastructure and severe health problems' to be found in these places.[3]

The CFTF saw no need in this situation to enhance the role of the public sector or empower an interventionist state. In what can be seen at the clearest statement of the ideological power of Blatcherism, the entire focus for recovery was placed at the door of multinational corporations and the foreign direct investment (FDI) that they controlled. In this view, the 'nomad capitalism' that Raymond Williams had warned of could be harnessed for the good of the old coal districts. For this purpose, however, they needed to be reconfigured, and this rested very heavily (almost entirely) upon the physical clearance of the old coalfield sites and the construction of appropriate premises.[4] Consequently, reflecting these new priorities, the local and regional government scene changed dramatically. In England new cross-cutting regional development agencies were set up, building on an established practice of drawing a range of stake-holders together, with representatives from education and civil society joining the trade unions and business representatives on committees. One North East (ONE) was established on this basis as a new regional agency to work alongside the Government Office for the North East.[5]

The situation in Wales was complicated by the devolution settlement, but while this led to differences between the two areas in governance arrangements, their economic priorities were remarkably similar. The Welsh Development Agency (WDA), which had been coordinating economic development since 1975, sat alongside the new elected Assembly and was later, in 2004, incorporated into the government apparatus. In both South

Wales and Durham, progress now depended on footloose international corporations on the lookout for profitable sites.

However, these new arrangements, with their emphasis on partnership working, made no direct appeal to the bedrock of Labour support in the coalfield districts. Indeed, in the North East the new regional development agency made clear that coalfield regeneration was not a priority in its emergent regional economic strategy.[6] This pointed to a weakness at the centre of the New Labour approach. Its commitment to globalisation, innovation and economic dynamism in a new knowledge-based economy was a world away from the realities of the old coalfield areas of Durham and the South Wales Valleys. And nowhere in the CFTF report was there any recognition of the anger and desperation being felt in these areas. What *was* recognised, alongside the prioritisation of FDI, was the need for community support, and this led to the government establishing the Coalfields Regeneration Trust. Chaired by Peter McNestry, the former general secretary of the supervisors' trade union NACODS, the trust was set up to provide funds for local community-led initiatives. Its remit was extended to Wales where the new devolved administration had introduced its own initiative, Communities First, also aimed at repairing the damage to communities caused by deindustrialisation. There was an expectation in both these schemes that, in some ways, community development would yield economic benefit in the form of jobs and employment. This wasn't always possible and in many places was patently unrealistic.

Special Areas Again?

As in the 1930s and the 1960s, the coalfields entered the 2000s as areas requiring special attention. This time, however, things seemed to be on the worst possible footing. In addition to the wholesale closures of coal mines, the areas had seen a dramatic reduction in steel production, with the imminent closure of the works at Ebbw Vale, and the further rundown of Llanwern, Redcar and South Teesside. Added to this was the closure of many of the new manufacturing plants that had moved there in the 1960s. The North East was particularly badly hit, having already seen the contraction of the textile industry and the closure of the modern Courtauld factory at Spennymoor. In South Wales, hopes of building a new economy around the car industry dwindled as doubts were raised over the future of Ford's axle plant near Swansea and BorgWarner's transmission plant just off the M4 at Kenfig Hill.

As policy makers in both areas sought to address these problems, they had looked abroad to Europe and the USA for examples of successful regional development strategies that they could emulate, recognising the need to go beyond the 'beauty contests' and auctions for FDI and the strategy outlined by the Coalfields Task Force. In this, an awareness of the history of both places as integrated industrial regions played a major part in raising hopes for creating 'regional innovation systems' and 'knowledge-based economies'. There was a belief that, with focused action from sophisticated local states, large international corporations could be encouraged to locate significant high-tech plants in these areas, which would link across to a chain of local suppliers. It was hoped that these private companies could be successfully *anchored* in the local economies, as had been achieved previously through the state-owned steel and coal industries. Once in place, it was argued, these companies would, by their nature, raise local skill levels, further embedding the plants in an 'associational economy'. Examples for possible futures were drawn from around the world. In the local implementation of such policies, the coalfield districts were to have a marginal presence. It was understood, however, that with the main corporations based around the A1(M) and A19 (in Durham) and M4 (in Wales) the supply chain of smaller enterprises would flourish further afield. In line with this, Ebbw Vale was identified as the site for a Welsh enterprise zone for the automobile industry.

In South Wales, the WDA embraced a new regional innovation agenda, drawing strongly from the example of Baden-Württemberg.[7] There were hopes of establishing an advanced manufacturing sector bringing highly skilled jobs in engineering, unlike the earlier generation of 'screwdriver plants'.[8] This was encouraged by the arrival of Bosch's car component factory at Miskin, building upon the established presence of Ford's engine plant at Bridgend. In the North East, Nissan was already well established with a chain of local suppliers, and this fostered the idea of creating clusters of innovative firms, which emerged as central to ONE's economic development strategy for the region. In this utopian thinking, such clusters would collaborate to create new products for twenty-first-century markets. The plan proposed bringing together new factories from inward investment, along with their supply chains, including new small firms as well as other inward investors, all drawing on research from the region's universities.

One North East claimed that implementing its strategy and developing clusters would generate 90,000 jobs in ten years.[9] As in South Wales, policy makers looked abroad for models of successful cluster development, and established NETPark in Tony Blair's constituency of Sedgefield on the southern margin of the coalfield, seeking to emulate the experience of the Research Triangle Park at Durham, North Carolina (whose growth had depended on defence contracts from the federal government, the significance of which seems to have been unappreciated by those promoting NETPark as a key plank in the regional regeneration strategy). The intention was to provide support for new firms as they developed their knowledge creation and R&D functions. Once established it was hoped that they would move to locations around the county as manufacturing units. To counter political opposition within the Labour county council, it was stressed that this would eventually benefit the rest of the old coalfield areas – another case of jam tomorrow.[10]

Repackaging the Coalfields

It was around these hopes of a new economy that local authorities and policy makers developed plans for the future of the North East and South Wales. However, in the talk of a new sustainable economy, there was no explicit consideration of the needs of the former coalfield districts. It was simply assumed that these would be met in the short term by the actions and policies of local authorities. This approach emerged as a reinvigorated form of an established orthodoxy, turbocharged by the hallmarks of New Labour: competition, allied to the operation of markets and audits.

A new state bureaucracy developed, engaged in the packaging of people and places, and selling them to large multinational corporations from all over the world. Revamped regional organisations melded with, and sat alongside, predominantly Labour local authorities to pursue the Blatcherite agenda of renewal. Many officials found themselves in roles where they were torn between their attachment to the past and the compulsion to move forward with FDI and the imperatives of globalisation and the markets. As one member of the East Durham Development Agency explained, 'We are in direct competition with Wales, Scotland, Europe and the former Eastern Europe, in particular.' His counterparts in South Wales understood things in the same way. In the words of one officer in Rhondda Cynon Taff:

> I come from Doncaster and South Yorkshire and I think they are a few years behind this area. In fact, I would say they are many years behind this area. Wales is very aggressive in its marketing . . . Like the Irish and Scottish . . . there is a lot of fighting going on for the few international inward investment projects.

There were no holds barred in the quest for new contracts and fresh investment. This often involved poaching firms located in other areas. As an official of Easington District Council put it: 'We've got to be slick and cohesive, and if you're not you're dead.' This encapsulated the new reality in the coalfield areas.

After decades when the two areas were linked through a nationalised industry and a national trade union, and had joined together in the common cause during a year-long strike, the inhabitants of South Wales and Durham were now at each other's throats, competing for jobs. They even fought over cricket and golf matches: the decision to award the 2006 Ashes test match to Cardiff rather than Chester-le-Street was viewed as a 'knife in the back' by the correspondent of the *Northern Echo*, who complained that 'The way we bend over to please the Welsh you'd think that they were the only people to suffer from pit closures.'[11]

In each area's sales pitch, however, this suffering was masked by an account of a buoyant, willing labour force, new premises, good transport links and ideal locations. The reality was left unspoken, except in bids to Europe for funding for training, skills enhancement and infrastructural support. Here, some of the negative consequences of the accelerated rundown of the coal industry and the absence of any concerted programme of reskilling broke through. When the North East made a bid to the EU for Objective 2 status in 1997, it explained that only 13 per cent of the labour force were employed as managers and administrators compared with a national average of 16 per cent, and that 'the Region continues to have a higher proportion of its workforce involved in lower skilled jobs.'[12] In South Wales, a bid to the EU's RECHAR programme emphasised that 'There is therefore a limited pool of people with experience in skilled technical or managerial work. Former employees of the coal industry often have skills which are specific to mining and which cannot be transferred.'[13]

The development agencies readily accepted that they had two distinct scripts through which to portray their region: upbeat and positive for the inward investors; downbeat and realistic for European funding agencies. Those who lived in these regions concentrated on the outcomes.

South Wales: Bargoed Colliery, 1973. Kjell-Åke Andersson,
Gruvarbetare i Wales (Helsingborg: Fyra förläggare, 1977).

Durham: Easington Colliery with Horden and Blackhall in the Distance, 1984. Keith Pattison, *No Redemption* (Hexham: Flambard Press, 2010).

'It's our pit': the Strike at Easington Colliery, August 1984. Keith Pattison, *No Redemption*.

'They will not starve': Canteen at Easington, 1984. Keith Pattison, *No Redemption*.

Penrhys Estate above Ferndale, Rhonda Fach, 1985

Paul Reas, *Fables of Faubus* (London: GOST Books, 2018).

SOUTH WALES MINER

Journal
the Nat
of Mine
South
No.2 Oc
Nove

CLOSURE PLAGUE KILLING VALLEYS

ABERPERGWM, ABERTILLERY, BEDWAS, BLAENSERCHAN, CELYNEN NORTH, CELYNEN SOUTH, COEDELY, GARW, MARKHAM, PENRHIWCEIBER, ST JOHN'S, TREFORGAN, WYNDHAM/WESTERN, ABERCYNON, CWM, NANTGARW . . . The list of closures lengthens daily.

In its vain search for short-term profits the Coal Board and the Government are destroying the Welsh economy.

Soon, our children will begin to wander the country in search of jobs. Just like the 1930s. Our life blood will drain away and our communities will die. We must not allow it to happen. This haemorrhage has to be stemmed.

Thatcher and her minions are reducing our economy to

The Grim Reality. *South Wales Miner*, 1985.

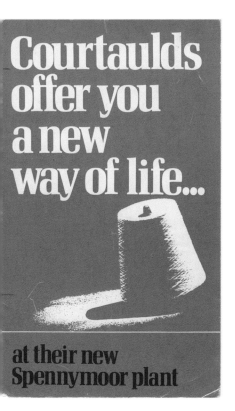

Durham: Recruitment Leaflet, Courtaulds, 1969.

South Wales: Contact Centre Supplement, *Western Mail*, 2013.

Durham: Searching for the New Economy. Photo by Ray Hudson, 2007.

Geraint Hodder, Roger Moseley, Billy Teague and Glyndwr Roberts lift the Red Flag as Tower Colliery is reopened. Tower Colliery Calendar, *Marching to the Millennium*.

Crowds gather at the Big Meeting in 2019: Photo Friends of the Durham Miners' Gala.

Manufacturing a Future?

Given all that was hanging on the promise of a new economy and a new way of living, the local press and television led with the successes as they occurred, often running prominent features in special editions and supplements. There was a constant emphasis on *high tech* and *modern*, to contrast with coal, which was presented as low tech and outdated. This was spelled out by the East Durham Development Agency: 'Yesterday it was coal. Today it's computer chips and microtechnology. Heavy industry out. High tech manufacturing and service industries in!'[14]

The North East had celebrated new plant locations throughout the nineties. These included Siemens (North Shields, 1997), Samsung (Wynyard, 1995) and Fujitsu (Newton Aycliffe, 1991), all supposedly following in the footsteps of Nissan's plant at Washington (1986) and other established businesses, such as NSK and Caterpillar (at Peterlee) and ThyssenKrupp and TRW (at Newton Aycliffe), which had come through earlier rounds of international business investment. These factories, which had chosen UK locations in the face of global competition, were part of the new high-tech micro-electronics revolution considered key to the region's future long-term economic well-being.

In South Wales, proximity to the M4 corridor was attractive for incoming businesses, such as LG, Aiwa, British Airways and Bosch, replicating the success of luring Sony and Ford in the late seventies. These contracts were greeted with headlines such as 'Attracting high-tech jobs' and 'At the cutting edge of high-tech engineering'.[15] The valleys attracted smaller units and Rocialle's sterile surgical instrument facility at the Cwm Cynon Business Park was a good example of this trend.

In spite of these successes, there was concern in both areas that the numbers of new jobs created were insufficient, that these new manufacturing projects were mainly locating in places outside the old coal districts and that they weren't leading to the creation of clusters of related high-tech activity, nor serving as centres of training pools in the ways that the old nationalised industries had done. As a local MEP in South Wales explained in 1999:

> And we have seen . . . a lot of inward investment coming into not just Cardiff but on the M4 corridor generally in South Wales – American investment, Japanese, Korean, especially with LG in Newport. And that is in sharp contrast to what has been happening in the Valleys . . . The Valleys have failed to attract either any substantial new investment into the area or actually succeeded in creating any indigenous growth.

This concern was not a new one. In his generally approving account of the changing economy that emerged after the closure of coal mines in the 1960s, Kenneth O. Morgan had commented on the 'growing concentration of economic activity and of employment opportunities in a narrow segment of South Wales – the coastal strip of southern Glamorgan'.[16]

On the coalfield districts of Durham and South Wales more jobs were being created, but these were insufficient: too few in number, predominantly low skilled, low value-added and frequently precarious. While this was often explained by the industrial inheritance of both areas, it was the case that low wages and assurances of good industrial relations had become an important part of the package offered to attract companies. This strategy carried the danger of reproducing these conditions and undermining the more ambitious and noble aims of creating highly paid high-tech work. In the business parks much of the land quickly filled with warehouses and the wrong kind of jobs, despite awareness that 'an overdependence on warehouse space may mean coalfield economies are particularly vulnerable to recession'.[17]

All this confirmed the view in Easington that the activities of government agencies had been limited, even inappropriate, and that the incentives paid to attract new companies had not been used to good effect.[18] One man called it a 'nightmare scenario'.

Talking with Easington lodge secretary Alan Cummings in his sitting room ten years after the Easington colliery had closed, he reeled off, at great speed, lists of local employers, their wage rates and their approach to trade unions and industrial relations:

> On the job front, you have got Walkers crisps, who seem to be a bad employer. They have used agencies to recruit, for lower wages, etc. There is also Charnos and Dewhirst who employ their own. The Japanese – NSK, Caterpillar Trucks. A lot of small firms . . . the German firm TWR, make seat belts, not very good payers. Samsung, the Koreans, Fujitsu and others at Newton Aycliffe aren't good payers. For these companies this area is seen now as the jewel in the crown. It's seen that way because of the low wages. It's nothing like what was in mining . . . there's a vast difference in the wages.

In Hirwaun, Tower Colliery veteran John (Trout) Davies assessed the local scene in a similar way:

> Apart from ourselves in Tower and I suppose Hitachi down by here there is fuck all in the Cynon Valley. Who is going to come to the Cynon Valley? You have got the units up in Hirwaun which are employing a number of people, but they are small factory units and with all due respect they are not even on full-time. At Aberaman Industrial Estates all you can see is 'To Let', 'To Let'.

Another man echoed these sentiments:

> Treforest is a skeleton of its former self really. About the nearest place is Nantgarw aero engine works . . . a lot of people work there. Hitachi up here, which has been a godsend to this end of the Valley, I don't think there's much else . . . you've got Asda's and Tesco's and places like that but they are junk. When you see the rates £4 and £5 an hour, when you multiply it it's

only £140, £160, £170 – it's not well-paid work is it? . . . You couldn't bring up a family on it or pay your mortgage on it, and again if you were only living in Abercynon and you landed a job in Aberaman, how would you get there?

These voices were far from isolated ones. People reflecting on the changes that had taken place during their lifetime – changes that had seen industry and manufacture closing and retail parks opening up – generally saw them as undesirable, a step backwards.

Renewed Vulnerability

As the configuration of this new economy emerged it was noticeable that – other than the insurer Admiral in South Wales – there were no examples of a major corporation locating its headquarters in either area. As in the sixties, the new manufacturing sites were effectively branch plants that carried out very little in the way of research and development. One of the founders of the Unemployment Centre in Aberdare felt that he spent his life watching developments repeat themselves:

It's the old story, if you were a large corporation there with branches out all over the place. If the main company is going through a difficult period, where is the first place you start pruning the tree? At its furthest points, at the ends of the branches. So there was always a very dicey economic base to these industries, and they were not basic industries.

This vulnerability became obvious as several of the large branch plants in both regions began to shed labour, and eventually shut down. As Chris Mullin observed in Sunderland in 1998:

Marks & Spencer is putting pressure on its suppliers to relocate to cheap labour economies . . . Bad news for Dewhirst workers, of which I have about 1,000 in my constituency. It comes on top of the proposed closure of Grove Cranes, Fujitsu and Siemens. If this process goes on all the progress of recent years will be destroyed, along with our hopes for the future.[19]

His fears were well founded. Across the North East, plant after plant closed. Older plants that had moved into the area in the seventies and eighties – including Dewhirst and Fisher-Price in Peterlee, Groves Cranes in Sunderland, Electrolux in Spennymoor, Rothmans in Darlington and Spennymoor, and LG Philips in Durham – all eventually closed. Among comparatively recent arrivals, Fujitsu's microprocessor plant at Newton Aycliffe closed down after only seven years in operation, and the new Siemens microprocessor plant in North Tyneside lasted just nine months, with the loss of 1,100 jobs. The Siemens facility had been hailed as a 'flagship for the North East's revival', but reports noted that the 'North East's jewel quickly lost its shine'.[20]

The closure of the Fujitsu and Siemens plants was the result of the collapse in the world market price for integrated circuits. Samsung's closure in 2004 at Wynyard, on the other hand, reflected a more familiar and endemic problem – that the North East was now in competition with lower-labour-cost areas in other parts of the world. Deputy managing director John Slider blamed the closure on falling world prices for computer monitors and microwave ovens, making it 'impossible' for the UK factory to compete with the cost of products made in Eastern Europe and the Far East.[21] Samsung's switch of production to Slovakia reflected deflationary prices on the high street for its products as well as wage differentials, with pay rates of up to £5.70 an hour in North East England compared to 50p in China and £1 in Slovakia. Two of its local suppliers, Woo One and Sync, had already relocated to Slovakia several months previously, Woo One having employed illegal Chinese workers provided by Asian gangmasters.[22] Hopes of the North East becoming a Silicon Fell evaporated rapidly. The region had lost many of its major investments, new and established, in the ten years before the 2008 crash; Nissan remained as the major survivor of the inward investment strategy, with established employment in its local supply chain bolstering the economy of north Durham and Washington.[23] In 2007, indicative of the extent of structural change in the North East's economy, in a region once renowned for producing things there were more people employed in retail than in manufacturing.[24]

And the job losses in manufacturing continued. A further 27,000 factory jobs disappeared in the following years, reducing manufacturing employment to 127,000. As a result, between 2007 and 2012, unemployment in the North East rose at a faster rate than in any other UK region. Commenting on the Samsung closure, New Labour Prime Minister Tony Blair 'deeply regretted' the loss of jobs, some of them among his Sedgefield constituents, but went on to say that 'it is part of the world economy we live in'.[25] Others saw things rather differently. Sunderland MP Chris Mullin's feeling of being 'entirely useless' was understandable, as was his realistic assessment that 'the plain truth is that Grove is owned by an American multinational and there is nothing we, the government or anyone else can do to stop them closing the place down.'[26]

Manufacturing in Sunderland, and across the old coalfield in towns such as Spennymoor and Peterlee, was in the doldrums, as it was in Newton Aycliffe, once seen as the engine for the new economy in the North East. Work was hard to find, and jobs continued to move away from the area as small and medium-sized firms decided to relocate. Cumbrian Seafoods, for example, founded in Maryport in 1997, had moved its main production facility to County Durham in 2007. It was subsequently taken over by Young's Seafoods Limited, which, in 2012, announced that its sites in both Seaham and Whitehaven would close in the next month, with the loss of up to 281 and 99 jobs respectively.[27]

It was a similar story in South Wales. Du Pont closed the old ICI factory near Pontypool, with its dramatic main building left standing as a monument to early post-war industrial design, amid the rubble and decay of a derelict business park. The old Hoover factory closed too after sixty-one years, and was converted temporarily into a film set for *Made in Dagenham*. As these exemplars of post-war reconstruction fell, more recent arrivals joined them. BorgWarner closed its transmission plant, and Ford sold the axle plant at Jersey Marine to the Linamar Corporation, which eventually closed it and moved production to Mexico, leaving trade union officials again complaining of workers being left on the industrial scrapheap.

As in the North East, factories that had been seen as operating at the cutting edge of a new technologically sophisticated post-coal economy closed their doors for the last time. The LG factory that had opened in 1996 with great fanfare – and at much cost, receiving a grant of £124 million from the WDA – closed in 2004. The Newport factory produced colour-display tubes for LCD computer monitors and colour-picture tubes for televisions, and by then employed just 400 people. At its peak it had employed 2,000 and had promised to increase this figure to 6,100. The company blamed an increasingly competitive market for its decision to cease production in Wales, claiming that falling prices for computer products, coupled with a rise in production costs, made it impossible to make a profit. The closure was an embarrassment to the Welsh Assembly and its attempts to attract investment to the region.[28] Seen locally as a textbook example of inward investment that failed to live up to the hype, the news came hard on the heels of the closure of Panasonic, also in Newport, as the parent company transferred production of car speakers to Asia with the loss of 280 jobs, as well as job losses at the factories of both Sony and Hitachi. And this was before the financial crisis of 2008.

Following the crash, hopes that South Wales could sustain a significant manufacturing base in the automobile sector took a further series of knocks. Blaenau Gwent, identified in Wales as an 'automotive enterprise zone', recorded the UK's highest level of unemployment increase as three component manufacturers announced closures. The situation deteriorated still further in 2010, when Bosch announced that it was to shift production to a new location in Hungary and close its large car components factory at Miskin near Cardiff, with the loss of 900 jobs. Bosch, as we have seen, was the critical 'anchor company' in the automotive supply chain and a central plank in the national economic strategy. The fact that the company had reacted so quickly to its first losses with the closure of the plant dented some of the more optimistic views of the stability of such branch plants within the new 'associational economy'.[29] Even more troubling was the fact that the Welsh government (at the time, a coalition of Labour and Plaid Cymru) had bent over backwards to offer its support. Amid 600,000 manufacturing job losses across the UK in the decade after 2008, total industrial employment in Wales fell to just over 155,000.[30]

There were fresh concerns over the future of Ford's engine plant at Bridgend, the other pillar in the Welsh auto sector. The Bridgend factory produced the Sigma engine that was exported to the EU as well as other global markets, including China and the United States. Ford was in the process of phasing out this model, along with production of engines for Jaguar and Rover. Hopes rested on the company's new Dragon engine, but in 2017 the labour force was dismayed to learn that Bridgend would produce these in much lower numbers: the planned capacity was reduced from 650,000 engines a year to 125,000 by 2021 and would supply only the EU market. As a consequence, there would be major job losses.[31] In explaining its decision, Ford referred to 'a fall in global demand and problems with efficiency including restrictive work practices specific to Bridgend'. The prospect of over 1,000 jobs being lost led Unite, the largest UK trade union, to ballot successfully for strike action at Bridgend. This earned some reprieve but it was to be short-lived. On 25 September 2020 the plant was closed.

These developments did not go without comment among the people who had seen the coal industry closed down for supposedly economic reasons. As the wife of an ex-miner in Hirwaun explained:

> Everyone thought that foreign factories were the answer. But I mean they don't care where they go next. I mean LG isn't the answer . . . they came to Merthyr, they had all the grants and everything and now they're gone. I mean, you talk about subsidised industries! They reckon at LG they have had something like £38,000 a job . . . They cribbed about supporting the coal industry in this country and everybody is having exactly the same only in different forms. Everybody is being subsidised to come here, but in different forms.

And what of coal?

> You go down to Neath and Swansea: there is always coal at that dock but it is coming in, not going out. Don't tell me it is cheaper to dig it up all the way over there in Australia and bring it across seven seas and sell it cheaper here. It doesn't make sound economic sense does it?

Once exported to all over the world, coal was now being imported into the UK. This reversal in many ways symbolised the change in the fortunes of the old regional economies. International markets had also badly affected the attempts to relaunch South Wales and Durham as new versions of the industrial regions they had once been, with so much resting on the investment decisions of multinational corporations.

CHAPTER TEN

'Just Jobs'

There's jobs and there's jobs. You work for a call centre, it's not the greatest job in the world is it? It's not like working for Fords . . . I must admit personally I am a little bit sceptical whether they are the type of jobs that we should be encouraging.
Spokesperson for English Partnerships, 1999

As the twenty-first century progressed it became increasingly clear that strategy documents promising the creation of successful, advanced industrial regions were not worth the paper they were printed on. The two regions were competing for new jobs and were not always able to pick and choose. Services, especially financial services, were expanding, and there was a growing need for new premises for the burgeoning call centres, the favoured mode of communication with customers and clients. Other kinds of work – in abattoirs and meat packaging, for example – also needed a home and these too gravitated towards the old coalfields, alongside the small branch-plant operations located on business parks and the warehouses that sprang up on sites adjacent to major transport routes. Here, at what was perceived as the low end of the job market, was where both areas found themselves.

Service Sector Salvation?

The Welsh Development Agency (WDA) had talked in 1999 of 'introducing new sectors of economic activity into the Welsh economy', and this goal was shared by the Government Office for the North East and the regional development agency One North East (ONE). Both the WDA and One North East hoped to attract and develop e-businesses, and also that the back-office call centre operations of the banks and insurance houses could be brought into or near the former coal districts.[1] As a result, these two areas became the focus for this kind of employment within the national strategy. In 2000 Britain led OECD member states in seeing call centres as a major source of technical innovation as well as providing employment growth to compensate for the loss of manufacturing jobs. The Coalfields Task Force had identified call centres as an important source of employment in the newly reconstructed economies of the coalfields, noting that 'they may offer opportunities even in more isolated areas'.[2]

By this time call centres had become the principal source of routine consumer communication for major corporations. Mainly located in the old deindustrialised regions, the industry employed almost 400,000 people in the UK in 2003 and there were hopes for significant expansion, towards a million employees by the end of the decade.[3] These call centres were most commonly associated with large specialist global corporations, mainly delivering for the retail and finance sectors (including banks, credit card companies, insurance companies, building societies, collection agencies and credit reference agencies).

This type of development grew in importance, with sites on the major transport routes of the A19 and A1(M) in the North East and in South Wales along the M4 corridor, Cardiff being a major centre.[4] In the Easington area, for example, at Peterlee's Bracken Hill Industrial Estate adjacent to the A19, a 500-seat development for Orange was greeted with much publicity in the late 1990s and expanded to over 1,000 employees, both male and female. This development was supported by the local author-ity, which, as with the manufacturing plants, was expected to facilitate training a compliant and flexible new workforce and provide transport for workers to and from the facility.[5]

By 2006, however, the call centre had closed, an event described in the local press as 'a bolt from the blue in an area with high levels of deprivation'.[6] The possibility that some of the workers might be able to transfer to Orange contact centres in Darlington and on Tyneside was scant comfort. As local Easington District councillor Hugh High commented, 'It is a devastating blow for the region. One of the reasons we built the business park here was so people would not have to travel out of the area to work.' It was symptomatic of the times that this closure coincided with French-owned Orange announcing plans to add a further 300 frontline staff to its base in India, angering unions. 'It's disgusting', said Lynn Browne, regional officer for the Commercial Workers' Union, which was not recognised by Orange but nevertheless represented many of the employees at Peterlee.[7]

The presence, further up the coast, of empty office blocks erected to house call centres on the Enterprise Zone of Seaham was a further stark reminder of the scale of international compe-tition for employment in this sector. This was often brought directly home to call centre workers, as at Thornaby in 2004, when staff at Npower, faced with the prospect of closure, voted by a majority of two to one to accept a reduction in wages of up to 25 per cent. Dave Harrison, from the union Amicus, said they had been expecting the cuts since the previous year after the company warned staff it could run cheaper operations elsewhere in the country:

We were told last August by the company that the cost of the call centre was somewhere in the region of 25 per cent above market rates. They needed to reduce the terms and conditions, not just the salaries . . . The other option was that they would close the call centres in Gateshead, Thornaby and Newcastle and open up elsewhere in the country . . . It was two hard choices really – one was lose your job, the other was have a reduction in your wages. The result of two to one was surprising in the sense it was so big. At least it has kept jobs in the North East.[8]

Despite such uncertainties attaching to work in call centres, for some people they still formed a relatively attractive source of employment. One call centre agent explained:

Well it's highly paid compared to other part-time work, such as shelf-stacking, which I'd done in the past, part-time work in shops and things like that behind the counter. And you got to sit down all day, and it was inside, and it . . . was convenient hours really.[9]

Such views reflect the depressed nature of labour markets in the North East, both on and off the former Durham coalfield, and the ways in which workers were lowering their expectations as a result. Even so, there were limits. The strain of this repetitive work was exacerbated by unsocial hours and heightened levels of surveillance. As the call centre industry became more firmly established in the North East, these pressures began to take their toll. A young woman, Carly explained:

When I started off, we didn't have sales targets, then they introduced three sales per day. Then we got individual sales targets for each individual product they had, so you had targets for bank accounts, savings accounts, loans, credit cards. I was quite happy to do this at the time, but then they decided to times the target by four. So what had been your monthly target then became your weekly target.

This increased pressure was unsustainable for Carly, as is clear from an exchange with her team leader:

I was on a call one day and had a team leader stand behind me saying 'sell them a loan'. I put the customer on hold and said to her: 'he's ringing to say his wife has died and he needs to make an appointment at the branch'. And she said 'he might need a loan for funeral expenses'. So, from that point on I said 'this is not for me'.[10]

In Wales, the call centres, now renamed 'contact centres', were recognised by the Welsh government as a distinct industry. As such, it had developed its own standards and award ceremonies, and was also seen as having a major role in regeneration strategies.[11] Admiral had moved its headquarters to Cardiff, where there were contact centres of ten other major companies: Conduit, British Gas, ING Direct, UK Barclaycard, Loans RCN Direct, Logica, BT, HSBC, Legal and General, and MOJ. One more company, EE, established a location at Merthyr, the only major centre placed on the old coalfield. In addition to its Cardiff base, Admiral has call centres in Swansea and Newport, where it overlooks the railway station, with each of its seven floors filled with rows of desks and computer screens all casting a green glow over the passing traffic.

Smaller companies with stand-alone sites, such as Save Britain Money, were based at the Enterprise Zone in Swansea. This centre and its entrepreneurial owner, Neville Wilshire, became the unlikely stars of a prime-time TV series on BBC3, *The Call Centre*. Some were caught off guard, taking it for a new soap opera. In fact it was a reality show that revealed Wilshire's unorthodox management strategies, including collective singing at the start of the day to build morale and his slogan that captured the cold calling element of the work: SWSWSWN – Some will, some won't, so what, NEXT! This mixture of organised fun and pressure seemed to typify the industry generally.

The journalist James Bloodworth spent some time working for Admiral for his book *Six Months Undercover in Low-Wage Britain*, and found it to be one of the better companies. He described the call centre in Swansea as 'huge, loud and boisterous' containing 'banks of hundreds of lightly partitioned desks', with 'scripts' for the workers to follow blu-tacked to white boards. All around there were the new slogans of consumer capitalism – 'Keep calm and drink Prosecco', 'Dream it, live it, love it', and so on. The weekly routine was broken up with occasional theme days when the workers were encouraged to wear fancy dress, and there was a fun day on Fridays when staff members were broken up into competitive teams. Beneath all this, he experienced 'a constant feeling that if you failed to meet your targets the mask of joviality would fall away to reveal a more hard-hearted capitalism.'[12] He had been told during his training that there would be 'a very Big Brother eye watching us at all times' – yet:

> The worst aspect of the job – and the downside to all work of this kind –was the sheer tedium of it all. You sat in a swivel chair from eight to five taking call after call after call from customers who were (somewhat predictably) unhappy with the amount of money that was leaving their bank account.[13]

This tedium mirrors the experiences of factory workers, and explains why call centres have been called an 'assembly line in the head'.[14] While assembly lines produce things, however, here we have tens of thousands of (often expensively educated) young people selling insurance and dealing with complaints. The Blair mantra, 'education, education, education', was supposed to generate skilled employment, jobs that would draw on the talents of the new workforce. It hasn't turned out that way. In Merthyr, working for EE, the talk is of good facilities but endless pressure: 'The first six months are great as you are not marked for value add (selling) but from then on it is non-stop, all shift with pressure.' Staff employed to offer technical advice seemed more contented, but for those involved in sales the comments all emphasised pressure: 'It's the worst retail environment I've ever worked in . . . Company does not care about you as an individual, you're simply a number to them.'[15]

But these were the jobs that were on offer, and they had come to proliferate in the old coal-mining regions, where – at least in policy discourse – they provided a quick and relatively cheap solution to the employment question. Given the low level of capital investment involved, however, these companies could be as transient and internationally mobile as the manufacturers. Workers became aware of this: they too withheld commitment, making use of a job for a while until something better turned up, or just leaving.

While seemingly offering a solution of sorts to employment problems, new jobs in call centres in South Wales, as in North East England, were to prove as vulnerable as those in manufacturing. This became very clear following the decision of Tesco to close its major multitasking call centre on the edge of Cardiff in early 2018, relocating the work to Dundee. Those job losses, coming on top of the haemorrhaging from manufacturing, led to a sense that South Wales, like Durham and the North East, was being engulfed by a deepening employment crisis.

Bad Jobs, Migrant Workers

In the decades that followed the mine closures, the destruction of the coal mining regime of production and the rundown of the old form of industrial capitalism, expectations of work and employment also adjusted downwards to reflect the new reality. We observed this in the experiences of the ex-miners: finding work in Durham and South Wales involved dealing with employment agencies and recognising the likelihood of zero hours contracts, low wages, tedium and uncertainty.

Even in these depressed conditions, it seems that there were limits and there were some jobs that people refused to do. There were a number of examples, but the clearest was at the St Merryn Meats factory, based at Merthyr Tydfil in South Wales, which has, unusually, been the subject of two studies.[16] Following the closure of the coal mines and the Hoover factory, both major sources of employment, the local labour market was extremely depressed. Merthyr Tydfil became the Welsh coalfield local authority with the lowest proportion of working-age adults in employment and the highest level of those claiming invalidity benefit. Under these circumstances, the announcement in 1997 that the company was to move its abattoir and meat-packing facility away from Cornwall and into the area was seen as a major boost to the local economy. Meat packing, like call centres, would be an industry suited to the conditions of the ex-coalfields. St Merryn had been provided with £15 million in grants and land from the Welsh Office and the WDA. William Hague, at that time secretary of state for Wales, explained that this provided 'Seven hundred well-paid jobs, here in Merthyr, exactly the right sort of jobs, in exactly the right place, it is something that we can all be very pleased and proud about.'[17]

Things turned out rather differently. After ten years almost no local people were employed in the factory, as they had come to take a very different view from Mr Hague of the work on offer there. As Stuart Tannock discovered:

> St Merryn has become a place that many locals in Merthyr tell their friends and family members to avoid working at if possible, as a collective memory has been built up of what work at the factory entails. A staff-person at a local welfare-to-work organisation, for example, explains that clients are asked, when they come in, to write down the jobs they ideally would like, the jobs they would not mind, and any jobs they absolutely do not want. St Merryn is the only employer in Merthyr that clients regularly say they do not want to work for. There are many other low-quality, low-wage jobs around, but none has attracted anything like the negative reputation of St Merryn.[18]

The reasons for this lay in the working conditions at the factory, and most particularly the way in which the workers were treated by supervisors and managers. From the very beginning, it seemed that by coming to a deprived area the company had taken a view that the labour force had nowhere else to go. As one ex-worker explained, 'Starting off, the company, St Merryn, were bastards. There's no other word for them. They were out and out bastards.' He provided a typical interaction between a worker and the manager:

> The manager would say . . . he wouldn't say it nice . . . 'Fucking get over there now and pack them fucking steaks now, you little bastard.'
>
> 'Whoa! Hang about mate, who the fuck do you think you're talking to here?'
>
> 'You, if you don't fucking like it, there's the door, make your fucking choice now'.
>
> 'Fuck you, I'm going'.

According to observers, the company's attitude has resulted in a high turnover of staff, depleting its potential workforce and leaving it without a coherent recruitment and retention policy.

> If they had treated the staff differently, we'd probably still be all Welsh over there, but they came here with bullyboy antics . . . 'Sack you? No problem, there's another fucking twenty behind you' . . . They get somebody else in. 'Fuck off, there's another nineteen behind you, that's no problem'. And dot-dot-dot-dot. All of a sudden, 'Fuck off. Oh, um, we haven't got anyone else behind him anymore. Oh fuck, what are we gonna do now? I tell you what, we'll get Portuguese in here'.

Given the resistance of local people to the conditions in the factory, it increasingly came to rely upon employment agencies for its recruitment, initially in the area and then from the fringes of the European Community. First Portuguese and then Polish workers travelled to this northern edge of the old coalfield, many unsure where they would end up on 'the road to nowhere'.[19]

Following the expansion of the EU on 1 May 2004, the UK, along with Ireland and Sweden, was in the minority of member states which, unlike Germany and France, granted workers from the new EU8 countries free access to its labour market. By 2006, 44 per cent of these migrant workers were in routine manual employment, compared to 19 per cent of UK-born workers.[20] Ian Fitzgerald, in his 2007 report for the Trades Union Congress and subsequent writings, examined the employment of Polish migrant workers in the construction and food processing sectors in the north of England, identifying that low wages and poor employment conditions were experienced by many.[21] He argued that good employers were being undercut by firms pursuing low-cost competitive strategies that were heavily reliant on the use of migrant workers. A study for the Home Office which covered twenty-nine employers in the North East recorded that:

> Employers of low-skilled workers reported that labour shortages were a primary reason for recruiting foreign workers. They had tried hard initially (through Jobcentres, local adverts etc.) to attract domestic workers but they were unwilling to take these posts, as often the conditions, pay, hours or nature of the work were unfavourable to them and migrants were more amenable to these conditions.[22]

In this light, the consequence of migration has not been to increase unemployment or to drive down wage rates but rather to produce a change in the very nature of the industrial structure, favouring not an innovative, investment-led economy of the kind aspired to by the Welsh government and ONE, but rather one that encouraged an increase in the *labour-intensive* production of goods and services. One Polish worker at St Merryn, reflecting on all this and the negative comments against immigrants in the town, commented:

> It's a crap job, everyone knows it . . . we haven't come to steal jobs from anyone, we just came to do jobs that no one else wants to do, and the thing is for us it's not the job that we want to do as well.[23]

Of course, these weren't the only 'crap jobs', and their persistence became an obstacle to attempts to raise the skills of local people, many of whom had come up against the harsh reality that skills were not what some employers wanted. As one training and enterprise council member reported to us in 2000, many local employers in South Wales didn't want a trained workforce. They would say:

> 'I don't need it, I don't need empowered young people, I need people to sit at this machine and do that, I don't want them thinking.' Two industries locally, textiles and construction, tell us that their standards are NVQ level 2 . . . So you've got two big industries locally saying 'I don't want you to have too many aspirations, because it doesn't suit my picture of the labour market'.

Once again, the question raised is about the quality of the jobs that were being created and how they compared with the ones that had been lost. The redundant miners had found to their cost that even two incomes could not compare with wages earned in the mine.

Counting Jobs

It is clear from the problems on both coalfields that the regeneration schemes set up to attract jobs to the mining districts had largely failed. As one man put it to us in South Wales:

The problem is that all big jobs left after the miners' strike. What was left was the small factories and mainly employing women on local jobs. Around my village the men were unemployed but a majority of women were working the factories.

By the first decade of the twenty-first century it was clear from the policies in place in South Wales that there was an unspoken acceptance of decline, and that the former coalfield areas would not return to their previous levels of economic activity. During this process, 'the coalfield' disappeared from public discourse to be replaced by 'the Valleys', where, in order to make a reasonable living, many young people moved away while others would commute to work at the cost of being 'geographically detached from their homes and the communities in which their social relationships are embedded'.[24] This new reality was recognised by a community development worker in the Cynon Valley who explained to us that while her remit was to provide local jobs, 'being realistic, we know that I am going to have to try and force people to travel down the Valleys to the M4 corridor to work, you have to be realistic about that.' This same acceptance was apparent in the revised regional economic strategy for the North East of 2002, which omitted, despite consultation, the key proposal by local authorities to make a special case for selective funding for coalfield areas.[25] Although the proposal was prominent in the Coalfields Task Force's report, it was never taken up by One North East.

A consistent pattern emerges: new jobs being created away from the old coal districts, often within commuting distance, near motorways (M4 or A1(M)) or urban complexes such as Cardiff and Tyneside. In Durham the new jobs were mostly found to the west of places where the mining jobs had been located. In South Wales the displacement was southward, but it was a similar pattern: *away from the mining areas*. Twenty years after the end of the strike and over a decade after the closure of the last pit, there remained a critical shortage of decent jobs in both areas. It became clear that the crisis caused by the closure of the mining industry was compounded by the loss of jobs in other industries.[26] This aggregate picture of failure registered in the deep feelings of many that the promised regeneration had not been delivered; as a result, the promise substantially to improve their lives and those of their children had failed to materialise. The new jobs were seen as inadequate and many of the newly established enterprises had proven to be less than stable. The new economy was producing jobs in some places and not others, and these were generally provided poorly paid semi- or low-skilled work, mostly in services. To all intents and purposes apprentices were a thing of the past. All this compounded a deep feeling of *loss*: of jobs, of an established way of life and of a community.

CHAPTER ELEVEN

The Fabric of Decline

*I looked at the line of spruce along the reservoir, in the valley
below; at the black barren tips climbing out of the sour bracken;
at the lines of houses, at odd angles, so bare and exposed, each row
seeming to finish in nothing, as if it had been merely interrupted.
Then below me, suddenly were the slate roofs of Pontythiw; the
grey arc of the by-pass . . . The people had to live between two
inadequate worlds, each harsh and unspectacular: simply a raw
transition, within which, unbelievably, there was the talk, perhaps
the practice, of community.*

Raymond Williams, *The Volunteers*, 1978

The coalfields of South Wales and Durham were made in the
countryside. There, they developed as a distinctive form of industry, away from the urban settlements that dominated most
accounts of the industrial revolution. In his biography of Aneurin
Bevan, John Campbell wrote of how:

He was in a real sense a country boy. The mining communities
are not truly urban but valleys with open hillsides in between
them . . . the mountain – more accurately the bare heather
moors – come literally to his doorstep.[1]

Nevertheless, when Bevan himself wrote of his upbringing in Tredegar, the emphasis was different. In his view:

> We were surrounded by the established facts of the Industrial Revolution. We worked in pits, steel works, textile mills, factories . . . We were the produce of an industrial civilisation and our psychology corresponded to that fact.[2]

By the beginning of the twenty-first century the mining villages of Durham and South Wales had become deindustrialised. The fact that they had also been officially declared *rural* areas did little to ameliorate this, for they had not, in truth, reverted to an agrarian past. They were stuck as *deindustrialised* or *re-ruralised* places not fitting easily into any map.[3] The loss of jobs was one thing, and with it the increasingly large numbers of older ex-miners left with a lot of time on their hands, a condition they shared with younger people. In addition to this there was the slow rundown of other parts of the local economy, the knock-on effect of the industry's rapid closure upon local suppliers and retailers. As people described these changes, they talked of shops closing, of boarded-up premises and of the loss of public services. Each of these had its effect upon daily life and social interaction. One man explained:

> Even the butcher's shop is shut, all the things that mean a lot to the community and are the heart of the community, they used to make people tick, like pubs and clubs, people are not doing that no more, people are not doing these things.

In previous discussions of coal-mining regions it has been argued perceptively that while the *communities* were established in and around the *occupation* of mining and the technical and physical demands of that industry, the *idea* of community can be retained in non-work activities, in ties of family and friendships, including those shared with non-miners. In his 1978 study of Durham,

Martin Bulmer was impressed by 'the persistence of traditional social patterns *and* the extent of social change'.[4] Forty years later, after so much upheaval, there was still talk of 'community' and of people finding ways to congregate and support each other on this new and difficult terrain.

Workless Communities

The mining industry was based on something we have called the coal-production regime. This involved a detailed relationship between work in the home and labour in the mine. The closure of the mines and the pressing need for women to find paid employment produced fundamental changes in social life and the ordering of community relations. The enduring features of traditional coal-mining communities revolved around the order that was maintained through the tyranny of the mine, a disciplinary technology that involved a carefully calibrated organisation of time and space. The mine, its shift system and the arduous nature of the work structured daily life. It was a way of life in which time was of the essence: to miss the last cage down the shaft was to miss a shift. In Easington Colliery the cage now stands still on a hill overlooking the village.

In South Wales, Dane Hartwell, who had been a prominent member of the South Wales NUM before becoming an official of CISWO, the Coal Industry Social Welfare Organisation, reflected on his life as a miner:

Work meant everything at that time. Work meant discipline. We weren't aware at that time that it was a form of discipline. You got up at half past five in the morning, you went to work, you had to be there at a certain time, you go down the pit, and then when you were down the pit, you had to concentrate on what you were doing and work very carefully because what you did or didn't do affected the people who were coming behind you. So, we had the discipline of work. That's something that's missed I think without the mines here today.

An older ex-miner, Thomas Jones, speaking at Tylorstown Welfare Hall and Institute, took a similar view:

In my day . . . when you left school you had a job to go into. You left school, and perhaps you took a week or a month off, but you were able to go directly into a job. So, it was a continuous thing. You got up early in the morning and you went to school, and you did your stint in school, and you came home and then you did what you liked. You left school, and you had to get up in the morning to go to work, you did your stint, and then you went home and did what you liked. There wasn't a whole lot of difference between school and work . . . It was continuous. Today, youngsters will come out of school and there's no work for them. So, what do we do? We can continue for a while to get up in the morning, and they might look for a job, but they can't find a job. So, what do they do? They stay out late in the night, getting up later and later in the morning. As time goes on you just have no incentive . . . to get up in the morning, because what's there to get up for? They're only going to be hanging around on the street. And this is it! They've got no money in their pocket. They've got no work. They've got no incentive.

In a world that, to an important degree, was made around work, the transition to uncertain employment was particularly problematic. In the Cynon Valley it was common to hear the complaint, made freely on television, that unemployment had become an inherited disease. But thinking of it in this way – blaming the victim – seemed unsatisfactory. It was issues like these which led to a voluntary centre being set up in Aberdare in 1981 to assist the unemployed. With a drop-in centre in the Methodist Church in the middle of the town, its trained advisers observed the ways in which employment changes were affecting local people. One of the centre's founders reflected in 1999 that:

> these are young people who have never ever done a day's work! But I think there are positive and negative things here. First of all, there are young people who would never put up with what my generation would put up with. They will say 'I'm not working for that!' But it manifests itself unfortunately in the worst extremes of total indifference to the older generation, to community pride . . . revulsion against society, but in the wrong way.

His concerns were shared by a community activist, further down the valley in Perthcelyn:

> I think what happens, they leave school, they got no money, then when they're eighteen years old they've got a small amount of money to live on, they can't really buy clothes and afford to go to a pub. And I think that's why you get so much drinking on the street, because it's cheaper to go to an off licence and drink it on the street than it is to go in the pub. So, then they start drinking on the streets, some people become abusive when they've had a drink and then some people say it's cheaper to go and buy some blow and they start off with the blow. Because people feel worthless, they haven't got a job or anyone.

There were similar stories in Durham, with the same emotions and the same language; the same worries over the rise in crime and the use of drugs. The village of Kelloe, just south of Durham City, changed considerably after the mines closed. Both the local pubs had closed and one man referred to it as 'a broken area' with 'a lot of young people growing up now with nothing to do . . . It wouldn't be this way if the pit hadn't closed.'

Places to Live

In the post-war period, a large proportion of the houses that made up the mining towns and villages of South Wales and Durham were provided by the local councils. In Durham, this housing sat alongside a system of company houses inherited from the practices of aristocratic coal owners. Together they formed a major part of the physical infrastructure of the mining towns and villages. This situation was radically transformed by the Thatcher revolution in a process of change that was carried forward under the Blair governments.

In Durham, the New Town of Peterlee became the main location for council housing and a major concern for Easington District Council. The town was named after the man who, in the inter-war years, had been both general secretary of the Durham Miners' Association and chairman of the Labour county council. It was built specifically for coalminers under the 1946 legislation as a 'new town'. Although controversial, it was to stand alongside nationalisation as a symbol of the state's commitment to the industry and its workers.[5] As such, the town was run by the Peterlee Development Corporation, which (under financial pressures that followed the IMF loan in 1976) handed responsibility over to the local council in 1978. While the council received grants from central government, these proved inadequate given the extent of the structural problems with the housing, and left a sour taste – a feeling that the rest of the housing in the district had suffered as a result of this unexpected change.

If the problem of leaking roofs and homes with inadequate insulation wasn't enough, the Right to Buy scheme, introduced by the Thatcher government and taken up by many Peterlee tenants, added to the general unevenness of quality and provision. Some of the consequences were explained by the local housing officer:

We have sold houses through the Right to Buy and then improved our own houses but not the Right to Buy ones and they have ended up with a substandard house compared to the ones that we have improved. So, you get a terrace now, some with flat roofs, some are half-baked schemes, some are fully re-modernised, and the skyline in some places looks absolutely horrendous. And there are some that we have not been able to modernise to the extent we would have liked to because they are connected to a property that has been bought.

Consequently, over an extended period, the local council moved from owning the majority of the District's housing stock to owning less than a quarter. This limited its ability to tackle housing issues on a large scale, and associated issues of community breakdown emerged. As a housing officer from Easington explained:

At the end of this terrace was this house that was in a terrible state, boarded up, privately owned, that had been bought under the Right to Buy, presumably the owner had left the country and the vandals had moved in and it was in a terrible state. On one hand, it is not our problem because it is not our house. But it is in our estate, and affects the neighbourhood, brings down the quality. Our tenant lives next door to it.

This was not uncommon, so much so that by 2006, 75 per cent of local authority-owned properties in Easington District were 'non-decent dwellings', failing to meet criteria that included being in a decent state of repair, having 'reasonably modern facilities and services and a reasonable degree of thermal comfort'.[6] Some of the properties owned by private landlords, which were the only alternative for those who failed to qualify for social housing, were in no better condition and often much worse.[7]

In South Wales there was a similar commitment to the building of council houses in the post-war period, when there was an acute housing shortage and an inherited number of sub-standard dwellings. Here, the topography of the area limited the space available for new development, as the narrow valley floors were filled with existing terraces and the fabric of the mining industry. As a result, towns at the heads of the valleys – such as Ebbw Vale, Merthyr and Aberdare – expanded north-ward on to the adjacent moorlands, into Garnlydan, Hill Top, Gurnos and Hirwaun. In the Rhondda we have seen how hous-ing estates like Penrhys were located high above Ferndale. Similarly, in the Cynon Valley, where the towns of Penrhiwceiber and Miskin sat in the bottom of the valley floor alongside the colliery, the new council estate of Perthcelyn was built high up above them on the top of the hill, at the end of a steep and winding road. While the geography was different, the pattern was the same as in Durham. At first many of these houses were rented by coalminers, and here too the Right to Buy scheme had created problems. Housing managers at the Rhondda Cynon Taff Council talked of 'pepper-potted' areas, where a mixture of housing (privately owned, privately rented and council) made it difficult to find a collective solution. Frequently too, as other options became available, people looked to move away from the estate to somewhere more accessible in the valley below.

To compound these difficulties, the NCB and then British Coal decided to abandon its commitment to colliery houses, adding to the general instability. The tight financial pressures imposed on the nationalised industries during the last years of the Callaghan government incentivised the NCB to withdraw quickly from the provision of housing for miners and their fami-lies. Tenants (miners, retired miners and the widows of miners) were offered 50 per cent discounts, 100 per cent mortgages and help with legal fees, and many took up the offer. However, 27,000 houses remained unsold and these became part of the pre-privatisation process. In the turmoil that followed the strike, British Coal announced that all sales and disposals should be speeded up and completed by 1988. In the end about 69 per cent were bought by miners and a further 20 per cent were sold to local authorities or housing associations at an average price of around £4,000. The remainder were sold on the open market, often through auction sales, for even less.

The manner in which these houses were sold off caused some resentment and created a number of serious problems in the coal districts, especially in Durham, where Easington had the second-largest concentration of colliery housing in the UK. There, the NUM tried to control the situation by setting up its own housing association, which was initially effective but hit financial problems, largely caused by the intransigence of the coal company.[8] The council's financial difficulties prevented it from buying as many of the unwanted houses as it would have liked. British Coal made no concessions, and in the absence of any oversight of the scheme, some of the worst housing in the district was sold at knock-down prices in auction to private landlords, many of them from outside the area.

These problems were exacerbated with the closure of the last mines in 1993, which prompted more people to leave in search of work and other opportunities. As a consequence, the housing situation in Easington was the reverse of that experienced in more affluent southern areas. As a housing officer explained:

> We have got many properties that are structurally sound, reasonable houses and nobody wants them. Nobody wants to move into that village because there is no work in that village because they are mining villages and not many people want to move into them as commuter villages.

The mines had closed, but their shadow remained in the houses and lives of the ex-coalminers and their families.

The coast was a different proposition, in easy commuting distance from the Tyneside and Wearside conurbations. In east Durham new executive housing for the managers of incoming multinationals was built alongside new estates with the aim of attracting people moving into the area as commuters to work in the urban centres. Slowly the social composition of the former coalfields changed. Seaham was the 'hot spot' for this kind of development in the Easington District. East Shore Village, built on the site of the former Vane Tempest Colliery, was described as being 'the ideal place to . . . attract a certain type of person'.[9] Here 650 new houses were built, with a further 190 constructed to replace demolished local authority stock at Parkside.[10] Further developments on the former sites of Seaham Colliery and the Port of Seaham – part of which became a marina – added to this dramatic change in the fabric of the built environment in the town and District. This process was extended through the provision of more modern retailing and leisure facilities. The Dalton Park development in east Durham was built on the site of the former Murton Colliery spoil heap, adjacent to the A19.

The coast was also an attractive location for managerial commuters in South Wales. But here it was located to the south, away from the coalfield and close to the developments along the M4 corridor. On the coalfield itself, however, there were similarities with Durham in the shape of new privately owned housing estates on sites proximate to the old colliery yard. Ebbw Vale was chosen by the Conservative government to host one of its Garden Festival sites in severely deprived neighbourhoods. Located on the site of the old Waunlwyd Colliery and on the slag heap of the steel works, it was an attractive success for a year. But the funding was short-term and the site quickly fell into disrepair, to be replaced by a large shopping centre populated by discounted factory outlets overlooking a new housing estate.

If there were 'hot spots', there were cold ones too. Both Rhondda Cynon Taff and Easington councils faced the major problem of empty properties and others in the private sector that were classified as unfit. In Easington these were mainly in areas of former colliery housing. Where previous policies had emphasised 'neighbourhood renewal', this was seen to have failed, given the low demand for 'sub-standard terraced housing'. Instead, a policy aimed at the renewal of the housing *market* – or 'housing-led regeneration' – was introduced, targeting parts of east Durham and the valley towns for housing demolition, and earmarking others for private housing development. Lee Williams of the Penrhys Partnership experienced some of the problems created by this policy:

> The fact that they're tearing down council houses has a weird effect on things around here. You know, things like doing up their council house. Some people will spend like £2,000 to decorate their flat, and some people will even spend a lot more. But around here they say, 'I don't know whether I should do it up or not', because you won't get compensation for doing that if the building gets knocked down.

Alexander Masters, in his visit to the ex-mining village of Bearpark, just to the west of Durham City, saw how the housing market and patterns of home ownership produced obvious signs of inequality, stoking tensions:

> Poor places with uneasy pockets of richness: a sports car garage; rows of new executive homes alongside the council estate . . . the Working Men's Club closed for good.[11]

New Arrivals

These changes, sometimes slow and incremental, sometimes taking place very quickly and unexpectedly, had a deep impact on daily life and upon the attempt to retain important and valued elements of the old industrial community. Since the Second World War, the coalfields of both Durham and South Wales had been home to local people, people who were born in the area. Here the mining towns and villages were made up of networks of families, and these kinship links underpinned the

idea of community. One man, brought up Tylorstown in the
Rhondda, remembers how many relations he had near to his
home:

> Community spirit, people think it's strangers coming together.
> Well, that's good and it does happen. But the nucleus of a
> community is the fact that . . . the families were there. Once
> the family started to break up, so did the community spirit
> start to break up.

Peter Blake, born and bred in Maerdy, taught in the school that
he had attended as a child, and eventually became the headmas-
ter. In the forty years that he was there, things had changed:

> When I started there were 444 children. Now, there's 186.
> Because people are moving out. We were a dormitory at the
> time. People lived in Maerdy and worked in Cardiff or
> Newport or Treforest. And they brought their money back
> here. Now, instead of working there and living here, they're
> living outside of the valley.

Terry Williams agreed, having seen the changes in his own
family:

> In the old days, if your family lived here, you settled in the
> village. Now, my two children, one lives in Essex and the
> other lives near Darlington. My stepsons, they have moved
> elsewhere too . . . living in Exeter. It's such a tiny population,
> and the younger people don't seem to want to stay in the
> village.

Maerdy had a resurgence during the strike, when its reported
status as 'the last pit in the Rhondda' brought in many visitors
and media publicity. But the mine closed soon after, and with it
the political involvement. As one ex-miner explained:

Well, there's no activity around here now, as there was in years past. Part of it is because there's no union activism anymore. The NUM promoted activity here. Now, there's no real political activity around here at all. The only time you'll see any political activity is when there's a vote for councillor or MP, and then it's just the week before. And it's the same old messages, same old rubbish. Most people just don't care anymore.

The village of Easington Colliery on the east coast of Durham was bigger than Maerdy, but until the mine closed in 1993 over 90 per cent of its households were families of miners living in colliery houses. The local NUM continued to function as an effective organisation, with Alan Cummings, the lodge secretary, involved in social issues within the village as well as dealing with employment tribunals and preparing claims for disability benefit. In his view, 'the whole complexion of mining communities has changed over the last few years: for the worse, in most cases. Most probably because of private landlords.' These were the faceless landlords who had bought two or three houses on the cheap, letting them out as slums on short-term tenancies without improving them. The people who took on these tenancies were often from nearby Hartlepool, where the rundown in council house provision had created a potential crisis for homeless people and for the Department of Social Services, which needed to find suitable accommodation. Easington with its relative abundance of private rental housing was a godsend. For the landlords, these tenants were, in Alan Cummings's words, 'like gold dust'.

This led to a considerable amount of scapegoating by council officials, who spoke in interview about 'the wrong sort of people' and those 'from the bottom of the heap' affecting life in the old mining communities of Easington. Bill Scorer of Easington District Council identified the closure of the colliery and the 'huge element of NCB housing which was sold off at auctions to absentee landlords in Manchester and London' as the root of the problems facing the District. 'There's been a huge influx of drug-related crime in the District to match that accommodation coming available', he noted. 'Now, you've got to put the two together.'

However, one housing officer made clear where the blame lay:

We have ended up with some of the communities starting to break down because of the importation of people from Tyneside, Teesside, who are being exploited by some of the private landlords in accommodation that is really substandard.

This was a commonly held view, shared by many of the long-established residents of the village. One woman, interviewed by Yvette Taylor in 2009, reflected on how Easington had become a place where 'you're neither one thing or another because of all the transient people who will never have their roots here'.[12] For her and others, though, the village, for all of its changes, had the strong pull of home. Alan Cummings agreed, considering that the core of the community still remained with the ex-miners, the lodge, the clubs and the welfare hall, and the fact that 'there is a large amount of families who have lived here all their lives, generations are still here, and long may it continue. That is a hope. That is the community.'

But the community was aging, and young people were facing uncertain futures. Reflecting on this, some challenged the idea that all the problems facing the community came from outsiders, with one woman insisting that:

These young people who are addicted, some from our own families, and good families you know, and if these young people get caught up in drugs it's horrifying . . . people from good families on drugs cause as much trouble as people from bad families on drugs.[13]

Katy Bennett spent some time with six single mothers living in social housing in the village, and looked at the situation through their eyes. They were aware of their outsider status, but she recorded that they had to deal with problems similar to those described by the established residents. Like them, they worried about crime and were nervous of strangers, of people who wandered the dark streets at night. Here, and everywhere, there was a fear of paedophiles. They had problems with the local authorities and of waiting on the telephone as their calls for assistance arrived at the call centre. Transport, too, was a problem:

> None of the women owned a car, so living a mile or two away from a significant person had a big impact on their lives as they coped with public transport and buses permitted to carry only two buggies at one time. It was not uncommon for several buses to pass a woman waiting with her child in a buggy at a bus stop before one with enough space would stop.[14]

Villages like Easington Colliery with a high density of miners living close to each other were unusual in South Wales, given its more mixed pattern of housing tenure and colliery closures. However, there were similarities. In South Wales, as the mines closed, many houses were vacated; new people moved in, and the issue of outsiders and 'the wrong sort' of people unsettling the balance of local communities was evident, but in a slightly different way. In the Cynon Valley the problems were experienced most acutely on the 'pepper-potted' council estates. Without the influence of the lodge, local people dealt with problems themselves or by complaining to local councillors. The Perthcelyn estate, high up on the hill above Penrhiwceiber and Mountain Ash, was one example. By the late nineties it had become a centre of multiple deprivation and a source of real concern for the Rhondda Cynon Taff council. The estate was made up of 270 social housing properties (council and housing association), 63 that had been acquired through the Right to Buy scheme and a further 93 privately owned dwellings. By 2000, 75 per cent of the children were in receipt of free school meals and the unemployment rate approached 30 per cent.

The pattern is a familiar one. It was the product of the closure of a major industry and the associated migration of economically active men and their families away from housing stock handled directly by the local authority, housing which was left empty. One woman, when asked if the place had changed much, echoed the view from Easington:

> Oh yes, not for the better, for the worse . . . all those flats used to be houses one time and they converted them into flats and the council don't care a damn who they put here.

Another agreed:

> I mean look at this estate – it's filled with big families that are unemployed, so I think the council must think, 'yes we'll perch them right up on the mountain by there which will isolate them from anywhere else.' But you know there are good people up here, 90 per cent of the people on this estate are good people.

This view of 'good people' trying their best to improve the situation but overwhelmed by the disruptive impact of a minority transient population is a common one. One woman explained how a lot of problems 'come from people that move from estates to estates to estates, they come to Perthcelyn, cause the trouble and go along again and leave the people to pick up the pieces'. Sometimes one individual can upset everyone:

> The boy that . . . we're having trouble with that now . . . he's into cars and motorbikes, stealing cars, all his friends that go there are druggies and thieves . . . I had another row with him the other day . . . and I told him, 'I'll get something done about you, because there's no way I'm moving' . . . Oh its terrible, you've got to live like that, decent people have got to live like that.

The underlying concern was that 'there's a lot of unemployment on the estate and a lot of drugs I think as well. High on drugs and drink, the drink a bit more than the drugs.' Some had had enough. One woman talked of 'moving away from here so we'll have a better chance and the children will have a better chance'.

Others tried to organise through a tenants' and residents' association.[15] Kate was one of these. Born on the estate, known and trusted by most of the long-time residents, she became involved in a project aimed at improving amenities there. She explained how she had recently had a conversation with her next-door neighbour, a man of seventy who has also lived on the estate for over forty years. She had asked him, 'Mr Griffith, how would you describe Perthcelyn now?' and he replied, 'It's the biggest and the best open prison in the world.' She found this shocking, especially as crime rates were falling in the area. In her view:

> They're getting fed up, they're sick and tired of the way they are being treated by the local authorities, they're sick of having to live in the environments that they're living in because there are still cars and motorbikes and things whizzing around this estate, and before long they are going to get up and they are going to rise and it's not just this estate. I heard it all through the valley.

Locking your Doors

Generally, and overwhelmingly, people feel that since the mines closed things have changed for the worse. One man spoke of a despair present 'everywhere in all the villages and towns through the Cynon Valley'. In Penrhiwceiber one woman vigorously explained how the closure of the colliery had 'broken the back of the community that existed when everyone worked together in the same place'. In Durham it was a similar story. Easington and Horden were very different from the places they had been when the pits were open, and people were quick to lament the loss of the lifestyle and community atmosphere they associated with the bustle of the pit. Then, there had been a lot of things to do in the villages, with entertainment in the evenings through the cinemas and clubs.

Over time, new ways of living emerged in these places, as practices that would previously have been considered out of the ordinary, some bordering on the illicit, came to play a more central role in economic activity. These involved working for employers off the books, for cash; providing a range of services (decorating, vegetable sales, hairdressing, babysitting, laundry, etc.) for cash; selling marijuana; various forms of scavenging; swapping, buying and selling on the internet; car boot sales; and so on. People took an easy-going attitude to these changes, but not to others. Burglary, car theft and vandalism were universally frowned upon and caused enormous conflict. Gwyn Owen explained how in his South Wales village 'nobody locked their doors and I knew all of my street and . . . there was no locking. It [locking doors] started prior to the strike but after the miners' strike it increased a lot'. Another man living in Maerdy concurred:

> When the colliery was open, before the decline of the community, I can remember when you didn't have to lock your door. You didn't have to lock your door at night because you were all family. If you wanted something of mine, and I had it, I would give it to you. All you had to do was ask. If I needed something that you had, all I had to do was ask. I could borrow it. But today, it's not like that. You've got to lock your doors now. Now you don't know your neighbours. They've built the housing estates, and they've brought people in from different parts of the valley, and you don't know who these people are. You don't know their backgrounds; they haven't actually been brought up in this community. You don't know them. So, now you've got a reason to lock your doors.

Again, this was a universal experience associated with the closure of the mines. In the Easington area, people mourned the loss of communities that had provided a strong feeling of security. They had once known that they could leave doors unlocked, and this had changed dramatically. In the past they felt that vandalism and petty criminality by young people had been dealt with by the men who worked in the pit, monitoring situations as they went to work – 'the benign police force', as one woman put it. She added that at that time they had little vandalism, no drug problem and little burglary, and children were safe playing on the street. However, the situation was very different without the mine, and 'it's not the same here anymore' was a commonly repeated phrase. One woman in Horden explained that she was very reluctant to open her front door at night, especially in the dark of winter, because of a fear that someone would come in through the back door and steal something. It seems that this had become a common practice for some young people in the village.

Everywhere we went, young people spent their evenings hanging around, in a park, on a street corner or on benches, wherever, drinking or using drugs, and often causing trouble. In Penrhiwceiber the youngsters would sit on the wall of the main street behind the bus stop. The place was known as 'the dole wall' and many elderly people found it a challenge to walk past it. In Easington one man remembered how he was attacked by a group of young boys on bikes as he made his way home from the club one night – they spat at him and called him names. The event still haunted him, and he had learned always to cross the road if he saw a group of young people ahead of him.

Looking Forward

There is no doubt that, following a programme that cleaned up the natural environment and removed all traces of colliery waste and despoliation, the old coalfields of South Wales and Durham have been physically transformed. Described as 'image development initiatives', these were quite extensive operations. The overwhelming motivation behind these efforts was the push to modernise and beautify the areas, making them more attractive to the external gaze of future investors, ecological tourists and outdoor pursuit enthusiasts. In the landscape of this new world, local people – young and old – benefited from being in the fresh air and enjoying an environment free of black coal dust. While many welcomed this, it would be hard to say that they had been fully engaged as a community. For many, the changes were experienced as another part of a process of erasure that was to become so complete that at the turn of the century it was possible to travel across both areas and be unaware of their coal-mining and industrial past. There was also some concern over the ways in which the new developments were controlled and organised. Access to the coast in Durham was much more regulated than it had been, and the forestation of the valleys in South Wales changed the open access to the mountains that people had once enjoyed.[16] At the same time, opencast mining expanded, (justified by contractors as a tourist attraction), producing protest and worries over noise and health issues.[17] So the transition was not an easy one, and it had not solved the other serious problems facing the people of these areas.

The new economy was leaving many of the young and old in its wake. Families were being stretched by the need for two incomes, and child care adjusted to the routines of the new employment regimes. Old community forms changed too, as key institutions including cinemas, chapels and miners' welfare halls continued to close. Alongside this, through the Communities First scheme in Wales, the activities of local authorities and the support of the Coalfields Regeneration Trust (CRT), numerous initiatives and programmes of work were set in place. The Dove community workshop, building on the activities of the Dulais Valley support group, offering new opportunities for local women, was an important development.[18] The determinedly independent Penrhys Partnership obtained significant funding from the CRT to establish an education and training centre located in the estate. In Durham the CRT also aided the development of the East Durham education trust, while in the west of the county the lodge officials of the old Sacriston Colliery were heavily involved in developing the amenities of the local colliery club as a community resource.

Processes of regeneration and commercialisation have seen much of the industrial landscape smoothed, or carted away to be preserved as tourist attractions in museums like Beamish and Woodhorn in the North East or the Big Pit museum at Blaenavon and St Fagans National Museum of History in South Wales. The Workmen's Institute at Oakdale was taken down and rebuilt at St Fagans, leaving the miners there with mixed feelings. The conversion of the old coal dock at Seaham Harbour into a marina is another example of how regeneration proceeded in part through a commodification of the mining past.

In the decade just gone, however, there has been a growing recognition of mining heritage, and community groups have formed to find ways of recognising and paying tribute to it through sculptures, murals and epitaphs. In South Wales the anniversary of mining disasters involving large-scale loss of life at Senghenydd and Six Bells provided an additional spur to memorialise the dead. In Senghenydd an Aber Valley heritage group was set up to raise the money for a memorial to the 512 men and boys who died in the two explosions at the Universal Colliery there in 1901 and 1913. Through grants, charity events and many individual contributions, funding was secured for a sculpture – *The Rescue* – and a memorial garden and wall of ceramic tiles made in local workshops. When it opened, the garden was filled with local people and trade union banners, including the DMA banner brought down by a Durham delegation.

Four years earlier, a Communities First project in Abertillery had organised a heritage group to discuss an appropriate memorial to the people killed in the explosion at the Six Bells Colliery. It obtained significant funding (£200,000), mainly from the Heads of the Valleys initiative, an organisation set up to assist in local regeneration. The project resulted in a major monument by the sculptor Sebastien Boyesen, *Guardian* – an enormous figure of a miner constructed from 20,000 horizontal steel strips. In his preparation for the piece, Boyesen consulted relatives of the dead, and through these detailed discussions came to realise that 'we were doing something that had much more resonance with the people. So often public art is decorative. This was much more than that.'[19]

Boyesen's words reflect a tension between large public projects and the perceived needs of the people. As one man said to us in Durham, 'Everything now is being done for the tourist. Nothing is being done for the people who live here.' While the public support for the *Guardian* had more than an eye on the potential for tourism (it was repeatedly compared with the *Angel of the North* in publicity), local people had been engaged in the process. In Durham this was achieved, on a mass scale, by the emergence of a multitude of collaborations like the one in Senghenydd, formed as local miners' memorial groups. In this area, people talk of 'our heritage' as a tradition embedded in hard manual work and the labour struggles of the past. Jim Coxon has documented the almost spontaneous ways in which groups formed around that idea and took on quite onerous commitments, often at the suggestion of just one person. Over a hundred memorials to the closed collieries exhibit artefacts of the mine, most often the pulley wheel and the tub, or take the form of murals, as at Seaham and South Hetton, the latter depicting the lodge banner. There are a small number of figurative sculptures commemorating the men who worked in them, most notably the 24-tonne statue of the working miner underground, encased in sandstone, at Fishburn. These are a recent phenomenon, one supported and inspired in part by the ongoing activities of the DMA and the memorial garden at its headquarters at Redhills. They have sprung, argues Coxon, from the way in which the absence of any visible reminder of the industry – its erasure – is felt and experienced by former mining communities 'as concomitant with the loss of their culture, heritage, tradition and identity'.[20]

CHAPTER TWELVE

Tragic Outcomes

We had a period in Seaham where the suicide rate of former miners was running at three times the national average. And the church, in Seaham, were really concerned about it, to such an extent that the parish priest from St John's actually did a publication in his church periodical.

David Guy, DMA president, 1999

When the mines closed, it was argued that the decline of the industry, with its dangerous working conditions and life-affecting diseases, ought to be welcomed and even applauded as a progressive development. A healthier community would be able to benefit from the restored countryside and its various amenities. But it was not to be. In fact, things turned out to be much worse. Census data make it abundantly clear that the former coalfields have some of the highest levels of ill-health in the United Kingdom. In South Wales 10 per cent of respondents to the 2011 Census said that their health was 'bad or very bad', and 15 per cent said that this placed a 'lot of limitations' on their day-to-day activities. The figures for Durham were slightly lower, at 9 per cent and 13 per cent respectively. In contrast, the returns for counties in the South East averaged 4 per cent and 7 per cent.[1] Ten years later little had changed and Horden in Durham had the highest percentage of people on health-related benefits in the UK. In Blaenau Gwent, over 10,000 people, one in six of the adult population, were being treated for depression with medication. The *Daily Mail* accused doctors of handing out anti-depressants 'like sweets'.[2]

On the Sick

The miners did not leave the scars of the pits behind them, and the insecurities of the post-mining world brought their own health problems. In this way the employment crisis exacerbated and extended the health crisis. As David Taylor-Gooby, a lecturer at East Durham Community College, observed in 1998, 'you can't work down the colliery for thirty/forty years and be healthy at fifty onwards'. DMA President David Guy concurred, and when drawing attention to the high incidence of osteoarthritis of the knees and related conditions among ex-miners, pointed to the years they had spent travelling on uneven roadways, often carrying materials, crawling along coal faces and working in cramped conditions, stooping or kneeling.

Everything inside a mine was hard – steel equipment and rock bumped against the human body with every move. Injury was commonplace, and to accommodate this within the management of the mine, older men were moved away from the hard work on the faces to other (back-bye) work underground and on the surface (on bank). When the mine closed these men were left damaged, and readily agreed to be signed off 'on the sick'.

Redundant miners had been encouraged by job centre staff to visit their doctors and, if possible, register for disability benefit, which would be more favourable to them in many ways than registering as unemployed. This move also benefited the government as it served to reduce local and national unemployment figures, minimising the apparent impact of the closures. This was important at a time when there was widespread criticism over the speed with which it had closed down the mines without a coherent policy for job renewal. It was this that started the debate over ill-health and unemployment, something that was made increasingly complex by changes in the benefit system.

Claimants for unemployment benefit were (and still are) required to attend a job centre regularly and to demonstrate that they were actively seeking work under the threat of losing their benefit. Invalidity benefit came without such requirements, although it increasingly required regular medical assessments. Many people in receipt of invalidity benefit, and feeling able to take a job, also realised that once back in work it would be difficult to return to their previous benefit status. As a consequence, those wanting employment needed some reassurance that any job they accepted would have a degree of permanence: that it was not temporary or agency work, or a zero-hours contract. As we have seen, work in the new economies of Durham and South Wales involved many of these forms of precarious jobs, creating high levels of risk for the potential worker for, as one ex-miner explained to us, 'Once you come off sickness benefit, you're never going to get back on it.'

As times moved on, and welfare payments came to be more politically sensitive than unemployment, many ex-miners in ill-health became fearful of having their status challenged and losing their benefits. Often, they became cautious about being involved in physical activities outside the home, as there had been (in all communities) examples of men being observed and reported, with consequent checks on their health status and their ability to work. With the Durham and South Wales areas registering among the highest rates of long-term sickness in the country, health and health benefits became a central part of the class struggle.

As a consequence, the regional offices of the NUM became actively engaged in supporting their members to negotiate the benefit system. In 1999, for example, David Guy in Durham found that:

The biggest amount of workload at present has been the servic-
ing of our members, who were either unemployed, or suffering from some incapacity whereby they can't work. Dealing
with DSS claims can range from industrial injury benefit,
mobility allowances, attendance allowances, housing benefit,
income support, and family income supplement for them that
are working but are on poor earnings.

Local lodges had over time built up close relationships with GP
surgeries, where the doctors were well aware of the history of the
mines and of local conditions generally. Ken Greenfield had
worked in the Easington District for decades and was a strong
presence on the East Durham Development Agency. Seen
through his eyes:

In this district, there are 14,000 people who aren't working
due to ill-health, long-term sickness . . . Arthritis, chest problems, knee and back problems, and they can't work. Many are
genuine, some doctors are sympathetic to families that they
have known for all their lives and have signed them off on
long-term sickness. It's difficult to prove that someone hasn't
got a bad back.

John Murphy, former local strategic partnership manager for
East Durham, put it like this:

We now have one of the largest proportions of people on IB
[invalidity benefit], and I understand that GPs were complicit
in this, looking at a lot of men, saying that they were not likely
to work again because of their age and that they were carrying
a few knocks. Then they signed them off for life.

Such references to 'a bad back' and 'a few knocks' had the effect
of trivialising mining injury and also of shifting attention away
from the real problems faced by the men who had spent their

working lives underground. Alan Cummings, the NUM lodge secretary in Easington, felt this strongly and when interviewed in 1999 he asked:

Why is it that more and more people are claiming incapacity benefit, ill-health benefits, disability living allowances? Why have we got all this increase? Why is people's health deteriorating at a time when we've got better medical care and better health products? There will be some people in the government who'll say what's happening here is that there are people who are 'swinging the lead', they're not genuine claimants. That's their answer to it. That isn't the answer to it! If society is so bad now, where we've got people who will resort to that type of thing, in order to make ends meet, that isn't the problem, it's what causes people to do that, is the problem, and that's what they should be tackling.

In 1999, we spent an evening in the workingmen's club in Blackhall with Barry Chambers. Barry had been a lodge secretary and remained involved with the activities in the area after all the pits had closed. During the evening, the issue of disability benefit became a constant theme, as one man after another came across and raised a problem with him. Men on disability benefit were facing tribunals to decide whether they were indeed unfit to work. In these discussions, preparing men for the ordeal of cross-examination at a tribunal, it was made clear that their questioners would assume that they were lying. As a result they had to exaggerate their condition in response to these assumptions. In such circumstances the truth was not at issue. This was the talk in Blackhall. Up the coast in Horden, at the Big Club, Irvin Lyons would have been having similar discussions. As would Alan Cummings further along the road, at the Colliery Club in Easington. In this way, the mining world continued after mining had ended. As Cummings explained:

We are the first point of contact in the communities for ex-miners to get advice, not just on compensation but many other important issues. Those people we help are genuinely, and I mean genuinely, appreciative of what we do for them. The lads know the way the union looked after them when the pit was working and since the pit closed, we have continued to serve the community, looking after members fuel interests, benefits, form filling etc . . . The pit's no longer there but the union is still functioning. Pits have always closed in Durham since time immemorial but there was always someone there in that village to look after the widows and pensioners.[3]

In 2004, 19 per cent of working-aged men in South Wales were in receipt of incapacity benefit; in Durham the figure was 16 per cent. In 2005, one of us gave a lecture addressing these issues to senior staff at the DHSS in London, explaining the ways in which local people understood their situation. This provoked considerable comment and one question appeared to be central: 'is it the case that these people feel that they deserve these payments as a right?' The answer involved a discussion of how people in the coalfields thought of their current situation, how this had come about and how they saw their prospects. It was pointed out that people still talked of Mrs Thatcher having 'stolen our jobs', and that they did feel that after many generations working the mines, with all the promises made, to be left on the scrapheap nursing the injuries of the mine, they were indeed entitled to welfare benefits. It was explained that this deep sense of injustice was magnified by the way the mine workers' pension fund had been taken over by the government after the privatisation of the industry and had not been returned. At that same meeting in 1999 in Blackhall, Barry Chambers had exclaimed, 'We must be the only industrial area that has to pay for its own regeneration through its pension fund.'

The Making of Ill-Health

Academic studies have established a close association between living on the former coalfields and suffering from long-term illness.[4] Yet we have seen how Christina Beatty and Steve Fothergill came to argue that much of the reported 'illness' in the coalfields could actually be seen as a form of 'hidden unemployment'.[5] Given the dominant voice of the *Daily Mail* on topics like these, this was a dangerous case to make, and one that was challenged by many health practitioners we talked with, who asserted that the people they dealt with were indeed ill or disabled. Moreover, there was a feeling that focusing on health issues through the lens of the benefit system simply added confusion to an important discussion. In response, Beatty and Fothergill suggested that:

> What appears to be happening is that where there are plenty of jobs the men and women with health problems or disabilities are able to hang on in employment or find new work if they are made redundant. But where the labour market is difficult – as in older industrial Britain – ill-health or disability ruins many people's chances of finding and keeping work. Employers are well able to recruit the fit and healthy instead.[6]

In difficult labour markets, therefore, where jobs are scarce, the weak and vulnerable are pushed to one side and onto benefits, and this process itself causes physical and mental harm.

Within the changed fabric of the old coalfields, the legacy of ill-health and early death persisted, with Durham and South Wales standing out as places with a high proportion of sick people reliant upon some form of sickness or disability benefit.[7] Some of these people (as we have seen) are ex-miners, but not all. One local authority official in East Durham talked of a prevalent 'urban myth', which assumed that once the miners had passed away, the high rates of ill-health would have decreased. However, looking at the statistics they discovered that this was not the case, as many people on IB [invalidity benefit] are too young to have been ex-miners.

Why then are young people in the old coal districts so much more likely to be suffering from ill-health than their peers in other areas? Investigating this issue in 1999, the head of public health in Bro Taff in South Wales discovered that 'across all of Wales the differential in the mortality rates between wealthy and poor areas has actually increased over the last ten years.'[8] This was at a time when medical experts had begun explore the *gradient* in life expectancy, measuring the differences in life chances associated with social class and also place of residence.[9] Some of these gradients were steep ones. Life expectancy in Durham City was ten years higher than in the villages of Easington twelve miles away. So too in South Wales; here the differences in life chances of people living in Blaenau Gwent lagged well behind those of people based down the A475 in Abergavenny and rural Monmouthshire. The quality of life also differed, with places of lower life expectancy also ranking high on the various indicators of deprivation.

These and other findings created an increasing awareness in Wales and the North East of the significance of ill-health and its concentration in the old coalfield districts. In pondering this worrying phenomenon, it came to be understood that the decline of the industry itself – with the loss of the amenities that came with an active mine and the various health and social services that had been provided by the NCB – had had an adverse effect on health. But it was also significant that the loss of these resources had been accompanied by a decline in local services and in the fabric of local communities. This was the view of Dr Arun Mukherjee, the director of public health for Cynon Valley, who saw the problem to lie in the ongoing consequences of the mine closures – the lack of jobs, the decline in the standard of housing and the general deterioration in living conditions and standards: 'So, all those things deteriorated over time.'

Concerns about the physical and emotional conditions of life in the coal districts framed a detailed study of health in the north of England that identified the Easington District as being singularly affected, standing out 'in its constantly poor health, on all three of our chosen criteria and across an almost continuous band of wards.' Many were permanently sick and babies were of low birth weight.[10] This was the reality of deindustrialisation, and it was a well-established pattern at repeated census returns that highlighted Mid Glamorgan, West Glamorgan and Gwent as having the highest rates of long-term illness in Britain, closely followed by Easington.[11]

Such statistics raised important questions relating to social and political aspects of life on the old coalfields. In this, the position of the ex-miner was obviously important, but as time went by the *direct* impact of mining receded and other factors were needed to explain the inherited elements of ill-health. A major investigation led by Professor Sir Michael Marmot of University College London made clear that 'social and economic differences in health status reflect, and are caused by, social and economic inequalities in society'. Furthermore, 'inequalities that are preventable by reasonable means are unfair. Action taken by the Department of Health and the NHS alone will not reduce health inequalities.'[12]

A Very Real Problem

Industrial decline, like old age, doesn't come alone; it is accompanied by many pathologies, with increases in levels of poverty and deprivation being the most significant. In Durham, David Guy, president of the NUM, outlined the situation in his Area, where at the turn of the century there had been cases of rickets and TB:

> We thought we'd eradicated these diseases and ill-health. They manifest themselves where there's been a lowering in the standard of the quality of life. And that's what's happening in this region . . . If you look at the children, and look at the type of diseases which are now prevalent in children, which weren't there ten, fifteen, twenty years ago, and ask yourself – really, why?

In 1980 the Department of Health commissioned a comprehensive report, known as the Black Report after its chair Sir Douglas Black, which firmly established a link between ill-health, death and social inequality.[13] It documented how poor people living in deprived areas were far more likely to be ill and to die earlier than wealthy people in affluent areas. But its 'findings and recommendations were virtually disowned by [Patrick Jenkin] the then Secretary of State for Social Services, very few copies of the Report were printed, and few people had the opportunity to read it.'[14]

Subsequently, an index of multiple deprivation, which brought together under one indicator an evaluation of the broad fabric of social and physical conditions and amenities available in each locality, was developed to categorise places in England and Wales.[15] Through this index it became clear that Easington and the local authorities at the Heads of the Valleys in South Wales were among the ten most deprived places in the UK. It was this pattern of deprivation that had, when filtered through the experiences of daily life and expectations, resulted in entrenched patterns of ill-health in these coalfield areas.

This was manifested in a variety of ways, most significantly in the emergence (and increased recognition) of mental health issues. Gerard Tomkins in Durham linked this directly to the decline of the mining industry and the associated increases in unemployment and poverty:

> But the things that don't come out in the mortality statistics is the mental health stuff, because I would say there is a high

level of stress – real stress, not worried executives high-pressure crap! It's that longstanding grind. There is a lot of reactive depression . . . [and] a high level of prescribing of anti-depressives, anti-depressants. We are the highest by some way in this region.

The 'longstanding grind' of being poor, and its impact on well-being and mental health, have been documented for decades.[16] The subject came to the fore on the coalfields in the nineties, as increases in the rates of suicide, alcohol abuse and the use of illegal drugs became a cause for concern amongst the medical authorities. As one doctor explained:

In the valleys there are pockets of population, particularly among the youngsters, where there is a drug problem and drugs-associated diseases like hepatitis B, hepatitis C particularly. Although that is not necessarily the overall picture there are identified areas where it is a problem.

These cases could have tragic outcomes, as a local church minister in Ebbw Vale explained in 2002:

In the space of six months about two years ago I buried five drug-related [deaths]. The youngest was 18 [years of age] and the oldest was a 27-year-old mother who lived in one of the streets up here. And I knew her parents fairly well, and she left a three-year-old boy for her parents to look after. It's a very, very, very real problem.[17]

In Durham three years later, Adrian Clarke and Alexander Masters documented the lives of young people addicted to drugs in former coal-mining villages in the west of the county. The violence and destruction of the strike set the stage for decades of family breakdowns and neglect. One young man explains that 'I wasn't too worried about addiction because I thought my life was shit anyway and didn't care much about myself', while a young single mother felt that she 'had nothing to look forward to and drugs were an escape from that feeling: life was more interesting with drugs.'[18]

These accounts describing a lack of self-worth, and with it the absence of any hope of a better life in the foreseeable future, show some of the consequences of a corroding industrial community. It's as if the decline in the mining industry, and the accompanying process of brutal conflict, left people damaged, weakening their capacity to care for others and also for themselves. A GP in the Rhondda Valley reflected on the way her practice had changed in the nineties:

> I think mental health problems are a worry . . . If I look at the practice that I've got, my child protection referrals have increased quite considerably. And also the amounts of drug and alcohol abuse have increased. I've been in this job about twelve years now. And those problems have increased quite considerably since those days . . . And there are a high number of people on benefit. And I think that it's hard for people to deal with things sometimes.

In a study of Ebbw Vale after the closures of the Marine Colliery and then the Corus steel works, Gareth Williams noted that there had been a noticeable effect upon the ways in which local people related to each other, damaging 'the resources for hope' that Raymond Williams had written about. He quotes an education welfare officer who explained that 'The changes in the area over the past thirty years have been tremendous. It had a feeling all of its own thirty years ago, a very strong community of miners and steelworkers . . . and now that's gone.'[19] A district nurse who had always worked in the area spoke in similar terms: 'That sort of comradeship has all gone. You knew who you could trust and everyone would help you, but that is disappearing, that sort of feeling is disappearing.'[20] A health worker said, 'Abertillery breaks my heart because it just was not like it looks now, it's just a dump.' The sadness of all this is amplified if we remember that ex-miners, breathless from the effects of their work underground, lived out their lives in places where, in the past, their condition would have been recognised and supported by neighbours, friends and fellow miners.

'Playing their Part'

As the coal districts declined through the nineties and into the twenty-first century, these concentrated centres of ill-health experienced a crisis in the health care provided by the state-run NHS. The national shortage of GPs was exacerbated on the coal-fields, where the unattractive features of the job (long hours and stress) were compounded by what became seen as negative features of the areas. GPs had to live locally, and invest in surgeries and other local property. Gerard Tomkins was tackling the consequences of this in Durham, where there was a crisis in the recruitment of GPs in the Easington District:

> Would you want to live here? I don't! It's not like hospital doctors where they come and they go and they can happily move on. They [GPs] make a substantial commitment, they make a lifetime commitment. When a young doctor wants to join a practice he or she has to buy into a partnership as you would as a lawyer or an architect, they need to borrow money to buy into the good will and so on of the practice. So that's one thing; secondly, they have to buy the premises. And virtually every medical practice in this area has substantial negative equity . . . all these things are positive disincentives to come into Easington.

There were similar concerns in South Wales and worries over the physical isolation of many of the ex-mining communities and a lack of transport. This, of course, could have been a central part of the agenda for regeneration, and to its credit the Coalfields Task Force had made recommendations to that effect. Had the subsequent practice of regeneration not focused so determinedly on job creation and responding to the needs of the large corporations, things might have been different. This was a missed opportunity, given that health professionals were keen to cooperate and felt the need for the health of the population to be linked with issues relating to economic change. Gerard Tomkins in Durham pointed out, 'We are trying to make a specific link between our health forums and any regeneration that is going on in the villages so that it is seen as part of the wider agenda all of the time.' But within the regeneration strategy, ill-health was underplayed, mentioned discreetly in pursuit of financial support from Brussels but hidden from prospective employers. As a consequence, far fewer resources were directed towards health in comparison to economic and housing regeneration. This failure sits oddly with the Blair government's flagship programme 'Saving Lives: Our Healthier Nation', with its clear aim 'to improve the health of everyone, and the health of the worst off in particular' and its emphasis on the need for a joined-up approach involving government, local communities and individuals.[21]

'Saving Lives: Our Healthier Nation' was an optimistic document. It promised a complex set of major strategic interventions by the state, with its various departments coordinating their activities around the NHS. In its overt acceptance of the findings of the Black Report – 'The life expectancy of those higher up the social scale . . . has improved more than those . . . lower down the scale. This inequality has widened since the early 1980s' – it promised a more open and dynamic approach than in the past.[22] 'Saving Lives' was to disappoint, however. For while the report drew a fine balance between the roles of the government, local agencies and individuals, its most striking feature was a poster-style contribution from the chief medical officer, 'Ten Tips for Better Health'. The way in which this was picked up revealed the true spirit of Blatcherism. In matters of health the *individual*, not agencies and institutions, was to take the lead. Individuals who ate the right food, stopped smoking, drank alcohol in moderation, took plenty of exercise, had safe sex and managed their stress level through conversations would be healthier and live a longer and happier life. They would also be 'playing their part' in the plan for a healthier nation.

This shift in emphasis – from a driving, reforming state to individuals looking after themselves – was critical. The 'Ten Tips' were to point the way for health campaigning over the next thirty years. There is no doubt that they were successful in many ways, especially in relation to smoking, and this had tremendous health benefits. However, it was clear from the beginning that individuals and families with greater resources (time, money, education) would be better placed to take advantage of the advice. People living in the old coalfield areas had less access to the kinds of lifestyle advocated in the posters and leaflets, and faced a much tougher environment. Here too the incentive (the promise of an extra ten years of life) might not seem much of a bonus to people who were struggling in the present to make ends meet, and to get from one day to the next. In this context a GP in South Shields observed that all of his patients suffered from the same thing: SLS – shit life syndrome. Poor housing, poor jobs, poor amenities, poor public transport. Shit life syndrome. Something more was needed.

Community Care

In Durham, Easington District Council had been absorbed into Durham County Council, which became a large unitary authority in 2007. The District Council, under the leadership of ex-miner Alan Napier, had taken care to support local community and education work. Worrying about the effects of the merger upon this activity, and with considerable prescience, it decided to establish an independent East Durham Trust. This received financial support from several bodies, including the Coalfields Regeneration Trust (CRT). As time passed, the East Durham Trust came to play a vital role in providing basic welfare support for the most vulnerable people in the communities along the east coast.

Malcolm Fallow, a local man with generations of involvement in the coal industry, took control of the East Durham Trust from its inception, and by 2016 was finding that the provision of food parcels had emerged as a central part of its activity.[23]

> Never ever do we come across people where we think 'do they really need a food parcel' or 'are they on the scrounge?' It's more the case that they should have come for a parcel two or three weeks sooner. This should not be happening in a country that is one of the top ten richest in the world.

Referring to the 'dignity issue' in the area, for people who are hungry but ashamed to admit it or to go to food banks, he works closely with his wife Glenda, a health visitor, who says, 'the first thing I ask is "have you eaten today?" And if I see that they need a parcel I tell Malcolm.'

Dignity has become a strong theme in life in the mining towns and villages, under the long shadow cast by the mine. It is linked to one of the critical, silent, problems that has emerged from deindustrialisation: the social isolation of ageing men, divorced from the world of work. We have seen how the traction of the routines associated with mining was particularly strong in these areas, giving a powerful meaning to work, and subsequently to its loss. This was understood in the local authority and it was this that led to the establishment of the East Durham Trust's most successful scheme, which was funded by Durham Public Health: the Cree Project – which soon became known as the 'men's sheds project'.[24] This provided sheds for men to use as meeting places, bringing together people with similar interests. Each meeting place had a 'shed champion', trained in knowledge of the various support agencies operating in the area and able to report issues and problems back to the trust. The project was so successful that it was extended across the county, and to women and young people. A similar scheme developed as Men's Sheds Cymru in South Wales, this time organised through a series of decentralised cooperative groups. Both projects operated at the basic level of human need and showed how the fundamentals of a civil society can be maintained and developed even in a context of recession and austerity. The same principles operated through health improvement in the Heads of the Valleys area in South Wales, where

> a commonly occurring theme was the need to make services needs-led and to work from the community up, rather than from the top down. We were told by many people about communities that did not trust officialdom or statutory services, so that there was very little wonder that people turned up late for medical treatment, already in an advanced state of illness.[25]

Maria Uren was the coordinator for the area. In her view the closure of the coal mines and steel mills was 'still raw'. For her there was a need for regeneration to impact more directly on the needs of local people, and as such she had supported programmes that focused on food cooperatives, walking groups and allotments. Reflecting on all these issues in Durham, Malcolm Fallow considered that:

> There was a certain spirit that came out of mining communities because they had to do things themselves. They created workingmen's clubs, trade unions and cooperative stores to help their communities. This created a culture of helping your fellow citizen ... [and] it's interesting how often we make references to the miners' strike of 1984–85 because the memory of those food kitchens is still very much with us. It's

amazing how many female activists there are in East Durham who are now parish councillors, school governors and community centre managers – women who are empowered in their own communities. And, if you talk to them about when they first got involved, more often than not they say the 1984–85 miners' strike.[26]

Further evidence, though of a different sort, of the strike's continuing legacy.

CHAPTER THIRTEEN

Monsters and Ghosts

Nationalization of mines simply makes a National Trust, with all the force of the Government behind it . . . We shall and must strenuously oppose this.

The Miners' Next Step, 1912

Given the nature of their work and the prevalence of physical damage, the coalminers have fought hard for compensation for industrial injury. After all the coal mines closed, pneumoconiosis and other pulmonary lung diseases persisted, as did many other injuries associated with work in the mine. Compared to those in other occupations, miners were found to have excess likelihood of death from chronic and unspecified myocarditis and also a high incidence of tuberculosis. Miners had a higher risk of dying than the rest of the population in all age groups, while deaths from bronchitis, emphysema and asthma were significantly higher than expected between the ages of sixty-five to seventy-four.[1]

Historically, in seeking redress for these injuries, mining trade unions in the UK have tended to focus on Parliament and changes in legislation rather than insurance or litigation. The post-war Attlee government had accepted the 1944 Act that established pneumoconiosis as an industrial disease and initiated the operation of a Pneumoconiosis Compensation Scheme. There were strict criteria over eligibility, and even after amendment this did not extend beyond men who were employees of the NCB at the time the disease was diagnosed. This was later to emerge as a serious problem for those 400,000 who had left the industry in the fifties and sixties, possibly with coal dust in their lungs.

Delay and Deceit over Pneumoconiosis

The NUM had largely ignored this issue until it was brought to its attention in 1970 by the case of an ex-Durham miner called Stanley Pickles, who had worked in the Clara Vale Colliery in the years after nationalisation. The mine had closed on 5 February 1966, and Mr Pickles developed symptoms while in his new employment. The Amalgamated Engineering Union (AEU) got involved, suing the NCB for negligence. The trade union's lawyers W.H. Thompson were greatly assisted by the ex-lodge secretary, Fred Hardy, who retained a detailed memory of the working conditions in the mine and was moved to support the claim, seeing its importance for all the men who had worked there. Through his knowledge of the colliery and its workforce he was able to identify key individuals to be called upon for testimony and support.

The resulting case was comprehensive, and the lawyers approached the court with some confidence. However, the case was never heard: it was settled at the door of the court in January 1970, on the instigation of the NCB's legal team, with compensation of £7,500 – far in excess of that available under the 1944 scheme. This well-publicised case produced anger within the NUM, with miners asking why their union hadn't taken similar action. As a consequence, several Areas, including Durham and South Wales, agreed to employ solicitors, with the view to identifying critical cases of ill health that could be pursued through the courts.

Geoff Shears had just joined Thompsons, and recalls taking the sleeper from London and waking up as the train passed the red-bricked terraces of the mining villages before arriving at Durham station. At the NUM offices at Redhills, he was surprised to find 'a hundred or so elderly men, some of them stooped, waiting outside the building on the driveway. Waiting there patiently with their cloth caps folded and held in front of them. Not wanting to go inside uninvited.' These men had come forward as 'having some dust' and were possible candidates for legal action. In preparing the Durham cases in readiness for trial, Thompsons went carefully through the documents disclosed by the NCB and found evidence of collusion between the union and the corporation over the real risks encountered in the local mines. A confidential letter to Sam Watson, dating from his tenure as general secretary of the NUM's Durham Area, explained that improved X-ray techniques had revealed that Durham miners had suffered a significantly higher incidence of pneumoconiosis than had previously been understood. This implied either that the levels of exposure to coal dust were higher than previously thought, or that the adverse effects were more insidious. This significantly strengthened the case against the NCB, and potentially the scale of compensation for which it would become liable. Shears remembers being shocked by the implication that Watson had colluded in supressing this information and avoided sharing it with the miners. The trial would be an opportunity for the lawyers to bring all the facts into the open.

The lawyers were surprised that in the move to litigation not one of the serving Durham NUM officials expressed any interest in the development of the pneumoconiosis cases. It was agreed however that the strongest would be processed and taken forward, with four selected to go to trial in the hope of creating a legal precedent. The Thompsons solicitors were encouraged by the view of their QC that the cases were extremely strong, with a 70–80 per cent chance of success, and the first cases in Durham were set down for trial.

There was a risk that, should the miners lose, it would be costly for the NUM. As the number of cases approached 4,000, the

union decided on a change of course, and in 1974, with Labour
back in power, it had 'approached the government to lobby for a
universal lump sum compensation scheme for pneumoconiosis
in lieu of legal action'.[2] In this, the South Wales Area, with its
long history of dealing with pneumoconiosis cases, played an
important role. Firmly committed to the efficacy of state-
regulated systems of compensation, it was also deeply sceptical of
the union's chances of success in the courts, notwithstanding
legal advice to the contrary. At a special Area conference called in
July 1974, D. C. Davies, the head of the area's social insurance
department, went as far as to express the view that 'we may as
well collect two million pounds from our members and throw it
in the sea, as we have no hope of winning the claims'.[3]

Nevertheless, as Shears recalls,

at the last minute, the NCB, the NUM and the government
intervened to stop the progress of the action – something
which they had no right to do without the consent of the men
– and negotiated a new Pneumoconiosis Compensation
Scheme. When this came in it paid out substantially less than
the cases would have been worth if we had gone to court and
won. We had estimated that one of the miners, a man from
Blackhall, could have won £24,000 in court, and he got some
£4,500 from the scheme. So, a massive saving for the Coal
Board and the government and the saving of a great loss of
face because everything we had found out would never emerge.

Settlements in line with the Pickles case would have exceeded
£300 million and there was every reason for government and
the NCB to accede to the NUM's request. The guiding hand in
the outcome, however, was Eric Varley, secretary of state for
energy, who was determined to distance the government from
an agreement that it had deliberately orchestrated, presenting it
as being between the NCB and NUM alone. If the government
had established a statutory scheme it ran the risk of raising

questions of equality with other industrial sectors, at huge cost to the government.[4]

This was the manner in which the new Coal Workers Pneumoconiosis Scheme was introduced by the NCB and accepted by the NUM in September 1974. The NUM agreed not to pursue the outstanding 4,000 cases or sue the corporation for the costs incurred in the preparation of the test cases for court, which were withdrawn. In return, ex-miners suffering from pneumoconiosis would be compensated – but, as ever, compensation would be restricted: only men with a minimum of ten years in the industry and widows whose husbands had died after 26 January 1970 would be eligible. The maximum settlement of £10,000 was rarely awarded (average settlements in the first three years of the scheme were below £2,000), and were much lower than equivalent compensation payments received by workers in other industries.

The scheme was generally regarded by the trade union as a step forward, and the union's biographer agreed, arguing that it 'removed uncertainty by making it unnecessary for miners or their dependants to use litigation in order to gain compensation'.[5] He also acknowledged criticisms of the scheme, however, both in terms of paucity of payment and the number of excluded potential beneficiaries, and he pointed to the prolonged refusal by government and the NCB to recognise emphysema and bronchitis as industrial diseases. Many people at the time thought it questionable whether the settlement was in the best interests of the affected men, and this concern was raised forcefully at the time by Arthur Scargill, who was then the compensation officer for the Yorkshire Area. As time passed, and following the mine closures, the inadequacy of the payments increasingly rankled with NUM officials and activists, who saw it as another poor pay-off for the union's support of the nationalised industry. They felt that they had learned a lot from this and, following privatisation, freed of commitment to the NCB, they turned once again to the courts for adequate compensation over the miners' other injuries.

Struggles over compensation for industrial injury had been a central concern of the NUM in South Wales, each lodge having its own compensation secretary, many of whom remained active after the closure of the mines. In Durham, under new leadership, the Area, long renowned for its rather pusillanimous approach, squarely faced the fact that, with its members out of work and experiencing significant ill health, something had to be done and a more militant strategy was needed. It began by following the example of Bill Etherington in the Mechanics, and engaged the labour law firm Thompsons as its solicitors. The firm had represented a number of the miners arrested during the 1984–85 strike, and this was seen as a continuation of that relationship. Removed from playing an industrial role, and already heavily involved in welfare issues, the NUM in both Durham and South Wales thus joined others in moving forward as litigants, looking to the courts for fairer levels of compensation for the other injuries and diseases affecting their members.

A Success That Has Helped All Workers

Throughout the nineties in both Durham and South Wales the NUM was registering numerous urgent problems experienced by ex-miners suffering from vibration white finger (VWF), a disabling condition brought on by the extensive use of pneumatic drilling equipment. Sufferers lose the sense of feeling in their fingertips, affecting their grip and making many everyday personal and domestic tasks difficult or impossible. British Coal would not deal directly with the NUM in the years that followed the strike, but had agreed that claims for occupationally induced deafness could be handled in line with a national compensation scheme that applied mainly to the shipyards. VWF had been recognised as an occupational hazard in the shipyards for some time and a compensation scheme had been agreed, so the South Wales Area attempted to establish an arrangement whereby miners' cases could be handled through a similar scheme. This proved less than successful, however – compensation payments were extremely low – and an agreement emerged across the Areas that cases should be taken to the courts.

In Durham, as they had previously done with pneumoconiosis, Thompsons selected a number of test cases to be taken to court. David Guy was especially pleased with the outcome, recording in 1999, 'We were recently successful, last year in Newcastle, winning a major claim against British Coal for the occupation disease vibration white finger, which has generated thousands of claims both through the DSS and against British Coal.' British Coal appealed in the summer of 1999 and had its case rejected, opening the door for discussions over a compensation scheme that would affect miners across the country. Shears was involved in these discussions and remembers the company's obfuscatory tactics, and its attempts to divide the various parties and undercut potential levels of compensation. Eventually a scheme was established, but there were delays over medical certification and settlements: it is these delays which the participants remember most clearly. 'When will we hear about the claim?' was a constant refrain. Under the agreement each Area used its own solicitors, and costs were covered by the scheme. Once in operation it became clear that extremely beneficial settlements were being granted to the injured ex-miners. By 2007, settlements averaged £15,100 in Durham and £10,700 in South Wales. These settlements were so far in excess of those received under the pneumoconiosis scheme that they focused attention on the whole question of *compensation* and the hidden costs endured by the men who had worked in the mines under nationalisation.

In Durham it was agreed that in order to sustain the fabric of the union organisation, its buildings, the salaries of its officials and its capacity to continue with future litigation, small deductions (7 per cent, capped at £1,000) would be made from successful claims.[6] This reflected the centralised traditions within the DMA, and not unexpectedly there was a different approach in

South Wales, with no such deductions being made. Speaking at the Durham Miners' Gala in 2008 as chief executive of Thompsons, Shears praised the DMA for taking the financial risk in fighting test cases at a time when the government refused to establish a compensation scheme. The union, he said,

> had risked everything so that its solicitors could prove British Coal was to blame for the miners' injuries and diseases over decades. As a result, the government's own figures show that the Durham Miners and Mechanics have the highest success rates and the highest level of compensation in the country – a success that has helped all workers.[7]

The union's success in bringing these cases to court and the establishment of the scheme had a huge social and financial impact upon the ex-miners and the coal districts in both Durham and South Wales. In Durham, Alan Johnson, the lodge secretary at Dawdon Colliery in Seaham, explained how the town had been affected:

> At first it wasn't so bad, there was a bit of redundancy money about and that kept families going for a while. When the money started to run out the village started to slide. We were going down and down. I know by the number of men coming to me with problems just how bad the situation was becoming. When we won the cases for Vibration White Finger it gave a lot of hope to folks in Dawdon. On Tuesdays and Thursdays my front room was open house advising men how to fill in forms – how to make a claim. The compensation scheme has brought tens of millions of pounds into this community and that has made a big, big difference. Of course, it's no substitute for the pit but I hate to think what it would have been like if it had never happened, but it did and we have the union to thank for that.[8]

But the impact was also broader and more deeply *political*. These cases and the ones that followed uncovered the highly negligent management of the National Coal Board. They identified, in a variety of different fields, how management at all levels had placed production and costs before the safety and welfare of its workforce. These were telling and disturbing judgments.

Breathless Miners

Pneumoconiosis, as we have seen, was established as an industrial disease and covered by the scheme established in 1974. At that time the NUM had agreed that the scheme would settle the issue of miners' chest diseases. Qualification under the scheme required a medical diagnosis, and many breathless miners failed the test, raising questions as to the cause of their ill health. In this way, pneumoconiosis became linked together with the neglected issue of bronchitis and emphysema or, as it became known, chronic obstructive pulmonary disease (COPD). This condition had been prevalent among miners in both South Wales and Durham, and was thought to be associated with the inhalation of shot-firing fumes on the coal faces. However, the cause of the disease was disputed. While doctors had agreed that underground fumes from shot firing could have been a contributory factor, others were to identify cigarette smoking as the main cause, and so compensation was strongly resisted.

In combatting this medical opinion, the union of the colliery overmen and deputies (NACODS) agreed in 1988 to fund a systematic survey of the medical evidence, and this was critical to the Industrial Injuries Advisory Council finally accepting bronchitis and emphysema as an industrial disease in 1993. The mining unions hoped that the Blair government would respond to this with a scheme similar to the one agreed in 1974. This was not forthcoming, however, and as a result the South Wales branch of NACODS decided to go to court and take eight test cases as part of its British Coal Respiratory Disease Litigation. Described as 'the longest and probably the most expensive personal injury court case ever to take place in Britain', it was marked by the extent to which British Coal fought to the last ditch rather than settle amicably.[9] The final result was hugely successful, but two of the plaintiffs were to die before the case was completed. The judgment by Mr Justice Turner at the High Court in 1998 was a watershed moment. He found that corporate management saw its role to involve 'the production of coal first and the taking of precautions in respect of health second', and that a 'leisurely approach' had been taken to the measurement of dust in coal mines. Thompsons represented one miner, with its solicitor Tom Jones announcing that the firm had 3,000 other cases on its books, and describing the judgment as 'legal history'. Peter Evans, the solicitor who represented five plaintiffs from South Wales, called the ruling a 'damning indictment of British Coal at all levels and throughout its entire history'. It was estimated that this would lead to the highest ever damages bill against a single employer.[10]

In its press release of 23 January 1998, the Department of Trade and Industry (DTI) accepted that:

> British Coal's conduct of its mining operations has resulted in many miners suffering from lung disease having their conditions made worse by coal mining dust. The government has accepted this, following the judgement given today in eight lead cases brought by former employees of British Coal, claiming compensation for various respiratory diseases.

In 1999, Durham Area president David Guy saw this as another 'major success' and was encouraged by the fact that 'It looks very much as if the DTI, who are now responsible for these claims, are going to negotiate a scheme whereby people will get compensation without too much undue hassle.' In fact, this turned out to be an optimistic assessment for, as with VWF, there were to be considerable delays in the process. These delays were so severe that by 2000 there was a strong belief in both coalfields that the process was being intentionally extended in the hope that people would die before they could claim the compensation. The *South Wales Argus* organised a campaign with a petition available for signing in all newsagents, urging the government to move things forward and provide justice for these injured mine workers across Britain. In a debate in the House of Lords there was enormous criticism of the delays, with Lord Clinton Davies feeling 'ashamed that my government have taken so long to deal with this issue'. Urging it to 'get a move on', he warned: 'If we do not, it will not be 40,000 who have died; it will be nearly 120,000. That is not acceptable for a Labour government. We shall be blamed – and rightly so – by the people concerned.'[11]

After more delays in what was clearly a complex bureaucratic process, a system was put in place that required all ex-coalminers seeking compensation to be medically examined in order to establish the extent and seriousness of their condition. It was for this purpose that the government set up a national programme of spirometry testing. However, with 120,000 cases under consideration and a potential total of 450,000, the public health service was presented with an enormous potential workload and there was the prospect of further lengthy delays. As a consequence, the miners' unions agreed that Healthcall – a private health company – should be brought in to handle the assessment, a move that led to considerable criticism, not least, as Alan Napier recalls, that 'them people, mind, have never been down a pit in their lives'.[12] Napier, who had worked in the Murton mine in Durham before becoming leader of Easington District Council, had considerable experience of the effects of work upon coalminers in later life. He remembers the Healthcall technicians shouting at the patients, and that they seemed determined to question the authenticity of claims – antagonised by the idea that miners were a special case. But the cases were processed, and when compensation was paid following the Turner judgment, it was again, and as a result of effective litigation, at levels far higher than those achieved under the pneumoconiosis scheme.[13]

Another Milestone

More was to follow. In South Wales and Durham, a number of coking plants had been built between 1950 and 1980. Often located close to collieries, they were designed to purify the coal for sale as smokeless fuel by burning it at high temperatures, creating sulphurous fumes in and around the workplace. The coke workers formed a group within the NUM, with a representative on the union's NEC. In South Wales they had become a militant group, and in March 1983, in the run-up to the ballot on strike action, a delegation led by Idwal Morgan travelled to Durham to convince the workers at the Fishburn Coke Works to fight against its closure and vote for the strike. They were unsuccessful: the coke works closed later that year, and the organisation of the Durham coke workers did not change in the ways that those of the miners and mechanics had. It was not surprising then, that in the 1990s it was South Wales that led in bringing British Coal to court.

The Phurnacite plant at Abercwmboi near Mountain Ash closed in 1990, eliciting a deep feeling that with the plant gone, 'everything has gone. There is no money in the valley, no money at all.' But there had always been worries about the plant and the impact of its processes upon the local environment and the health of its workers. These fears were realised when there was an increase in the number of cases of lung cancer appearing among members of the redundant labour force. After considerable upheaval and local distress, the cokemen's union was finally able to bring a negligence claim against the company. Hugh James solicitors identified eight of the 183 former Phurnacite workers to bring as test cases, and their claims were eventually upheld at the High Court in 2012. The ruling by Mrs Justice Swift found convincing evidence that diseases of the lung, namely COPD, emphysema, chronic bronchitis and lung cancer, could have been caused by the processes at the plant, which she described as 'very poor right up to the time of the closure'. In a telling judgment she noted:

Overall, I found that the attitude of the management to the safety of its workforce appears to have been reactive, rather than proactive. I decided that the operators of the plant were in breach of statutory duties owed to their employees throughout the period of its operation. There were many measures that they could have taken to minimise or eliminate altogether the risks to their workforce had they chosen to do so. Thus, I found that the claimants had succeeded in establishing liability on the part of the defendants.[14]

This success came after many years of the trade unions trying to hold British Coal to account for the working conditions in the plant. Reflecting on this, Bleddyn Hancock of the mining deputies' union NACODS, which had supported the claimants, said, 'The people of the Aberdare valley have long known that the filth of the Phurnacite plant damaged health. Now many men and their families will be compensated for the devastating effects of respiratory disease and lung cancer.' The success of the Phurnacite litigation encouraged the union to take forward a group action being brought on behalf of another 260 coke workers and their families in South Wales. A test case was heard at the Royal Courts of Justice in July 2018 under Mr Justice Turner, with evidence of extreme working conditions (working in a sandstorm with no face masks or protective equipment) contributing to severe respiratory diseases, including chronic bronchitis and lung cancer. Here, British Coal admitted a breach of duty by failing to protect its employees from exposure to dust and fumes. Kathryn Singh of Hugh James solicitors saw this as another 'pivotal milestone' that justified the fight of the cokemen and their families. The test cases had established guidance that could be applied to 173 unresolved claims from ex-workers, including more than 100 who were employed in South Wales by government-owned British Coal at Coedely, Nantgarw and Cwm coke plants.[15]

Over these twenty years that followed the end of coal mining and coke production in South Wales and Durham (and elsewhere), the workers and their families were compensated for their pain, inconvenience, suffering and distress – but it had taken a long time. Ironically it was only after the demise of the nationalised industry that the trade unions were able to obtain justice. It was ironical too that a corporation entrusted to produce coal and coke 'on behalf of the people' should have been found so neglectful of its own people. The words of Justice Turner are worth repeating here. British Coal and the National Coal Board had put 'the production of coal first and the taking of precautions in respect of health second'. It was a damning indictment.

Justice and Fair Play

In considering the ways in which the coalfield districts have survived the loss of industrial employment, too little attention has been paid to the miners' own organisation, and the role it has played in sustaining communities, providing help and assistance to retired and unemployed coalminers and obtaining significant financial redress in compensation for the legacies of ill-health and the negligence of the National Coal Board (and British Coal) as an employer. In financial terms alone, miners could feel that the greatest amount of support they received after the closure of the coal mines came from the diligence and organised strength of their trade union representatives, who continued to be active long after the industry had effectively closed down.

Throughout, there has been a strong sense of injustice and a stress on the need to provide redress, to right past wrongs inflicted upon the coal industry and its workers by different governments. The treatment of the accumulated wealth of the Mineworkers' Pension Scheme was felt to be particularly unjust. When British Coal was privatised the government of John Major had agreed to underwrite the fund, ensuring miners would receive their pensions, but allowing the government to take 50 per cent of any surpluses. It seems that the union saw this arrangement as acceptable, with the government offering more security for the fund than any alternative arrangement. Nevertheless, questions were raised in 2008, by which time over £3.5 billion in surpluses had accumulated to the government.[16] This ongoing transfer of capital from the pension fund to the Treasury had continued unchecked under the New Labour government, in spite of evidence from its own actuarial report. This report had assessed the future risks to the scheme and was content that the distribution could be altered to provide 85 per cent to the miners and 15 per cent to the government. That this was not acted upon led journalist Rachel Heeds to note that:

> Investment surpluses from miners' pension funds have been used for compensation schemes which were due to miners for conditions such as vibration white finger and pneumoconiosis, a potentially fatal condition, caused by their work in mines. This compensation should have been entirely independent from pension funds. Miners were effectively paying their own compensation.[17]

It was in response to this that a UK miners' pension scheme association was set up in 2011, under the banner of Justice and Fair Play, and organised a petition to Parliament with the aim 'to right the wrong of the 50/50 sharing of surpluses, to a more realistic percentage which reflects the guarantors' risk, and recover all monies that rightly belong to the mineworkers of the UK.' With over 8,000 members, its concern has been to re-examine and reverse the decision that led to 50 per cent of all the growth in the pension fund being embezzled by the Treasury. At the time of this decision, British Coal insisted that Union of Democratic Mineworkers (UDM) representatives would be included in all meetings, which, given the NUM's policy on non-engagement with the UDM, meant that its representatives were in effect excluded from discussions. Arguments still rage over the implications of this.

Separately, meanwhile, the outcome of the final inquiry into the Hillsborough disaster in 2012, with its critical view of the South Yorkshire police force and exoneration of the Liverpool football fans who had died, spurred a campaign to petition yet again for a public inquiry into the events at Orgreave during the Miners' Strike. As Rachel Heeds commented:

> For many, life in the mine was still lived out in argument and conversation. The strike too, was always remembered and nowhere more clearly than in the long-standing Orgreave Truth and Justice Campaign. This was set up in order to get 'justice for miners who were victims of police lies and cover-ups at Orgreave in June 1984'. Something which the organisers see as representing one of the most serious miscarriages of justice in this country's history . . . [and that] has never been adequately addressed. It is important that the truth is established and that the police are brought to account.[18]

The call for a public inquiry was rebuffed by Conservative home secretary Amber Rudd, however, and this refusal led to a 'Death of Justice' rally being organised in Sheffield on Halloween night, 31 October 2017, the first anniversary of Rudd's decision. The campaign website noted, 'We all know it's the old monsters and ghosts of the Tory party who were responsible for the injustice then, that denies us justice now.'[19]

The legacies of work in the mines and the experiences of the 1984–5 strike are still prominent in the daily life of the coalfields, kept to the fore by the remains of the miners' trade union organisation and by the tenacity of informal groups and campaigns driven by a keen desire for justice. This persistence reveals how deeply mining and industrial life was embedded in these local communities, and how in this transient age there remains a deep sense of history and past struggle.

CHAPTER FOURTEEN

Building from the Past

Emerging new forms of resistance to the brutalities of global capitalism must coexist with older forms, scrounged from the dustbin of history.

James Ferguson, *Expectations of Modernity*, 1999

In their year-long strike in 1984–5, coalminers and their families displayed extraordinary powers of resistance, self-organisation and belief. Subsequently, colliery closures, combined with a weak employment recovery, ill health and outward migration, weakened the capacities of the coal districts of Durham and South Wales to respond to the challenges they faced. Among the wreckage caused by the destruction of the coal and steel industries, however, there remained strong remnants of the solidarism of the past. These remnants are found in many places, some small and seemingly mundane, others more public and of greater apparent significance.

Trade union membership is one indicator. This had fallen precipitously across the country since the rundown of manufacturing industries began in 1979. At that time trade union membership reached its high point of 13.2 million, estimated as being between 51 per cent and 58 per cent of all workers.[1] Forty years later membership has fallen to 23 per cent, but there are great regional disparities. In the North East and Wales, union density stands at 29 per cent and 30 per cent respectively, while in contrast only 19 per cent of South East England's labour force is in a trade union.[2] Collective sentiments and behaviour remained embedded in former coalfield regions in ways that have yet to be eroded by the acid of the market.[3]

Holding on at Tower

Tower Colliery, near Hirwaun on the northernmost scarp of the South Wales coalfield, provides one example of how these collective sentiments endured through determination, leadership and a deep attachment to the mining industry. In 1993, after enormous pressure from management and against the recommendation of the lodge committee, the men agreed to accept the closure of the mine. Subsequently each committed £8,000 of his redundancy payment to buy it back, reopen it as Goitre Anthracite and run it as a form of cooperative, drawing on past traditions of non-statist socialism.[4] This daring approach – and the geographical prominence of the site – made it famous, and it was seen by many as a beacon of hope, a triumph of imagination and a demonstration of what could be done. The mine welcomed visitors from all over the world. On one of our visits, we met up again with Paul Robeson Jr, standing in orange overalls in the pit yard after a visit underground. There was a visitors' centre as well as an open-house canteen, which was also the base for a local credit union, set up to challenge the loan sharks that had come to dominate credit in the local villages.

The story of Tower has been documented in books and academic journals, as well as in the popular press.[5] It has been celebrated as opera and in French cinema. We have seen how, in the maelstrom that led up to the privatisation of the coal industry, the workforce at Tower was put under enormous pressure to accept redundancy payments and to vote for the closure of the mine. In an extended process their number dropped from over

600 to 250 of some of the most deeply committed coalminers in South Wales. One of their leading advocates, Dai 'Doscow' Davies, chairman of the NUM lodge in the new company Goitre Anthracite, explained how, as pit after pit closed, the men who refused to leave the industry were moved on to other pits, and Tower was the last:

> So we finished up with hardcore people in Tower who were desperate to be miners in the mining industry for as long as they can and that is why, when . . . it was put up for sale, the people here had the bottle to go for it and that is why other pits in Yorkshire and the Midlands didn't. Because there were hardcore people in Tower who wanted to stay in the mining industry no matter what. Even at their own expense – putting money in themselves. There was a lot of things they could do, they could have let the colliery go and it would have been bought by somebody else like they did in Yorkshire . . . but you had a hardcore of people here, the most awkward bastards in the British Coalfields – us stuck up here in Tower!

Tyrone O' Sullivan agreed, adding that at the pit before the closure there was

> a very radical leadership, a leadership that was still out there doing things, we are still getting people from Solidarity and El Salvador and Nicaragua and so on to the pit, to the canteen. There are other pits that wouldn't dare do that, we are still getting Arthur Scargill down, I mean everybody says 'he is the kiss of death, never invite Arthur Scargill to your pit, don't show you are militant.' Bullshit! Better to frighten them off, not offer to lie down and get killed.

This leadership and the coherence of the lodge committee were critical in the process that saw the resistance to the colliery closure being organised and transformed into a political struggle for ownership of the mine. It was not an easy task. Trade unions in the UK have generally been lukewarm in their support of producer cooperatives. It was argued that they would inevitably be under pressure to compete and would gradually take on the form of capitalist firms, often surviving by extracting greater effort through the commitment of their members – the so-called 'sweat equity'.[6] This was certainly the position taken by the NUM and endorsed at its annual conference in 1992. At that time, Arthur Scargill had been re-elected as president and, in his speech at the conference, he viewed cooperative ventures as naïve in failing to appreciate that they would need to operate in 'the hostile capitalist environment'.

But Scargill's approach had been tried, and the mass strike had failed to deal with the harsh reality of the closure programme. As it continued to roll destructively across the coalfields, miners and their supporters began to take an interest in takeovers, but Tower Colliery, in the form of Goitre Tower Anthracite, proved to be the only long-term survivor.[7]

The period when the mine was to be closed remains highly charged in the memory of these men and especially so for the leadership cadre. They remember the details of the events, the drama of the decision and the powerful sense of achievement that surrounded the successful purchase of the mine. Their success was all the more pleasing for the way it proved so many people wrong:

> So, we said 'right oh, what we will do, we'll buy it.' And they said 'what do you want to buy it for, you're a bloody twp [fool], what do you want it buy it for, you can't buy this colliery.' That was Mr Cox, the manager, and he was one of the guys who wanted to buy it: 'Aye, aye well you know I am an Engineer and I can.' That sort of attitude. Now we had worked here for thirty-four years, the boys had worked here all those years, they know about the reserves, they know about the mine.

Anyway, they didn't like it and we put a bid in and we had
Price Waterhouse in London, the top accountant in the
country and everything like this. They thought 'well the
stupid bloody miners, what do they know about bloody
business and things like this, sledges like this, who the hell
are they?'

Anyway, they were embarrassed, weren't they, every time
they tried to put us down, they were embarrassed. Then we
marched from here to London and got the publicity and
everything, by now they were totally embarrassed.

But it hadn't been easy; it had taken a lot of courage and the
miners had had a lot of help. In their assessment of the success
of the Tower venture, Waddington and his colleagues credit the
open outlook of the leadership group, seeking help and assistance where they could. At a TUC conference, Tyrone
O'Sullivan met up with Fairwater Consultants, the
TUC-sponsored agency for worker cooperatives, and this led to
the formation of TEBO, the Tower Employees Buy-Out team.
They went to Barclays Bank, which insisted that the initial
£2,000 per worker should be increased to £8,000, and that in
the new management structure there should be a five-person
company board composed of three managers and only two
trade union directors. They accepted these terms. More remarkably, they went to Price Waterhouse – the accountants who had
acted to organise the sequestration of the NUM's funds during
the strike – to assess the financial viability of their bid, and
approached leading Thatcherite John Redwood (then secretary
of state for Wales) for his support. This pragmatic approach
also led them to include Philip Weekes, the ex-Area director of
the NCB, as chairman of the new company.[8] According to the
Waddington study, 'It was this carefully calculated approach to
organisation and strategy that ultimately served to impress
Rothschilds, the Government's merchant bankers, and the
Department of Trade and Industry.'[9]

In this, of course, they were in competition with the previous management of the mine, the same management that had orchestrated its closure.[10] However:

> The DTI had actually informed the management at Tower Colliery that they could not take the pit because they were the people who had said it was non-viable, uneconomical and with geological problems and that is why it should close. So, if they were going to buy it, how could they? They would have been in the meetings. They had manipulated the situation that it would shut. So, you could forget about getting pissed boys, as you are the ones who have caused it to fucking close! 'You are the ones that were telling the British government that it is non-viable. What do you want to buy it for?'

Revenge was sweet, but also hard-headed. Because, as the miners knew, 'If we had collapsed after three months, there would have been pats on the back and hand claps. "They can't run the business but aren't they wonderful the salt of the earth."' The TEBO team was determined to make the mine succeed. They knew that they needed a team of qualified managers and supervisors who would have to come from British Coal. In this they were 'looking for straight men, not yes men'. On one thing they were clear – they would not employ a finance manager who had worked for the NCB or BCC, seeing them to be expert in making the case for the closure rather than the development of the mine.

They took a hard-nosed and realistic approach to the potential reserves and planned to eke them out, over as long a period as possible. They knew that as the mine had closed it no longer had the benefit of the established contracts with the power generators, and that it would not be easy to develop new markets for the anthracite – but they knew that it could be done. Their main aim was to save the pit and keep jobs there for as long as possible. In this, they needed to retain the support of the rank-and-file members who had been through a traumatic time.

Having accepted that the mine would close and having received their redundancy payments, they now faced the choice of whether to take a chance and buy into the collective owner-ship of their workplace. One man remembers:

When the first redundancy came out, I think if you finished you could go out with say £14,000 or £15,000. Well most of my butties took that money and run because they thought there was no future in mining and they didn't think there was any more money on the table. Now I was lucky enough, I was single, but I didn't need the money so that's probably the only reason that I stayed on and I didn't go with them . . . But that money was a fool's money, fool's gold – because it never lasted them, because they always kept dipping into it because they had such a low-paid job, and within twelve or fourteen months it had vanished. It never lasted with them and they've never done anything with their lives since then.

So this was their last mine and we fought them all the way, they offered us . . . another £9,000 on top of our redundancy which [for me] was then £29,000 and they offered us more money. Remember all that had been happening from 1985 up to 1989. All these pits closing, and all of a sudden you go home to your wife, 'I've got £32,000 coming to me and they've offered me another 9.' More money than you'd ever seen. Now of course some did take it and then they offered another £9,000 . . . when we turned them down again . . . they were gobsmacked. Now the papers started saying that they were going to take the money off us. Now you imagine the women in the house now, all of a sudden now they have got £40,000 coming to them and then the next day the papers are at them . . . you can see the backbone of what kept the miners there and it was a lot of women that made the decision for the future of these kids: 'right, you stick it out.'

Stick it out they did, as committed families, and on January 2 1995, forty-eight years after vesting day 1947, and a year after privatisation, there was a new vesting day and the Tower Colliery was reopened. It was no longer part of a nationalised industry but it was, as its banner declared, 'back in the hands of the work-force'. The Tower workers with their families and supporters sang 'The Red Flag' as their MP Ann Clwyd cut the red ribbon with these words: 'Today is better than 1947 when the industry was nationalised. Now it's a people's pit. The miners and the community have shown the way – when you are prepared to fight you can win.'

Then it was back down the shaft for hard graft: producing coal.

> So we bought the mine, we came back here on January 2nd, and on January 5th we were producing coal . . . and they told us it would take eight months before we got any coal out of here . . . and we were producing something like 280,000 tonnes a year and £23 million, with a £2 million profit a year, not many multinational companies that were producing that kind of thing.

On the back of that success the company declared an interim Christmas dividend of £500 and increased wages by £23 per week, leaving funds to purchase a shearer-loader cutting machine. Glyn Rogers had been chair of the old lodge committee, and was centrally involved in the new concern as a director taking responsibility for personnel issues. He remembers, 'the first year was excellent. The second year wasn't too bad, but of course there were slight problems, geological problems, sales problems.'

Such problems were not going to go away. The men remained members of the NUM, and as such were both union members and shareholders. Their elected management representatives often felt that they were caught in a crossfire, 'being shot at all the time'. They kept reminding the men that they were having to compete in 'the nasty vicious world that is outside' while telling themselves that 'we have to survive for all the people who support us outside . . . because we are lightning rods to them.'

Yet the presence of the 'real nasty vicious world' outside goes some way to explaining the success of Tower and the way the leadership group was able to retain the commitment of the men to the project. Glyn Rogers remembered:

> In the first year . . . everybody was walking on air because . . . they didn't like the outside world and they realised that at the colliery, where they were working, they were nigh on their own boss, so it is a lot easier to work in a colliery without somebody standing over you.

This reference to the quality of alternative employment – its low wages and tedium – crops up repeatedly in the accounts that these men give of their reasons for 'taking a chance'. The period between closure and reopening had given many of the younger men a taste of what was on offer away from the mine. But there was also an idea that under the new ownership working in the mine had to be different from what had gone before. The removal of the incentive scheme was a big step forward.

What Tower offered was a life that was different from what had gone before: a job with decent wages and good people to work with. Tyrone O'Sullivan reflected upon this, and upon the idea that working in a cooperative meant that you worked harder:

> Do people work harder because it is their own company, well I say they don't, not in my industry, because the coal is not any softer because we own the thing. They have always worked hard, but I do think there is perhaps 5–10 per cent benefit. If you do it properly there are advantages of becoming owners, by talking to people and getting them to talk to you, yes, they work just as hard as they used to before but now they are pass-ing their knowledge on to you as well – and not only that, we

listen. We used to pass the knowledge on before in my day but nobody listened, but the things they say to you now, you are listened to.

The new cooperative operated on the principle that the men were shareholders at meetings and when they weren't working, but the work in the mine needed to be controlled by the authority system vested in the management and the directors. For Tyrone O'Sullivan this meant that:

> Tower is something special in many ways, we had the right lot of people . . . to come into a pit being a shareholder and still accepting taking instructions and orders is still a hell of a strong discipline, miners have it. They had to have it because in the past, if you didn't have it, it would kill you. We have trained to be disciplined to work on our own.

At another time he put it more directly: 'The structure is the same as British Coal because you have to have discipline. When you pass through the gates you're an employee not a shareholder. But the atmosphere is different.'[11]

This formulation didn't solve everything; forming a cooperative hadn't magically changed people. Its very existence created issues for trade unionism. Dai 'Doscow' Davies reflected that under British Coal you knew where you were:

> You knew who the enemy was, the fucking manager of British Coal . . . I can tell you now from my heart, to be a trade union leader now within this cooperative is blowing my head off, because you have got to let it go, you think you have got no enemy in here but you have, because you have got different thoughts to what they have got and, they are directors, they have the responsibility, to get this company to run in the most efficient manner . . . Now some people have tried to wear two hats here, shareholder, union – you cannot do it. I said

yesterday 'look, I will conduct myself the best way I can as chairman of the NUM, I am managed by my members and by my lodge committee to achieve certain things and that is what I have got to do and fuck the company'. Not to the extent of bringing them down because we will bring ourselves down. Now . . . they think I am the enemy within and I think they are the enemy within, but the great thing about it, for all the problems and for the mental stress it gives you, is that all our problems and issues can be dealt with here. There is no Area production manager to deal with, no Area director, no minister up in London to fucking deal with, it is all within here, it is all in this fucking colliery by here.

Clearly, life in the Goitre Anthracite wasn't a rose garden, and the change in ownership structure didn't resolve personal tensions and the kinds of problems that come through hierarchies and complex decision-making. It would also be wrong to think of the workforce as starry eyed, all equally committed to the future of the cooperative as an *ideal*. For the elected directors and the men who had been centrally involved in achieving the purchase of the mine, there was always a worry. They remember that at the last meeting, when Tower was under the axe, the members *did* vote to close the colliery against the recommendation of the committee. There was a fear that if they faced the threat of a takeover that this might happen again.

The experience of the cooperative can be seen as a process within which self-centredness, seen as the product of capitalist market relationships, is slowly eroded, if not completely broken down. Tyrone O'Sullivan remembered the importance of the annual meeting, and how he, as chairman of the company, and the directors answered questions from the workers and shareholders who hold them to account. On one occasion it was noticed that the company had donated £40,000 in sponsorships, which amounted to £150 from each of them. One worker got up and asked about this money – what was it for, what was it spent on?

So Ken Davies, a great lad, a guy who was down the pit with me today, one of the directors, he started reeling off how sponsorships involved all activities of young children, a disabled riding school, local athletics £1,000 per year, several bands, junior rugby teams, drug and alcohol abuse, anything that gets the kids involved and away from drugs and we were going to give even more money to help the community, £500 here, £200 there. And in the end the boys said: 'right I've heard enough, he's doing a wonderful job; marvellous.' I was so proud. You see he wanted to have a go at us, to catch us out. He thought, 'I'll get the bastards now with this £40,000.'

While agreeing with this, Glyn Rogers remained concerned that the men had become complacent, thinking that 'the final battle was fought to get the colliery back and that they won the war'. As he put it, 'People don't have the time anymore.'

This tension between running a mine as a cooperative going concern and maintaining a widespread political/revolutionary presence in the community was a central one. It was exacerbated by other changes that were taking place in the aftermath of Thatcher's Britain. As everything else closed down, Tower began to stand out as something apart. In spite of the wider role that it played in the Cynon Valley, through recruiting workers locally and through its various sponsorships, there were detractors.

In small valley communities like the Cynon Valley you see all the jealousy of people who are successful and so forth ... You've got people who are trying to make a success for themselves as coalminers, most of us had had the bottle ... we took a bit of a chance. But ... I have heard it said, 'oh Tower Colliery this' and 'Tower Colliery that', talking down about it. A lot of them people are the ones who hear Tower on the news and they are the people who are drawn into thinking that we are something different because we got up off our asses and said 'right we are going to have crack at this.'

To these men who had always worked hard and who had taken a chance with their money and their futures, such criticism was hard to take, but probably inevitable. While there are limits to what can be expected of a cooperative enterprise, the experience of Tower signals the possibilities of achieving far more if such activities were located more broadly in regional and national economic policies and community development.

The venture lasted for fourteen years. When it finally closed in January 2008 with its reserves exhausted, it had outlived almost all of the NCB's other coal mines, including most of those in Nottingham. At the closing ceremony, Rhodri Morgan, first minister of Wales, said the miners at Tower had been 'inspirational'. For him it was 'a story of confidence among the workers in their own ability and in the future viability of their mine.'

Durham: The Miners' Big Meeting

In 2003 a delegation from Tower travelled up to Durham to take part in the annual 'Big Meeting' or gala that was held there every year on the second Saturday in July. Several of the delegates had attended the Centennial Gala in 1983. That year, when they had been on strike, they had visited the coalfield for support; they were invited back and strongly encouraged to return for the Big Meeting in July. They had been impressed on that occasion and expressed sadness that they hadn't been involved before. In 2003, however, they were amazed by the size of the event, the enthusiasm and support, and the fact that it was continuing ten years after the mines had closed.

This event – the Durham Miners' Gala or Big Meeting – is another example of the continuity of a collective spirit associated with coal-mining trade unionism. Perhaps more than anything else, it brings out the deep historical roots of Durham mining trade unionism that contribute to it as a unique event, unlike anything found in any other coalfield or among any other group of workers. Its nineteenth-century origins, the Methodist

influence in its banners and the near-medieval setting of the City
of Durham were elements which helped to produce an extraordinary working-class occasion: a combination of parade, family
reunion, political gathering and revivalist meeting. On occasions
it morphed into a state parade, and always there were elements of
carnival, with women dressed as men and miners dressed up as
toffs or dancing with each other. It is an occasion like few others.

The gala dates back to 1869, when the newly formed Durham
Miners' Association decided to mark its presence in the county
with an annual meeting to be held in Durham City on a Saturday
in the summer. The first meeting took place two years later in
1871 at Wharton Park, at that time on the edge of the city. Later
and in subsequent years it took place on the racecourse in the
city centre on the second Saturday in July. It was an occasion for
the people of the mining villages to march together through the
city behind the banner of their local lodge to music played by
their colliery band. It was also an occasion to listen to the speeches
of their leaders and invited guests and, sometimes, for the only
time in the year, to meet friends and also family.

Jack Lawson, as MP for Chester-le Street, provided this
account from 1932:

> It is exhilarating to march with your band and banner . . .
> Banner after banner, band after band, followed by the members
> of the lodges and their wives. From remote places on moor
> and fell and from the huge collieries near the towns, they have
> marched: down from the boundaries of the coalfield and up
> from the centre they have come . . . since eight in the morning
> they have been coming into the city of Durham and even at
> noon the apparently endless march goes on.[12]

Durham banners are ornate and still bear a trace of their roots
in nineteenth-century Primitive Methodism. Their presence was
noted from the earliest days: made of silk measuring 8 x 6 feet and
with images painted on both sides, they were unmissable – and

in 1872 the *Durham Chronicle* remarked, 'The display of banners was a very prominent and pleasing feature of the demonstration. Altogether there were upwards of 70 flags on the ground ... The greater proportion of them were indeed artistic productions, both in design and execution.'[13] For the local miners, the banner created a sense of identity. They were also material objects with an emotional attachment. David Guy remembers:

> We were told as children to memorise our banner so if we got lost we could find our way back to its safety. As we grew up the banner took on a more important place in our lives. It represented our history, the past struggles and achievements of our parents and grandparents and of course the bitter disappointments.[14]

The motif painted on a new banner was always a matter for considerable discussion, given its importance not just for the lodge but for the local community; its unveiling was a significant event, often conducted with a religious solemnity. Every lodge had a banner to serve as an emblem for the lodge and its people. Given some of the ways in which it was seen and spoken about, the banner *was* the people.[15]

While the *form* of the Big Meeting was changeless, the *content* of these occasions altered over time in response to the underlying political and social reality. In the post-war period, under the leadership of Sam Watson, the gala was developed and used as a mobilising force to support nationalisation and the Labour government. In 1946 it was estimated that a quarter of a million miners and their families marched through the city in the first gala after the war. On that occasion, the platform included Clement Attlee, Aneurin Bevan and the US ambassador, Averill Harriman. Michael Foot spoke there the following year, and when interviewed in Tredegar in 1980 he remembered:

I started there in 1947. That's when I shared the platform with Arthur Horner. It was strange because the Durham Area emerged as a right wing within the union and the Labour Party, but I was elected to go there regularly. The Durham Miners' Gala . . . in those days it was absolutely sensational. There were so many lodges you see and they had to start bringing them in at half past eight in the morning. The whole city absolutely throbbed with the thing from early in the morning right through until you left. And you left absolutely drunk with it – the music, the banners and all in that beautiful city. It overwhelmed you really. In those days it was, far and away, the best working-class festival that there was in this country. Far and away the best. It was just marvellous.

Watson was aware of the capacity of this 'working-class festival' to move people and form part of a political project. Under his guiding hand, leading figures from the Labour Party came to dominate the occasion, first Attlee and then Hugh Gaitskell, with other guests including the American, Israeli and Yugoslav ambassadors who were regularly invited to witness the spectacle. With all this in place, and at a time of cold war, the parade was presented to them as a *demonstration of free people*.

The closure of the pits in the sixties and the huge reduction in the number of coalminers diminished the size of the Big Meeting, and the leadership of the miners' union accepted this as a fact of life. Once a mine closed it was no longer expected that the lodge banner would be paraded through Durham City in July. However, these banners still had significance. Some, including the famous one at Chopwell, were put on permanent display in the local community centre, while others (for example, the one at Dean and Chapter) had a less noble fate, being left to disintegrate, unattended and uncared for. On gala day, their absence was missed; the parade was supplemented with girl kazoo bands, and the NUM Area leadership began to refer to its importance for the tourist trade. This was looked upon with scorn by men like

George Alsop, who had been lodge Secretary at Chopwell and a member of the Communist Party:

> It used to be a really big day. A big political day and a right booze-up too. But the last time I was at Durham I saw a contrast. It's more of a carnival now. Everybody's in bands – brass bands, jazz bands. It hasn't got the political significance it had. You used to go the Durham for your rights, more or less, for your political rights. But today it's treated more or less as a carnival.[16]

The carnival element was always there, but only as a part of a much bigger picture, a picture that was fading. Attempts to reinvigorate the occasion through the involvement of other trade unions and associations were rebuffed. Dave Ayre's father was a miner and he 'used to carry me on his shoulders to the Big Meeting in Durham when I was a baby'. As secretary of the Wear Valley Trades Council, he had also become concerned for the future of the gala:

> through the trades council we wanted to expand it by including other trade unions and trades councils, because there aren't many miners' lodges left now, except round the coast. But the NUM won't have any other union representation; they want it kept as a *miners'* gala.[17].

But things were to change. The appointment of Ian MacGregor and the year-long strike that followed were decisive factors, assisted, coincidentally, by 1983 being the gala's centenary year. In commemoration of the original event, the closed lodges were asked to parade again with their old banners, while lodges from other Areas of the NUM were also invited to attend. Arthur Scargill and Neil Kinnock (who was standing for the leadership of the Labour Party) were the main speakers. It was an occasion that visually demonstrated what had been lost with the mine closures of the past. It galvanised many for what seemed certain to be a struggle ahead. While carnival elements were ever present, it clearly resembled the 'big political day' that George Alsop had lamented. It also set a pattern and the tone for the future approach to the gala.

During the strike (as on previous occasions of war and industrial conflict) the gala was cancelled, replaced with a demonstration that again and even more forcefully brought together the symbolic power and emotional strength of the occasion. As a demonstration it was decided that all Areas of the NUM and all trade unions should be invited to take part in support of the strike. This was achieved through a radical change in the composition and tenure of the executive committee, brought about by rank-and-file organisation across the east coast lodges. The demonstration was a tremendous success, and emphasised the power of the occasion and the extent of trade union solidarity. After the strike, the closed lodges – Horden, Sacriston, Herrington – were encouraged to get involved, along with others that had closed before the strike. The East Hetton lodge banner continued to parade, with the miners living there demonstrating their commitment to their local community as well as to their new lodge at Easington Colliery.

This pattern continued as other lodges closed, but in 1993 the combined closures of Easington, Dawdon and Westoe created a crisis. By this time the Durham and Northumberland Areas had merged into one North East Area, with the Ellington Colliery in Northumberland operating under the ownership of RJB Mining. Dave Hopper remained as general secretary of the new Area until Ellington closed in 2005. But deep mining had ceased in County Durham, and it was clear that a decision needed to be taken about the future of the Big Meeting. The expectation was that, with neither mines nor miners, the gala would end. One problem was money, but there were other worries too. Some miners, like Mick Carr from Horden, felt that it would be wrong for the gala to continue, as it would lack authenticity; he worried that it would fizzle out, or be kept going to feed the egos of a few. 'No Miners – No Gala' was the slogan of a group that would gather in protest at the Colpitts pub in Durham on gala day. However, as Mick Carr's friend David Temple was to point out:

> On July 10 1993, the local mining communities poured onto the streets of Durham in greater numbers than had been seen for twenty years. Again, many old banners, frail and faded from the winds of past galas, were lifted from their resting places and brought out into the streets . . . The message was unmistakable – this is our Gala; it expresses who we are; it must go on.[18]

This proved convincing evidence of the potential for the gala to be authentically reconfigured as a permanent event, outlasting the mines but building on the culture and politics of mining.

Once committed to this future, the Area leadership and executive committee faced the problem of replacing their depleted reserves with a new source of income that would allow the gala to continue, and the trade union to remain as a viable organisation, most especially in relation to fighting compensation claims. They received some early help from Michael Watt, a New Zealand businessman who, before making his fortune, had worked alongside ex-Durham miners in the 1980s. Having enjoyed their company and been moved by their talk of the strike, and also of the Big Meeting days in Durham, he offered a grant to the union to cover the costs of the gala through until 1999.

The final closure of all mining of course meant that the National Union of Miners could no longer be recognised by the Registry of Friendly Societies as a trade union in the North East. It was in this context that the Durham Miners' Association and the Durham Colliery Mechanics' Association were re-established as organisations set up to support and seek compensation and legal redress for their members. An affiliated membership scheme was set up, with an annual subscription fee of £20 for ex-miners.

This allowed the union to continue to support miners in employment tribunals and to take forward the compensation work discussed earlier. As we have seen, it was agreed with the members that deductions would be made from successful claims and these provided the financial and organisational structure that allowed the gala to continue and to grow. This growth was exponential: on the one hand, more and more people and community groups from the North East began to attend, and on the other, the event began to attract trade union delegations and community groups from across the UK. By 2003, the gala had become a national event that extended beyond the coalfield and the miners. This transformation mirrors the achievements of the earlier period, but in a different political context.

In many of the villages where mines had closed, some remnants of the lodge structure remained. Following the most recent closures, like Sacriston inland, and those on the coast, lodge officials remained in post as a source of social support, legal advice, leadership and organisation. At Easington Colliery, Alan Cummings continued to be an active lodge secretary for decades after the mine had closed. He also sat on the executive committee of the DMA alongside Lawrence Claughan of Sacriston, taking an active role in defending members in employment and medical tribunals. Men like these were determined to continue supporting the gala, and other ex-mining villages began to follow, reviving their old banners and marching in Durham City.

Many villages, however, were without banners, or their banners needed repair. To help them, banner groups and partnerships began to be established across the west of the old coalfield, in a pattern that mirrored the developments of the support groups during the 1984–85 miners' strike, and often linking in with the other local heritage groups. Encouraged and supported by the DMA, these groups met with the aim of accumulating funds locally (through raffles and other events) and applying for aid from the Heritage Lottery Fund. This fund had been criticised for the lack of support it had given to poorer areas, and particularly the old coalfields, but there followed many successful applications from Durham. In 2001, the New Herrington Miners Banner Partnership was the first of these to obtain funding and commission a replica banner. The lodge secretary was centrally involved and made it clear that:

> Part of what we do is about letting Thatcher and her like know we are still here. They closed the pits and took the jobs, but every time we take that banner out, we are saying to them 'we're still here, and we are still fighting for our communities.'[19]

Under the new leadership, DMA officials and executive members regularly attended meetings, offered advice and coordinated the involvement of new banners in the annual parade. Each year new banners appeared from the lodges of mines long closed, and their reappearance pointed to a new development in the organisation of solidarity and collective behaviour. On many occasions, the DMA linked up with local community workers funded by the local authority, or by one of many charitable funders and organisations. These workers were most often women, and concerned with dealing with issues of community development, and the problems of dislocation and lack of employment in the old coal-mining areas. The banner groups provided a focus for their activities, while also linking them with the lodges and the organisation of the old trade union. In providing advice on making funding applications they added a new level of expertise, helping the communities to help themselves. The groups also provided a focus for other activities (local history, photography) with potential to engage people of all ages, linking up with the many other heritage projects that were emerging. In reflecting on the situation in South Wales, David Adamson has questioned the capacity of the trade unions to engage with the lives of disaffected young unemployed people.[20] These developments in Durham, built around the banner and the Big Meeting, demonstrated that a (defunct) trade union could build on the past and build bridges across a fragmented working class.

In these and other ways, the changes represented a cultural revolution. In Durham the Redhills Miners' Hall had been changed beyond recognition. It had once been an austere place, the centre of the trade union, where rules were made and enforced. Dave Hopper remembered, as a young miner, approaching the building with a mixture of 'fear and awe'. After the closures of the sixties and through the seventies, Redhills, like the industry itself, had been in decline. Visiting it, you were impressed by the architecture, the statues of the old leaders that stood on plinths along the driveway, and by the silence that evoked a sense of reverence. Barry Chambers remembered an occasion in 1981 when he was involved in a fierce discussion on the ground floor of the building: Harold Mitchell, the president, came to the top of the stairs telling them to be quiet because 'this is not a miners' hall'. Barry felt that this said it all, because 'that is just what it is. It is a bloody miners' hall.'

Again, the strike changed everything. Redhills was the political centre during those twelve months and under the new leadership it retained this openness and became a much livelier and more inviting place, often bearing banners in support of local and national campaigns. It became a centre for film – *The Happy Lands* and *Still the Enemy Within* were both screened there to large audiences – and for exhibitions and discussions of mining history and culture. In all this, the strike remained a constant reference point, and contributed to a political shift in the *content* of the Big Meeting.

For decades the guest of honour at the Big Meeting had been the leader of the Labour Party, accompanied by other guests chosen from within the Labour elite and sympathetic international dignitaries. Under Watson it had been carefully stage managed and crafted, so that Durham in July became an important date in the calendar and one where, through informal conversation at dinner on the Friday night, important discussion took place. This was to change. Neil Kinnock spoke again in 1985, but the muted reception to his speech and the obvious antagonism felt by many led him to refuse further invitations, and this pattern continued under the leaderships of Smith, Blair and Brown. Instead, guests and speakers began to be drawn from beyond the political elite, with internationalism of a different kind bringing visitors from Cuba and Chile, Spain and Australia.

Trade union membership was in decline, and national leaders had become open to the idea of developing links with social movements as a way to widen their support. In this context the re-emergence at Durham of the gala as a platform for left-wing ideas and discussion was both timely and welcomed by the activists who travelled north (and south); in our conversations they often spoke of having their 'batteries recharged' and of experiencing 'something unique'. It was an enormously successful collaboration that saw the gala transformed from a small local meeting of coalminers into a broad-based national trade union and working-class celebration. Showing the capacity of this event to transcend both Durham and coal mining, the Union UNITE always had a large delegation. Retired official Eddie Roberts remembered that attending the gala provided union activists with a sense of hope, a break from the feeling of isolation: 'You realise that there are so many people out there who do actually think along the same lines as you. This is a very important role that the gala plays, whether consciously or otherwise.'

Solidarity

It is clear that on both coalfields mining had a deep and lasting meaning that extended beyond the closure of the mines. At Tower the men took a chance with their money in order to save the mine and also to be able to work in a job that had a sense of purpose, alongside people they knew and got on with. It was a gamble but one that was worth taking. Given the lead, they all followed with their £8,000. In 1998, Glyn Roberts, Tyrone

O'Sullivan and Phil White were sitting in the office block, talking about potential new markets for anthracite, about the visitors' centre, the strike, picketing and about TEBO. Everyone agreed that the lead that they gave at Tower was seen by many as inspirational. The same was true of the decisions taken by the new leadership in Durham and the support it gave to the continuance of the annual Big Meeting as a collective display of solidarity and support. Both initiatives drew upon critical elements in working-class experience, in which the strike played a vital part. These men still talked with pride of the year that they resisted the plans of the Thatcher government. In Durham, David Temple explained in a note, 'I often think how poorer our lives would have been without that year. If we had just faded away without a fight, I am sure there would now be no Gala to boost our sense of well-being each year.'

The militancy involved in the strike and in the politics of the leaders at Tower and Durham was one that built on ideas of solidarity, not just as a means to an end but as a value in itself. A value based upon friendship, family and community, something anchored in specific, familiar places. At Tower a common phrase used in dealing with British Coal and then transposed into the cooperative was 'free and fair', something that spoke to the common decency that William Morris recognised as a necessary basis of a good socialist society. All of this was evident in Hirwaun and Durham in the first decades of the new century and fed into discontent with the policies of the main political parties and the feeling that things needed to change. In 2014 Dave Hopper expressed the view that 'we have to start all over again. We have to take the union into the villages and organise social support up from the bottom in ways that can take the labour movement forward again.'

CHAPTER FIFTEEN

The People Speak Out

I could hear the lords and ladies now from the grandstand, and I could see them standing up to wave me in; 'Run' they were shouting in their posh voices, 'Run'. But I was deaf, daft and blind and stood there where I was . . . out of gladness that I had got them beat at last.

Alan Sillitoe, *The Loneliness of the Long-Distance Runner*, 1959

In December 2015, Kellingley Colliery in North Yorkshire was capped with concrete, sealing off the UK's deep reserves of coal. Following the demise of Maltby, Hatfield and Thorsby earlier in the year, Kellingley had been the last of the old NCB mines in operation.[1] Known locally as Big K, it had opened half a century earlier to feed the electricity-supply market. Now its shipments to the Drax power station were replaced with Russian imports, while the mine's owner, UK Coal, shifted operations to a sister company, the property developer Haworth Estates.

Here we can glimpse some of the interrelations between deindustrialisation and globalisation: domestic production is replaced with imports, while finance and property speculation thrive. These processes have produced a situation in which the UK has become an asset-based economy rather than one concerned with the production of material goods. By 2019, manufacturing contributed just 10 per cent of UK gross domestic product compared with 23 per cent in Germany and 17 per cent in Italy. This had a huge impact on employment patterns and the composition and nature of the working class. In 1981, the manufacturing and mining sectors employed almost 6 million workers, accounting for 22 per cent of all jobs. By 2019 they accounted for less than 3 million, or 8 per cent of the national labour force.[2]

Tony Benn, who had been a Cabinet minister in the Wilson and Callaghan governments, said afterwards in conversation that one of his deepest regrets as a politician was that he 'didn't recognise deindustrialisation sooner and fight harder to stop it'. What followed under Thatcher accelerated the process. The removal of capital export controls, drastic cuts in the top rates of taxation, then the demutualisation of the building societies and the loosening of stock market controls under the Financial Services Act 1986, saw:

> American, German, Dutch and French firms [pour] into the City to snap up sleepy partnerships or poach their brighter talents. The cult of get rich quick linked the Big Bang with what became known as the 'Lawson boom' of the late eighties. The associated stereotypes, the yuppie in the black suit, the Cockney futures trader, the 'phone number' bonus, the Porsche and the Cotswold manor became icons of Thatcher's Britain, cruelly contrasted with the unemployed miner and docker.[3]

This was to be more than a blip in the trajectory of the more generalised growth and prosperity that had characterised the post-war period.

Rather than break with the downward slide, the governments of Tony Blair and Gordon Brown accelerated it, further weakening the welfare system and enthusiastically endorsing the beneficent power of the markets. In those years, 'globalisation' was on the lips of every Cabinet minister as an unstoppable current that the working class had to learn to swim with, on peril of being washed away by the tide of History. Ethan Kapstein of the Council on Foreign Relations in New York noted around this time how 'rapid technological change and heightening international competition are fraying the job markets of the major industrialized countries'. However, 'just when working people need the nation state as a buffer from the world economy, it is abandoning them'.[4]

In a speech to the Confederation of British Industry (CBI) in 2000, Blair made it clear that the view of the state as an engaged actor within the economy was a thing of the past. In opposition he had worked to remove from the Labour Party's constitution a commitment, under Clause IV, to take large parts of the economy into state ownership. In government he spelled out that this policy needed to be replaced by one that saw the modern state as a facilitator for foreign inward investment, providing the necessary infrastructure and labour force. This was presented as both an essential requirement for and an unavoidable consequence of globalisation and something which confirmed the new portability of 'work' and the increasingly transient nature of working relationships. He re-emphasised this throughout 2002, most clearly in his speech at the Labour Party conference where he explained how 'globalisation and technology open up vast new opportunities but also cause massive insecurity'. The role of progressive politics was to build reforms 'around the needs of the individual as consumer and citizen' while at the same time reforming public services and the welfare state.[5]

In this way, the *worker* was removed from politics, and *insecurity* embraced as the new condition of economic life. Making plain the troubles that Kapstein had identified so clearly, the welfare state itself was targeted for change, and weakened further in a process begun by Thatcher: as time passed, benefit payments were increasingly subjected to surveillance, cuts and restrictions. Moreover, a politics of low taxation enforced the need for the state as employer to make cutbacks and borrow from the employment practices of the private sector. In a curious inversion of post-war logic, the *private* became the exemplar for the *public*, and working for the state (in benefit offices, hospitals or universities) meant being subject to many of the practices of corporate industry.

Given this retreat and redefinition of the role of the state, the experience of Durham and South Wales through the 2000s was one of continued decline – if not from a golden era, then at least from a time when life had seemed more predictable and it was possible to imagine a future that involved material progress. The New Labour years also contributed to a sense of being marginalised, different, excluded from the mainstream and in some sense unworthy. The emphasis in Whitehall was not upon social class but upon the socially excluded, accompanied by the calumny that they were in some way or other responsible for their predicament.

Into Austerity

The financial centre in London had formed an essential plank of New Labour's approach to the economy. In his Mansion House speech in 2002, Gordon Brown praised the audience of bankers for how

> you have taken globalisation in your stride, its risks and opportunities, and have become ever more international in your reach. What you, as the City of London, have achieved for financial services we, as a government, now aspire to achieve for the whole economy.

He went further in 2007, when he congratulated the lord mayor and the City for their 'remarkable achievements' in an 'era that history will record as the beginning of a new golden age for the City of London'. Moreover, 'I believe it will be said of this age, the first decades of the twenty-first century, that out of the greatest restructuring of the global economy, perhaps even greater than the industrial revolution, a new world order was created.'

That was true, of course, but not entirely in the way that Brown expected. Later that year the golden age began to fall apart, as Northern Rock branches opened to queues of savers wanting to withdraw their small deposits. The failure of Lehman Brothers in the USA in September 2008 then threatened the whole financial system with meltdown, averted only by enormous state support. The exact level of this support has been difficult to establish, with the IMF suggesting at one point that it could be as high £1,183 billion, while the National Audit Office gave a lower estimate of the full cost of the state rescue at £850 billion. Careful and conservative estimates established that when the dust had settled the cost to the taxpayer would total £550 billion *at the very least*, or nearly £10,000 for every person resident in the United Kingdom. The scale of the state rescue was twenty times the £28 billion devoted to closing and 'regenerating' the coalfields.[6]

Durham and South Wales contained some of the most deprived areas in Great Britain. It was upon these communities that the axe of austerity fell most heavily under the Cameron governments of 2010–16. It had often been said of the coal districts that they shared all the problems of the cities but with none of the benefits. In these small, often remote settlements, many of such leisure activities as were available relied upon the local authorities. These included swimming pools, youth clubs, leisure centres and the amenities associated with parks and gardens. By 2016 Durham County Council had been forced to make £180 million worth of savings, with another £64 million due by 2020. Sunderland was in a worse position, its cuts totalling £317 million.[7] As a consequence, council staff were laid off, leisure centres and youth clubs closed, refuse collections became less frequent, and bus services were withdrawn. Chancellor George Osborne also took aim at 'welfare dependents', describing workless households as skivers, with the curtains drawn, asleep, while others left for work every morning – pernicious imagery reinforced by endless TV exposés of 'benefits street'. Housing benefit was restricted to the minimum number of bedrooms needed for the occupants, and disability benefit claimants were subjected to draconian testing.

Much to Cameron's own surprise, the 2015 general election was won outright by the Conservatives, largely thanks to the near total collapse in support for their Liberal Democrat coalition partners. The victory, however, was pyrrhic in its consequences for the prime minister. Throughout his premiership he had been under pressure from a strongly organised group of Eurosceptic MPs to reopen the question of European Union membership. This pressure had increased with the strong electoral performance of UKIP under the leadership of Nigel Farage. To quell these difficulties, in 2013 he had promised an in/out referendum in the next Parliament if he could form a majority Conservative government. His hope and expectation had been that the coalition would continue and that a Lib Dem veto would save him from releasing 'the demons', as he called them.[8]

The Brexit Upset

'We're out!' With these words and a wave of the hands, BBC news anchor David Dimbleby reported the verdict of the people in the Brexit referendum of 23 June 2016. Although the polls had indicated a different outcome, a Leave victory had looked likely from the moment the Sunderland result (61:39) came in shortly after midnight. The UK had voted to withdraw from the European Union, and while the core support for leaving had been in the south and east, it was the working-class vote in the north of England and in South Wales that tipped the balance. In the old coalfield areas, the result was a landslide. Six of the ten constituencies in Durham recorded Leave votes of over 60 per cent, as did Blaenau Gwent and Torfaen, with smaller majorities elsewhere.

The Brexit vote revealed things about the way Britain has changed, and how these transformations have affected class relations. Many people in London, in their surprise and shock, talked of not knowing *anyone* who had voted Leave. The sociologist Frank Furedi found colleagues at the University of Kent expressing a similar view, and proposed that this was 'the nub of the problem. It seems that too many academic supporters of the Remain campaign have talked only to people like themselves.'[9] More generally the metropolitan response was of anger, with the Leave vote often attributed to ignorance and a lack of education which, taken together with xenophobic leanings, was seen as an adequate account of how this remarkable result had come about.

For more perceptive observers, however, there had been straws in the wind that indicated that this was a far from adequate account. In June 2007, Gordon Brown had spoken at the annual conference of the GMB union and declared that 'it is time to train British workers for the British jobs that will become available over the coming years.' One of the concerns being expressed in that trade union at the time related to the way in which freedom of movement was interpreted within the EU, with companies that obtained contracts in the UK able to post their own workers to the jobs. This happened at the Lindsey Oil Refinery in North Lincolnshire in 2009, when the local union organised a strike in protest against the posting of Italian and Portuguese workers to the site. The strikers carried placards proclaiming 'British Jobs for British Workers!' Similar strikes were to take place at the Grangemouth Oil Refinery, the Aberthaw power station in South Wales and at Wilton, near Redcar.[10] In each case the slogan was the same. It was a real problem for the trade union leadership, and never clearly addressed by the Remain campaign.

By contrast, in the Leave camp, especially on its UKIP wing, the question of free labour movement within the EU was elided with that of migration from the wider world – of legitimate asylum claims from people in war zones – under one word, *immigrant*, on posters and leaflets depicting an inward flood. This strategy was clearly adopted with the intention of causing fear, particularly among people in places already struggling economically.

In the 2015 general election, UKIP had taken second place in the four Durham constituencies with the highest density of ex-miners, the Conservative Party strengthening ominously in the others, especially to the west of the county.[11] In every constituency in South Wales, one or other of the nationalist parties, Plaid Cymru or UKIP, finished as runner-up. This pattern continued into the Welsh Assembly elections in 2016, with UKIP winning seven seats. Forms of nationalism and right-wing popularism were on the rise, aggravated by deep feelings of resignation and a sense of hopelessness and sometimes anger that all the jobs had gone and places had been forgotten, with many promises broken.

Under the circumstances, the Brexit vote shouldn't have come as such a surprise. People complained of being taken for granted by the Westminster parties. Talking with people in Blaenau Gwent it became clear that few who voted Leave did so with any expectation of significant gain for them or their town. German sociologist Jürgen Habermas explained it as a vote for identity over interest, but in Blaenau Gwent it seemed less clear than that; more like a reaction to the series of injuries – the sequential acts of material and symbolic violence – that had been inflicted on these people and their households over the previous thirty years.[12] Seen from this perspective, there was a strong class element to the referendum. Decades earlier Alan Sillitoe's short story *The Loneliness of the Long Distance Runner* (1959) had described a world of us and them, in which a Borstal boy refused to win the long distance race for 'them'.[13] He got nothing for himself except the satisfaction that they hadn't won either. The parallels with 2016 are clearer than may at first glance be supposed. In its analysis of the referendum result, the Electoral Reform Society was extremely critical of the way the vote was organised, but concluded that:

> what these numbers tell us is that people had by and large lost faith in established political figures as opinion-leaders – except where those figures might be said to be kicking against the Establishment . . . Traditional theory on campaigning in refer-endums is that such figures can command considerable alle-giance owing to voters' tendency to follow political party cues. But such was the culture of mistrust in the EU referendum that the 'big beast' approach appeared to have, for the Remain side at least, the opposite of the desired effect.[14]

Convinced that their vote had become meaningless, given the coalescence of the major parties on so many issues, this was an occasion when many people felt that their votes *would* add up, and it was with this in mind that they gave voice to their discon-tent. One man we talked with in Blaenau Gwent refused to use a pencil to record his vote, insisting on a magic marker pen 'so that they couldn't rub it out'. His offer of the pen to others was happily accepted.

Central Control

In 1966, before the Aberfan disaster, the Labour Party polled 61 per cent of the vote in Wales. Four years later this had fallen to 52 per cent; it continued on a downward path, election after election, reaching 37 per cent in 2015. The economic policies of New Labour were combined with increased centralisation of decision-making within the Party. A new approach to the selec-tion of parliamentary candidates came to the fore with the selec-tive imposition of women-only shortlists to boost female repre-sentation in the House of Commons. The Party hierarchy felt that these would be particularly appropriate for old industrial areas in need of modernisation. In South Wales the impending retirement of the left-wing MP for Blaenau Gwent, Llew Smith, ahead of the 2005 general election was seen as an appropriate moment to introduce change into the valley towns. Blaenau Gwent was based on the old Ebbw Vale constituency that had been represented by Aneurin Bevan and Michael Foot, and had always ranked as one of the twenty safest Labour seats in the UK.

News of the shortlist was not well received in the town. Llew Smith gave vent to a prevalent view that it was 'a fix by the young kids and the New Labour chattering classes who run the party in Cardiff'. The objection was to the *imposition* of a list rather than a list *per se*. David ('Dai') Davies, trade union convenor at the steelworks, pointed out that a recently vacated seat in Leeds had not had a women-only list imposed, allowing Gordon Brown's adviser Ed Balls to be selected for the constituency.[15] There was also a suspicion that the intention was to impose someone from London on the constituency rather than recruit a local activist. Events were to prove this correct, and eight of the twelve members of the constituency executive committee stood down in response to the selection of Maggie Jones, a London-based trade union official and senior member of the Party's National Executive Committee.[16]

It was in this context that Peter Law ran as an independent candidate in 2005. Law was a sitting member of the Welsh Assembly, where he held a Cabinet post. Seen in the constituency as 'Labour through and through', he had a strong personal following and it was no surprise when he overturned a 19,000 Labour majority to win by 9,000 votes. Subsequently the requirement of an all-women shortlist was removed, and when Law died of a brain tumour in 2006, Owen Smith was selected to stand in the by-election as Labour candidate in his stead. But with wounds still to heal, Dai Davies, who had been Law's friend and campaign manager, ran as an independent with the support of the Blaenau Gwent People's Voice Group. The independent won again, albeit with a reduced majority of 2,000. Not until 2010 would Labour regain the seat, revealing how potentially friable the Party's base had become when a strong local candidate stood against the impositions of a remote and uncaring London.

Heartlands?

While not quite as dramatic as its collapse in Scotland, the decline of Labour in its electoral heartlands in the north of England and South Wales is significant enough (Table 7). On the Durham and South Wales coalfields, where it was once common place to say that Labour votes were weighed rather than counted, Labour's share of the vote dropped, notably in 2015, to below 50 per cent in four constituencies. There was only one seat, Easington, where it still exceeded 60 per cent. This pattern continued into the Welsh Assembly elections in 2016, when the Labour vote barely reached 50 per cent in the Rhondda and Cynon Valley. In Blaenau Gwent, it slumped to below 40 per cent. The 2017 general election produced a blip in Labour's favour. Had it not been for the revival of the Scottish Tories, Theresa May would have been forced to resign as prime minister and the socialist Jeremy Corbyn would have formed a government as leader of the largest party.

Table 7. Labour Party share of popular vote in general elections (percentages), 1966–2019

	North East England	Wales
1966	61.1	60.7
1970	57.5	51.6
1974 Feb	51.0	46.8
1974 Oct	52.2	49.5
1979	50.2	48.6
1983	40.2	37.5
1987	46.4	45.1
1992	50.6	49.5
1997	64.0	54.7
2001	59.4	48.6
2005	52.9	42.7
2010	43.6	36.2
2015	46.9	36.9
2017	55.4	48.9
2019	42.6	40.9

Note: North East results 1966–92 are those for the Northern standard statistical region, which included Cumbria.

May's narrow escape weakened her decisively and opened the door for the right-wing populism of Boris Johnson. There was a similar but opposite response within the Labour Party, where on the parliamentary backbenches the thought of a Corbyn government was anathema, a view that was shared by much of the national press. Under constant fire from its many opponents, there was no coherent effort by the Corbyn leadership to build on the platform of 2017.[17] As time went by, with one sequence of parliamentary votes following another, the issue of Brexit emerged more centrally than it had at that general election. Having been told that leaving the EU would be the simplest of matters, many Leave voters began to feel that their vote had been ignored and that *they* – the political class – were not going to allow Brexit to happen.

At the same time, the policies of austerity continued, and things were getting worse in the towns and villages of the old coalfield areas. In October 2019 the Coalfields Regeneration Trust called for the establishment of a national coalfield day, under the banner of 'Forgotten Communities', to raise awareness of their plight, and for a new tranche of funding to be ringfenced for the coal districts alone. Chairman Peter McNestry pointed to 'deep rooted issues around employment, skills and health and wellbeing', and the need for politicians to 'take the necessary action that is so clearly required'. As he acutely observed, 'Many of our communities may well be the key battleground for the next general election, which appears to be coming sooner rather than later.'[18]

He was right in this assessment, but the general election of 12 December 2019 produced the result he must have dreaded, with Labour losing a significant amount of support generally, and particularly across the old coalfield areas. In South Wales, in spite of the Party's vote dropping well below the level of 2015, Labour did retain all its seats. In Durham, however, where trends were similar, the consequences were more severe. In every constituency, over half the vote went to a combination of the Conservative and Brexit parties. An area with a history of strong local leadership was unlikely to be sympathetic to a neutral stance on the key issue of the day. This was the talk in the clubs in the Easington constituency. Brexit and a perceived lack of leadership crowded out any discussion of the Labour manifesto. It was the west and south of Durham though, denuded of mining in the sixties, that saw the most dramatic shift. In three seats – Bishop Auckland, Durham North West and Sedgefield – the Conservative candidates won. This was a remarkable turnaround. The loss of Sedgefield, the former constituency of Tony Blair, was a dramatic one, especially given the hopes that people had entertained there for a new economy. In Durham North West, home to Chopwell, the 'little Moscow' village, and to the former steel town of Consett and the coking coal pits of the Derwent Valley, a massive swing to the Tories saw a local activist, Laura Pidcock, lose the seat that she had held since 2017.

In considering these changes, Bishop Auckland is an interesting example. It is a medium-sized town in the west of the Durham coalfield, previously one of the safest of Labour constituencies, represented until 1959 by Hugh Dalton, chancellor of the exchequer in Attlee's post-war government. In addition to the town of Bishop, the constituency contains settlements such as Spennymoor, famous for 'pitmen painters' such as Norman Cornish and one of the Wilson government's designated growth centres after the closure of the Dean and Chapter Colliery in 1966. Bishop was once seen as a place that spoke both to the past and the future. In the sixties, it was here that families of miners in the closed collieries were moved by the Labour council onto new estates that some referred to as 'labour settlements'. In 1966, 22,000 people voted Labour in Bishop, giving the Party 65 per cent of the vote. These were halcyon days. From 1970 onwards, Labour never took more than 50 per cent until the Blair landslide of 1997, when its support leapt by over 5,000 to 65 per cent of the poll. Blair had spoken to a packed gathering in Spennymoor after his first election to Parliament, when he talked of a new future beyond socialism. This again proved short-lived: in 2001, 8,000 voters deserted the Party. Another 3,000 left in 2005, and by the Brown defeat of 2010 support for Labour had dropped to 39 per cent, though this was still 13 percentage points ahead of the Tories. In 2017, however, while Labour gained 4,000 additional votes, its total of 21,000 was just 500 more than those given to the Tory candidate: Bishop Auckland had become a marginal seat – and in 2019 it fell to the Conservatives by 8,000 votes.

In Neath in South Wales, situated to the west of the coalfield at the mouth of the Neath Valley, near to the M4, the 1966 election was again a high-water mark, with 31,000 people giving Labour 80 per cent of the vote. By 1970 the Party's vote had dropped by 3,000. It then ebbed and flowed somewhat until the elections of 1992 and 1997, when, with the high-profile Peter Hain as MP, it increased to around 30,000 votes and 70 per cent of the total. But in the elections of the twenty-first century the Labour vote fell consistently – so much so that in Hain's last election in 2010 it had almost halved to 17,000, or 46 per cent of the vote. In 2017 it jumped by 4,000 to 57 per cent of the vote, the Tory vote also rising by 8 percentage points. In 2019, however, Labour returned to a relatively medi-ocre performance on a par with 2015, mustering a majority of 6,000, less than half its winning margin under Corbyn two years earlier.

What Had Happened?

There is little doubt that the election was dominated by Brexit and that this effectively crowded out discussion of other issues. The issue posed major problems for Labour, whose voters and constituencies were split between Leave and Remain. In 2017 the Party had promised to honour the result of the referendum, but in two years many things had changed, most notably in the strong support within its parliamentary ranks for a repeat of the vote. The final compromise was an unpalatable one, and many saw it as a major reason for the loss of seats in the so-called Red Wall extending from the North East across the Pennines into Lancashire and into North Wales. In their investigations of the election result, researchers at Cardiff University found that when asked the question, 'As far as you're concerned, what is the single most important issue facing the UK?', respondents invariably answered 'Brexit'.

Figure 1. 'What is the single most important
            issue facing the UK?'

Source: Richard Wyn Jones and Jac Larner, 'How Wales Voted in December
– and Why', Wales Governance Centre webinar, Cardiff University, 23
September 2020.

It is likely that a survey in the North East would have obtained
the same result. The effects of this on voting were not necessarily
straightforward, however, and as we can see from Table 8 the
result varied between the two areas. The 2019 general election
vote broadly mirrored the EU referendum, but with some noticeable inconsistencies. In the Durham constituencies with the
highest Leave percentages – Easington, Houghton, South Shields
and Washington – the Labour vote held up. What these had in
common was that they all included the most recently closed coal
mines, where a strong semblance of political organisation around
the DMA lodge continued. The seats that were lost were all in
the west, where the mines had closed in the sixties. In South
Wales, where the decline of mining was more evenly spread, the
decline in the Labour vote was clear, but less dramatic. Here too,
the strongly Leave constituencies, such as Blaenau Gwent,
Rhondda and Torfaen, saw a decline in support but not as sharp
a move to the Conservatives.

Table 8. Constituency results of 2016 referendum and 2019 general election (percentages)

Durham

	2016 Leave vote*	2019 Labour vote
Bishop Auckland	61	36
City of Durham	43	42
Durham North	60	44
Durham North West	55	42
Easington	66	46
Houghton and Sunderland South	65	41
Sedgefield	59	47
South Shields	63	46
Sunderland Central	55	42
Washington and Sunderland West	65	43

South Wales

Blaenau Gwent	62	49
Caerphilly	55	45
Cynon Valley	57	51
Islwyn	59	45
Merthyr Tydfil and Rhymney	58	53
Neath	54	44
Rhondda	60	54
Torfaen	61	42

*Source: C. Hanretty, 'Areal Interpolation and the UK's Referendum on EU Membership', *Journal of Elections, Public Opinion and Parties*, 27:4, 2017.

Clearly other, more long-term forces were at work in the election. Reflecting on her defeat, Laura Pidcock wrote a perceptive open letter to her constituents in Durham North West, in which she explained that:

what was acutely obvious throughout my time as the MP, was that there was a hard core of people who were bitterly angry with me before I had even opened my mouth: angry at the political establishment; angry at the expenses scandal; angry at being left behind, angry that their life was not as good now as it was; angry that their communities had not been invested in and that there was no longer a buzz and a sense of community about the place. At many doors, there was a mixture of fury and apathy at successive governments (and I very much include New Labour in that).[19]

Across the coalfields, the sense of a loss of community had been exacerbated by discontent with seemingly small decisions taken by Labour-controlled local authorities about specific local issues, which had built up over time to create substantial disillusionment. In Durham, Mary Stafford carried her activism during the Miners' Strike into her involvement with a local heritage educational group in Lumley. After the election result, she reflected on how the people in her village had wanted to set up a boxing club as something that would involve young people. However:

The idea was blocked, primarily by Labour councillors. I think they thought that boxing was a dangerous sport, not the right thing and not to be encouraged. This led to a massive reaction. A residents' group was formed and it led eventually to the election of an independent councillor. I sometimes think now that people perceive the Party being more concerned with its own interest and preoccupations than with those of the community it represents.[20]

In Blaenau Gwent a radical change in waste and recycling collections caused turmoil with domestic arrangements, leading women residents to organise a demonstration outside the council offices. The decision to close the famous cinema in Brynmawr was another incident which caused upset, its rescue by the actor Michael Sheen accorded greater significance than any EU investment. Issues like these contributed to the Labour-controlled authority being called by some not Blaenau Gwent but 'Blind and Bent'. Throughout the election campaign, the Party and its local and national leadership were attacked on Facebook. As one man put it: 'social media had a big impact on this election because people won't put up with it any more.'

This pattern affected both coalfield areas: long-term decline, a lost community and an atrophied local Party peopled largely by elderly men, dealing with levels of austerity not seen for generations. All of which was exacerbated by a deep sense of neglect and of being neglected, of many small things building up over time into an irresistible tsunami of discontent that swept through these places. This provides a concise summary of how many of the residents had come to understand their lives and the paucity of hope in former colliery towns and villages. In times past, welfare halls like those in Easington and Ferndale had hosted crowded meetings of Party and trade union leaders. During the strike of 1984–85 they were at the centre of events. 'I've noticed how the whole base of the Labour Party has dissolved under our feet, as it were, in old strongholds like Neath and right across the South Wales Valleys,' observed Peter (now Lord) Hain. 'Those organic links between big trade unions in mines and heavy industry and so on, and then social clubs, welfare clubs, rugby clubs and so on, that organic link between the Party and those community roots has basically just dissolved.'[21] With this sense of loss and dispossession came a smouldering resentment and an unwillingness to follow the Party in the way people had done before.

Conclusions and Reflections

That's how it was then! Everything that grew took long to grow; and everything that ended took a long time to be forgotten. Everything that existed left behind traces of itself, and the people lived by those memories, just as we nowadays live by our capacity to forget, quickly and comprehensively.
                        Joseph Roth, *The Radetzky March*, 1932

The end of the era of coal-based industrial capitalism has been a painful one, and the pain lingers in the memories which keep the past alive on the old coalfields. People remember how, for all its dangers, coal had underpinned a collective way of life that was stable, and which had given them a real sense of worth. The closures took much of this away, along with a sense of hope: that things could still improve; that there would be better times ahead. This hope was, of course, central to the modernising boom of the post-war era, and its slow unwinding – finally coming apart in the financial crisis of 2008 – has had a lasting effect on everyone. But it is the people of the old industrial areas, especially the people of the coalfields, who have been hit the hardest.

Within the broader process of British industrial decline, the toppling of King Coal was a significant moment. Coal had powered the first industrial revolution and laid the basis for successive economic transformations spanning two centuries, employing over a million workers at its peak. Its decline was not quite so gradual, and the denouement of the 1980s and 1990s was a dramatic one. In this book we have outlined some of the traumatic consequences of this decline, along with their broader political and social significance.

The final closures occurred under private ownership of the mines, following the Major government's overturning of the Nationalisation Act of 1946. At the time, nationalisation had generally been seen as a progressive development, the route to a more secure future for the workers and their communities. This was certainly the view of the NUM. There were many problems though, and, certainly during the 1960s, the rapidity of colliery closures, combined with tragedies such as that which befell the village of Aberfan, created the impression of an uncaring employer remote from the aspiration of producing coal 'for the benefit of the people'. Many miners became disillusioned, and this feeling intensified under Thatcher, when over the course of a year-long strike the full panoply of the resources of the state and nationalised industry was used to defeat them. The pace of the subsequent closures, achieved in no small part through the power of money and the mobilisation of fear, was seen as an illegitimate use of state power, facilitated by state ownership. As such there was little public mobilisation of opposition to the privatisation of those mines that remained; nationalisation was not mourned.

The organisation of underground workers into an industrial trade union had produced a powerful political force in the UK, harnessed for parliamentary purposes to the Labour Party. This profoundly shaped the nature of working-class involvement in mass politics through the twentieth century. The rise of imported oil and nuclear power in the sixties, along with other technical developments around gas turbines and the subsequent emergence of labour militancy, all contributed to the rapid closure of the industry. With the end of the mining industry and the defeat of the NUM, a political space opened up for the emergence of New Labour and a form of politics that embraced financialisation and the globalisation of manufacturing supply chains. By engaging with and embracing these processes, Blair and Brown turned their back on the Party's past and its heartlands. According to their campaign song, things could only get better. In reality, New Labour proved incapable of dealing with the social ramifications of deindustrialisation and the deep inequalities that were integral to its political project.

These developments were keenly felt on the coalfields, where the mine has always cast a long shadow. For many people, the destruction of the industry and the manner of its ending seemed unjust, and chimed with a suspicion that democracy itself was in decline. Most critically, the closures weakened peoples' sense of living their lives as active citizens, able to participate in the political process through their own institutions and to influence outcomes. In the age of coal-based capitalism, the miners had been centrally placed within the national economy, and able to fashion a social democracy in which working people like them had a say and a stake. Their decline marks an ending on many levels, and this has registered politically first in the Brexit vote and subsequently in the election landslide of a populist Tory government under Boris Johnson.

Tim Shipman's account of the EU referendum upset, *All Out War: The Full Story of How Brexit Sank Britain's Political Class* (2017), quotes Sam Adamson, the young woman remembered for her televised celebration of the Sunderland result:

> I definitely feel that the working-class people got their voice heard. It shook our then Prime Minister. It shook the Labour Party. For the working-class people it was 'now you've heard us what are you going to do about it?'[1]

The answer seems to have been 'not a lot', and it was the sense that Westminster would rather set the Leave verdict aside which added to the anger spilling out in the general election of 2019. What is at issue is the erosion of the historical identities of people living in these so-called backwaters, and the ways in which their day-to-day experiences and sense of self have been diminished over recent decades by wrenching economic changes and the centralisation and hollowing out of the political parties. This 'structure of feeling', to use Raymond Williams's term, reflects an unambiguous loss of power and significance.

The deindustrialisation of Britain, the closures of its mines and factories, has been powerful and inexorable, and we have seen how our two coalfield areas, despite their different political traditions and identities, have followed a very similar path of economic deterioration. Notwithstanding the devolution settlement which provided Wales with a degree of self-government, the economic outcomes – of closures and failed regeneration strategies – have been analogous. This suggests that the deep impact of mining and the manner of its ending was such that any politically led transformation needed far greater resources and more determination than were available. It has also been clear that any meaningful involvement in these matters by the people affected by them has been minimal, with policy development characterised by official obfuscation and delay. For more positive change to take place on the former coalfields there would need to be a much greater degree of devolution to Scotland, Wales and the regions of England, locked into a very different and deter- mined national economic strategy that could provide the resources for change.

Without such a change, there is no doubt that both Durham and South Wales face a grim future. In both areas, the old towns, villages and new estates are emerging as commuting settlements, with those residents who have secured employment, many of them having moved into areas of new more affordable housing, travelling into the major urban centres around Cardiff, Swansea, Sunderland and Newcastle, limiting their engagement with their home communities. There, living in different parts of the settlements in the older housing of the coal-mining era, many households continue to find themselves dependent upon ever-shrinking welfare benefits, assisted increasingly by emerging local initiatives that retain elements of old community life. This support (through the men's sheds, food banks and clothing banks) has been vital, particularly for the elderly and for the ex-miners and their families. Furthermore, it was the NUM's persistence, in spite of a loss of membership, with compensation claims through the courts that produced significant amounts of financial relief. It was the miners' pension funds that under-pinned this, as well as providing much of the regeneration fund-ing. All this emphasises the ways that people in these areas have survived of necessity through their own efforts and those of their own organisations, rather than through inadequate state support.

The NUM has been a major force in British trade unionism. More than any other union in any other industry, it developed a political form of unionism that extended beyond the workplace into the local community and wider society. It was commonly said that in South Wales the NUM *was* civil society, and many felt that its demise would create a major social void. Yet it seems that remnants of the forms of community organisation typified by the lodge, though damaged, have been retained and repro-duced in daily life in both coalfields. Despite all the challenges, elements of coal-mining community have survived the trauma of mining's demise. In this, they testify to the deep roots that mining and industrial life had within local communities and the popular culture. The sense of loss encountered everywhere shows that nothing comparable has emerged in the post-industrial world, and that without it people feel, in the words of one ex-miner, like 'kites without a wind'. Recuperating this situation and building a new and better world has become the challenge of our time.

The context is not likely to be propitious, however. The COVID-19 pandemic has revealed and widened deep social and spatial divisions in the UK, as poverty, with all its implications for the lives of millions of people, swells alongside the fortunes of a small class of billionaires. Constructing the basis for a more socially progressive alternative will not be easy or straightforward. There is no doubt that this must involve the public sector, and with it a strategy for greater public and collective ownership of significant parts of the economy. The experiences of the miners and mining communities in South Wales and Durham have made very clear that this change has to go beyond the traditional form of nationalisation. That approach, at one time heralded as progressive, turned out in practice to be a Trojan horse that undermined the industry and communities that had been built in and through it. The nationalised industry came to cast a dark shadow across the landscape and lives, undermining local government and democracy – not through *too much socialism* but because the approach was *not socialist enough*. This lesson needs to be learned in any attempt to chart a different path in the future.

It has often been said that 'history is a great teacher but there aren't many students'. It's the same with 'lessons', and in this case a particularly difficult one. Political parties have their in-built trajectories that are increasingly difficult to shift. It was with this in mind, and with it the sequential loss in support for Labour from within the working classes, that Raymond Williams had seen hope in the miners' strike in 1984, not least in the ways that different kinds of communities had mobilised support.[2] For him this was not 'the last kick of the old order'. Properly understood, he argued, it could be seen as 'one of the first steps toward a new order'. During that strike the collective organisation of miners, their families and supporters provided meals, food parcels and Christmas parties. These activities were sustained by external bonds of solidarity across the country, linking the coalfields with universities, urban centres and small rural towns and villages, all brought together in a common cause against injustice and an emergent 'nomad capitalism' that sees everyone and everywhere as expendable. Since then, those 'first steps' have gone in different directions, to the extent that people in these different parts of the country have come to be seen as polar opposites – members of different tribes, separated by employment, education and age. But there *are* features that they share in common, not least on the labour market where the experiences of unemployed members of cabin crews and retailing establishments bear a striking similarity to those of manual workers in the old industrial regions.

So rebuilding the labour movement and establishing the 'new order' is not going to be easy, but the old coalfield areas have a part to play that does not simply involve waving the union flag. They remain key centres with a history of trade union membership and the deep experience that accompanies this. These organisations have the capacity to coordinate the strengths of community-based activities, linking them with workplaces and providing a conduit through which locally based experiences could be shared nationally and more widely. And with a more devolved political structure within the UK, it would be easier for new forms of ownership to be encouraged and developed. Furthermore, there would be a deep symbolic significance in the areas once ruled by coal playing an active role in the creation of a new, more equitable and sustainable economy based upon renewable sources of energy. As the words emblazoned on a miners' banner proclaimed: The past we inherit – the future we build.

Acknowledgements

The Shadow of the Mine is based on materials that we have gathered together over the past forty years, some ourselves and others with different research teams and colleagues This has involved the collection of documentary materials, field notes, observations and endless conversations alongside various extended programmes of recorded interviews and surveys.

In Durham in the seventies and eighties we benefitted from working closely on projects with David Sadler, Frank Peck, Frank Ennis, Andrew Cox and the late Terry Austrin. At the time of the major strike in 1984–85 we were closely involved with the local communities, the NUM and also with the local authorities affected by the closures that followed. Later, Lone Krogsgaard Hansen and Susanne Schech helped with interviews in and around Consett in North West Durham and, later in the nineties, we established the Coalfield Research Programme in Manchester and Durham. Based on two linked projects funded by the ESRC and Joseph Rowntree Foundation. Andrew Cox, Katy Bennett, Emma Hollywood and Tim Strangleman organised and conducted interviews with key decision makers across the coalfields. This material was analysed and published in seven Discussion Papers. These are included in the 'List of Sources' at the end of the book.

In 2000, Amanda Smith helped us with fieldwork interviews and questionnaires with ex- miners in Horden and Easington on the Durham coast. Meanwhile in Cardiff, Julian Hunt conducted interviews with ex-miners working at the Pot Noodle factory before commencing his PhD, while Martin O'Neil and Di Murphy did fieldwork interviews in Penrhiwceiber, Hirwaun and the Cynon valley. Derek Kilmer kindly made available to us the transcripts of the interviews he undertook in the Rhondda valleys in 1998 for his doctoral research at Oxford University.

All of these people have our warmest thanks.

For many years we have worked with, supervised and examined many research students who produced PhD theses that have dealt with the coal industry, its workforce and coalfield places. These are an invaluable and hitherto underused resource. Along with others we have read, they are included in the 'List of Sources'.

In the preparation of this book, we were greatly assisted by Chris Orton at Durham University who drew the maps. We are indebted to Keith Pattison, Raul Reas and Kjell-Ake Andersson for permission to use some of their wonderful photographs.

This book has been a long time in the making and over the years Geoff Shears has been a great support with his expert advice on issues of industrial injury and compensation. Other friends have shared their expertise, reading the drafts (sometimes more than once) and particular thanks go to Chris Jones, Simon Clark, Steve Davies, David Howell, Gareth Rees, Theo Nichols, Helen Sampson and Kostis Hadjimichalis. Hilary Wainwright's belief in the project helped us see the way to our publisher Verso. There we are indebted to our editor Tom Hazeldine for his commitment to the book and to the continuous improvement in its structure and to Duncan Ranslem for his patient care with the text, and for calmly bringing it into production.

Finally, our thanks for love and support to Helen and Geraldine who have also lived with this book for many years.

Huw Beynon, Llanellen
Ray Hudson, Durham
April 2021

A Note on Sources

In this text we have benefited greatly from reading theses that have been written on the coal-mining industry, the strike of 1984–85, the closure of the mines and the consequences that followed. We were involved in many of them as supervisors or examiners. They form an important collective body of work and we list them here.

PhD THESES

Allen, Meg, 'Carrying on the Strike: The Politics of Women Against Pit Closures', Manchester University, 2001.

Anderson, Gail, 'Housing-led Regeneration in East Durham: Uneven Development, Governance, Politics', Durham University, 2015.

Atkin, Michael, 'The 1984–85 Miners' Strike in East Durham: A Study in Contemporary History', Durham University, 2001.

Blakeley, Helen, '"A Second Chance at Life": Love, Labour and Welfare on a South Wales Estate', Cardiff University, 2011.

Brannan, Mathew, 'Workplace Resistance in a Call Centre Environment', Wolverhampton University, 2004.

Doring, Heike, 'From the Margins to the Centre and Back:

Trajectories of Regeneration in Two Marginal English Coalfields', Cardiff University, 2009.

Greenwood, Ian, 'The Process and Consequences of Industrial Restructuring and Plant Closure: A Case Study from the UK Steel Industry', Leeds University, 2009.

Grundy-Warr, C., 'Engineering Links within the Coal Chain', 2 vols, Durham University, 1989.

Howells, K. S., 'A View from Below: Tradition, Experience and Nationalisation in the South Wales Coalfield 1937–1957', Warwick University, 1979.

Hunt, Julian, 'From Despair to Where? Coal, Capital and the New Economy', University of Wales, Cardiff, 2004.

Jones, Nerys Anwen, 'Coal Was Our Life', University of Wales, Bangor, 1988.

Jones, Stephanie, '"Still a Mining Community" Gender and Change in the Upper Dulais Valley', University of Wales, Swansea, 1997.

Lloyd, Anthony, 'Life in a Northern Town: Call Centres, Labour Markets and Identity in Post-Industrial Middlesbrough' Durham University, 2010.

Lloyd-Jones, Sarah, 'A Map of Transition in the South Wales Valleys', University of Wales, Cardiff, 2005.

McCrindle, Jean, 'The National Organisation of Women Against Pit Closures', Oxford Brookes University, 2001.

McIntyre, Patricia, 'The Response to the 1984–85 Miners' Strike in Durham County: Women, the Labour Party and Community', Durham University, 1992.

Morrell, V., 'Ice, Sea, Coal Common Themes: Interpreting the Cultural Representations of Scott, Dunkirk and Durham Coal Miners in the Context of Decline', University of Huddersfield, 2017.

Parry, J., 'Class and Identity Processes: Restructuring in the (Former) Coalmining Communities of the South Wales Valleys', University of Southampton, 2000.

Renouf, J, 'A Striking Change: Political Transformation in the

Murton Miners' and Mechanics' Branches of the National Union of Mineworkers, County Durham, 1978–1988', Durham University, 1989.

Smith, Amanda, 'Constructions of "Sustainability" and Coalfield Regeneration Policies', Durham University, 2004.

Strong, S., 'The Production of Poverty: Politics, Place and Social Abandonment in Blaenau Gwent Wales', Cambridge University, 2017.

Thomas, M., 'Coalfield Restructuring and the "Enterprise Economy": A Sociology of Re-industrialisation', Cardiff University, 1990.

Wadwell, James, 'Coalfield Regeneration and Improving Best Practice', Durham University, 2005.

Wass, V., 'Colliery Closure and the Re-employment Experiences of Redundant Miners', Cardiff University, 1992.

Warren, Jonathon, 'Living the Call Centre: Global, Local, Work-Life Interfaces', Durham University, 2011.

Yoo, B., 'Welfare Politics and Social Policy of Coal Workers' Pneumoconiosis in Britain and South Korea', Edinburgh University, 2009.

MPhil THESIS

Clapham, M., 'The Effect of the 1984–85 Miners' Strike on British Industrial Relations', University of Bradford, 1990.

COALFIELD RESARCH PROGRAMME

In the Preface we acknowledged our debt to the researchers who have worked with us over the years on various projects relating to the coal industry, particularly the ESRC, which funded 'Social Exclusion or Flexible Adaptation? Coal Districts in a Period of Economic Transformation 1997–2000'. At various points in the text we have drawn upon discussion papers produced during that project. All are available at huwbeynon.com.

DISCUSSION PAPERS

DP1: H. Beynon, A. Cox and R. Hudson, 'The Decline of King Coal', 1999.

DP2: K. Bennett, H. Beynon and R. Hudson, 'Different Places: Representations', 1999.

DP3: K. Bennett, H. Beynon and R. Hudson, 'Working Together to Achieve More: Strategies for Facilitating Regeneration', 1999.

DP4: H. Beynon, R. Hudson and T. Strangleman, 'Rebuilding the Coalfields', 1999.

DP5: H. Beynon, R. Hudson and T. Strangleman, 'Retraining the Workforce', 1999.

DP6: H. Beynon, R, Hudson and E. Hollywood, 'Regenerating Housing', 1999.

DP7: H. Beynon, R. Hudson and E. Hollywood, 'Health Issues in the Coal Districts', 1999.

Notes

Introduction

1. A. R. Hochschild, *Strangers in their Own Land: Anger and Mourning on the American Right*, New York, The New Press, 2016, p. 5.
2. Ivor Thomas, *Coal in the New Era*, London, Putman, 1934, p. 32 A similar view was expressed in the United States, where Lewis Mumford went so far as to characterise modern industry as the age of 'carboniferous capitalism': L. Mumford, *Tecnics and Civilization*, New York, Harcourt Brace, 1934.
3. George Orwell, *The Road to Wigan Pier*, London, Penguin, (1937) 2001, p. 18.
4. Orwell, *The Road to Wigan Pier*, p. 30.
5. John Wilson, *Memories of a Labour Leader*, London, Caliban Books, 1980, p. 96.
6. Mark Benney, *Charity Main: A Coalfield Chronicle,* London, G. Allen and Unwin, 1946, p. 101.
7. Tony Hall, *King Coal: Miners, Coal and Britain's Industrial Future*, Harmondsworth, Penguin, 1981, p. 46.
8. Bernard Hare, 'Going Under', *Guardian*, 13 September 2006.
9. E. P. Thompson, *The Making of the English Working Class*, *Harmondsworth*, London, Penguin, 1968, p. 12.

1. Two Coalfields, Two Labour Traditions

1. M. J. Daunton, 'Miners' Houses: South Wales and the Great Northern Coalfield, 1880–1914', *International Journal of Social History*, 1980: 143–76.
2. An account of the transition from putter to hewer is provided by Jack Lawson, *A Man's Life*, London, Hodder and Stoughton, 1932.
3. W. S. Hall, *Durham Colliery Mechanics' Association: A Historical Survey 1879–1929*, Durham, J. H. Veitch and Sons, 1929.
4. For details see H. Beynon and T. Austrin, *Masters and Servants: Class and Patronage in the Making of a Labour Organisation*, London, Rivers Oram, 1994, pp. 149–53. See also Lewis H. Mates, *The Great Labour Unrest: Rank-and-File Movements and Political Change in the Durham Coalfield*, Manchester, Manchester University Press, 2016, p. 45.
5. These were both achieved by Acts of Parliament in 1910 and 1912, the second after a major national strike.
6. Wilson, 1990, p. 284. Despite these words, there was a difference of intensity: it seemed as if Liberalism had entered the very bones of the DMA.
7. G. D. H. Cole, *A History of the Labour Party from 1914*, London, Routledge and Kegan Paul, 1948, p. 85.
8. Such expansions of the workforce were sometimes brought about by disputes. The Marquess of Londonderry responded to the coal strike of 1843 by transporting strike breakers from his Irish estates, explaining that he did so in order to defend 'the majesty of the law and the rights of property' and to do 'my duty by my family and station'. D. Roberts, *Paternalism in Early Victorian England*, London, Routledge and Kegan Paul, 1979, p. 135.
9. H. Francis and D. Smith, *The Fed: A History of the South Wales Miners in the Twentieth Century*, London, Lawrence and Wishart, 1980, pp. 10–12.
10. The term was developed by Michael Burawoy to consider the ways in which labour processes within the workplace combined with external market forces to produce different kinds of authority relations. Here, we extend the consideration of external forces

to the realm of social reproduction, achieved in this case through the Mines and Collieries Act 1842 that banned the employment of women (and boys under ten years of age) underground. See Michael Burawoy, *The Politics of Production: Factory Regimes under in Capitalism and Socialism*, London, Verso, 1985.

11. Ned Cowen, *Of Mining Life and Aal its Ways*, Durham, n.p., 1973.

12. Lewis Jones, *Cwmardy: The Story of a Welsh Mining Village*, London, Lawrence and Wishart, 1937, p. 4.

13. J. B. Priestley, *An English Journey*, London, Victor Gollancz, 1934, pp. 336–7.

14. Anthony Jones, *Welsh Chapels*, Cardiff, National Museum of Wales, 1984, p. 46.

15. Lawson, *A Man's Life*, p. 69.

16. Jonathan Rose, *The Intellectual Life of the British Working Classes*, London, Yale University Press, 2001, p. 237; see also Hywel Francis and Siân Williams, *Do Miners Read Dickens? Origins and Progress of the South Wales Miners' Library 1973–2013*, Cardigan, Parthian, 2013.

17. House of Commons Debate, 22 November 1920, vol. 135, c3.

18. See David Smith, 'Tonypandy 1910: Definitions of a Community', *Past and Present*, 87: 58–184.

19. L. H. Mates, *The Great Labour Unrest: Rank and File Movements and Political Change in the Durham Coalfield*, Manchester, Manchester University Press, 2016.

20. For details see ibid.

21. George Askwith, *Industrial Problems and Disputes*, London, John Murray, 1920, p. 209.

22. These included the Sankey Commission (1919), the Buckmaster Court Inquiry (1924) and the Samuel Commission (1925).

23. Noah Ablett was a beneficiary of the education programme at Ruskin College, Oxford. The Central Labour College in London was also popular among the miners.

24. For details see David Douglass, *Pit Life in County Durham: Rank and File Movements and Workers' Control*, Oxford, History Workshop, 1972.

25. Union membership was to decline from 1919 until nationalisation in 1947.

26. Arthur Horner, *Incorrigible Rebel*, London, McGibbon and Kee, 1960, pp. 56–7.

27. For discussion see B. Supple, *The History of the British Coal Industry Vol. 4, 1913–1945*, Oxford, Oxford University Press, 1987.

28. Quotes in D. Howell, '"All or Nowt": The Politics of the MFGB', in A. Campbell, N. Fishman and D. Howell, eds, *Miners, Unions and Politics, 1910–1947*, Aldershot, Scolar Press, 1996, p. 47.

29. Both quotations taken from W. R. Garside, *The Durham Miners, 1919–1960*, London, Allen and Unwin, 1971, p. 184.

30. W. R. Garside accuses the officials of 'lethargy'. Garside, *The Durham Miners*, p. 198.

31. Julian Symons, *The General Strike: A Historical Portrait*, London, The Cresset Press, 1959, p. 134.

32. N. Edwards, *History of the South Wales Miners' Federation*, Volume 1, London, Lawrence and Wishart, 1938, p. 140.

33. Garside, *The Durham Miners*, p. 226.

34. See Alan R. Griffin, *The Miners of Nottinghamshire, 1914–1944*, London, Allen and Unwin, 1962.

35. D. Gilbert, 'The Landscape of Spencerism: Mining Politics in the Nottingham Coalfield, 1910–1947', in A. Campbell, N. Fishman and D. Howell, eds, *Miners, Unions and Politics, 1910–1947*, Aldershot, Scolar Press, 1996, p. 180. The term 'buttie' was also used in South Wales, and is still in common usage; however, there it was not linked to a separate occupation and hierarchy within the work force.

36. R. Page Arnot, *The Miners: Years of Struggle*, London, George Allen and Unwin, 1953, p. 495.

37. The new union stressed in non-political status and became known as Spencerist or non-pol. It lasted in Nottingham until 1937, when it merged with the NMU to form the Nottingham Miners' Federal Union (NMFU), which, with Spencer as president, was affiliated to the MFGB.

38. For details see Francis and Smith, *The Fed*.

39. Will Paynter, *My Generation*, London, Allen and Unwin, 1972.

40. Edwards, *History of the South Wales Miners' Federation*, Volume 1, p. 141.

41. Dick Beavis, *What Price Happiness? My Life from Coal Hewer to*

Shop Steward, Durham, Strong Words, 1980, pp. 22–3

42. Edwards, *History of the South Wales Miners' Federation*, p. 141.

43. In both coalfields the large local authorities had by now come under Labour control. A miners' agent, Peter Lee, had become chairman of Durham County Council as early as 1919. There, and later in Glamorgan and Monmouthshire, miners were involved in developing forms of municipal socialism, with important developments in local policies on education, housing and public health, pushing back on what Lee described as 'this system of gold and greed'. For details see J. Lawson, *Peter Lee*, London, Hodder and Stoughton, 1936.

44. Quoted in Garside, *The Durham Miners*, p. 342.

45. Pilgrim Trust, *Men Without Work*, Cambridge, Cambridge University Press, 1938.

46. Wal Hannington, *The Problem of the Distressed Areas*, London, E. P. Publishing, 1976 (1937), p. 27; Michael Foot, *Aneurin Bevan: A Biography, Volume 1, 1897–1945*, London, Faber and Faber.

47. J. Jenkins, 'Hands not Wanted: Closure and the Moral Economy of Protest, Treorchy, South Wales', *Historical Studies in Industrial Relations*, 38, 2017: 1–36.

48. Quoted in N. Fishman, 'Heroes and Anti-Heroes: Communists in the Coalfield', in A. Campbell, N. Fishman and D. Howell, eds, *Miners, Unions and Politics, 1910–1947*, Aldershot, Scolar Press, 1996, p. 106.

2. State Ownership

1. Quoted in H. Francis and D. Smith, *The Fed: A History of the South Wales Miners in the Twentieth Century*, London, Lawrence and Wishart, 1980.

2. Keith Middlemas, *Politics and Industrial Society: The Experience of the British System since 1911*, London, Andre Deutsch, 1979, p. 98.

3. For details see Carl Grundy-Warr, 'Engineering Linkages in the Coal Chain', PhD Thesis, Durham University, 1989.

4. NUM (Durham Area) *Annual Report, 1946*.

5. Mark Tookey, 'Three's a Crowd? Government, Owners and

Workers during the Nationalisation of the British Coal Mining Industry 1945–47', *Twentieth Century British History*, 12:4, 2001: 493.

6. For details see Tookey, *ibid* and R. Page Arnot, *The Miners: One Industry, One Union, A History of the National Union of Mineworkers 1939–1946*, London, George Allen and Unwin,1979, Chapter 4.

7. *Durham Advertiser*, quoted in David Temple, *The Big Meeting: A History of the Durham Miners' Gala*, Washington, Tyne and Wear, TUPS Books, 2011.

8. Nina Fishman, *Arthur Horner: A Political Biography. Vol. 2: 1944–1968*, London, Lawrence and Wishart, 2010.

9. See Huw Beynon and Terry Austrin, 'The Performance of Power: Sam Watson a Miners' Leader on Many Stages', *Historical Journal of Sociology*, 28: 4, 2015: 458–90; and S. Cohen, 'Labour Party Anti-Communism and its Limits: The Case of Sam Watson', *Socialist History*, 44, 2014: 41–61.

10. Will Paynter, *My Generation*, London, George Allen and Unwin, 1972, p. 9.

11. J. Rex 1960, 'Weekend in Dinlock: A Discussion', *New Left Review*, May/June:42–45.

12. This was a system where a series of parallel bords or headways or rooms were driven into the seam. These would meet up with another headway driven at right angles to produce a series of squares or pillars of coal which supported the overlying strata. In contrast, longwall mining involved the driving of just two parallel roadways into a panel of coal.

13. William Ashworth, *The History of the British Coal Industry, Volume 5: 1946–1982 – The Nationalized Industry*, Oxford, Oxford University Press, 1986, p. 74.

14. In South Wales, manpower had fallen from 135,901 in 1937, to 107, 624 in 1946; in Durham, from 114,480, to 107,346.

15. George Pepler and P. W. MacFarlane, *The North East Area Development Plan*, interim report presented to the minister of town and country planning, 1949, copy in Durham University Library.

16. Durham County Council Planning Committee, Minutes, 14 August 1950, p. 2.

17. Quoted in Kim Howells, 'A View from Below: Tradition,

Experience and Nationalisation in the South Wales Coalfield 1937–1957', University of Warwick PhD Thesis, 1979.

18. Letter from Sam Watson to A. L. Horner, 23 September 1948.

19. Norman Dennis, Fernando Henriques and Clifford Slaughter, *Coal is Our Life: An Analysis of a Yorkshire Mining Community*, London, Eyre and Spottiswood, 1956.

20. See Colin Hughes, *Lime, Lemon and Sarsaparilla: The Italian Community in South Wales, 1881–1945*, Bridgend, Seren Books, 1991.

21. In June 1919 there were to be race riots in Cardiff and also in Newport and Barry. See Neil Evans, 'The South Wales Race Riots of 1919', *Llafur: Society for the Study of Welsh Labour History*, 3:1, 1980: 1–20.

22. H. C. W. Roberts, HM Chief Inspector of Mines, *Explosion at Easington Colliery County Durham: Report on the Causes of, and Circumstances Attending, the Explosion which Occurred at Easington Colliery, County Durham, on the 29th May, 1951*, Cmd 8646, London, HM Stationery Office, September 1952.

23. Written by Durham miner Robert Saint after the explosion at the Gresford Colliery in North Wales in 1934. For its significance see Peter Crookston, *The Pitmens' Requiem*, Newcastle upon Tyne, Northumbria Press, 2010.

24. Dennis, Henriques and Slaughter, *Coal is Our Life*.

25. A. McIvor, and R. Johnston, *Miner's Lung: A History of Dust Disease in British Coal Mining*. Aldershot: Ashgate, 2007: 54.

26. Francis and Smith, *The Fed*, p. 441; Arthur McIvor and Ronald Johnston, *Miners' Lung: A History of Dust Disease in British Coal Mining*, Aldershot, Ashgate, 2007, pp. 148–9.

3. Power Politics

1. A. Robens, *Ten Year Stint*, London, Cassell, 1971.

2. Unsurprisingly, the classic studies of colliery closures in the period were conducted in these two areas. For South Wales see John Sewel, *Colliery Closures and Social Change: A Study of a South Wales Mining Valley*, Cardiff, University of Wales Press, 1975; for Durham see Department of Employment and Productivity,

Ryhope: A Pit Closes, London, HM Stationery Office, 1979; and M. Bulmer, 'The Decline of Mining: A Case Study in Spennymoor', in M. Bulmer, ed., *Mining and Social Change: Durham in the Twentieth Century*, London, Croom Helm, 1978, pp. 235–63.

3. William Ashworth, *The History of the British Coal Industry, Volume 5: 1946–1982 – The Nationalized Industry*, Oxford, Oxford University Press, 1986. Employment in the Yorkshire and Nottingham mines increased significantly in this period.

4. D. Kelly, 'The Process of Mechanisation in British Coal Mining since 1945', *Economic Studies*, 4, 1969: 136.

5. *Colliery Guardian*, October 1968: 663.

6. Quoted in *Colliery Guardian*, 15 December 1967: 693.

7. NUM Durham Area, Annual Report, 1964: 8.

8. In 1964 the government had assured the trade unions of holding production at 200 million tons, increasing with economic growth. In 1965 George Brown, in producing his Coal Plan, accepted that this had not been met and that production was likely to fall to between 170 and 180 million tons by 1970 – the actual figure was 147 million tons.

9. Quoted in Andrew Taylor, *The NUM and British Politics: 1944–1968*, Aldershot, Ashgate, 2003, p. 191.

10. Will Paynter, *My Generation*, London, Allen and Unwin, 1972, p. 151.

11. In 1977, NUM's Executive Committee, under the leadership of Joe Gormley, agreed to implement an incentive payment system, despite its having been rejected by the membership in a ballot. This, together with the NEC's refusal even to consider Paynter's reform of the NUM's structure, given the 'vested interest of union officials who objected to being disturbed from the thrones of their little empires' proved to be disastrous for the union in the 1980s. Paynter, *My Generation*, p. 149.

12. Ibid., p. 135.

13. Ministry of Power, *Fuel Policy*, Cmnd 3438, London, HM Stationery Office, 1967.

14. Richard Crossman, *Diaries of a Cabinet Minister*, Volume Two Lord President of the Council and Leader of the House of Commons, 1966–8, London, Hamish Hamilton 1977, p. 451.

15. NUM Durham Area, Annual Report, 1963: 11.

16. In fact, Seaton Carew is located off the coalfield.
17. Robens was forecasting that government policy would lead to the loss of 300,000 jobs in the coal mines by 1980, and the end of coal mining in Scotland, Wales and the North East. Crossman, *Diaries*, pp. 571ff.
18. *The Times*, 13 November 1967.
19. Ibid.
20. Robens, *Ten Year Stint*, p. 12.
21. For details see Brian J. McCormick, *Industrial Relations in the Coal Industry*, London, Macmillan, 1979, p. 108.
22. The origins of this approach lay in the response to the depression of the 1930s among capitalists in the North East (R. Hudson, *Wrecking a Region*, London, Pion, 1989, pp. 18–19). It was reflected in the 1944 White Paper on Employment Policy (Ministry of Labour, 1944, para. 29), which noted that 'there might be some small and isolated villages, especially in mining areas, which owing to permanent changes in industrial conditions [offered] no hope of sound economic revival. In these rare cases the population [might] have to be re-established elsewhere'. It was perhaps most forcefully stated by Pepler and MacFarlane in the unpublished but nonetheless influential North East Area Development Plan, an interim report presented to the minister of town and country planning (1949, p. 167, emphasis added): 'Some of the mining towns and villages are so derelict and so badly situated that it would not be reasonable to expect new industries to establish themselves there to take the place of mining . . . To make some of these places really habitable would cost a great deal of money *and would be a disservice to the inhabitants*, as it would tend to anchor them where either now or before long they would have no prospect of earning their livelihood.'
23. John F. F. Robinson, 'Peterlee: A Study of New Town Development', PhD thesis, Durham University, 1975.
24. Teresa L. Rees, 'Population and Industrial Decline in the South Wales Coalfield', *Regional Studies*, 12, 1978: 69–77.
25. The plant was eventually built at Halewood in Liverpool, where there were no large-scale engineering industries competing for labour. See Huw Beynon, *Working For Ford*, Harmondsworth, Penguin, 1973.

26. Gwyn A. Williams, 'Mother Wales Get Off My Back', *Marxism Today*, December 1981: 18.

27. Thirty-one years later another secretary of state – Ron Davies – fulfilled a pledge to return the money. This was paid without interest, a further slight that was later made good by a donation from the newly devolved Welsh government. In all this time the people of the village were left to deal with things as best they could – by supporting one another, with looks and tears, or sometimes in silence, by not talking about it at all. For further detail about the Aberfan disaster see Ceri Jackson, 'Aberfan: The mistake that cost a village its children', BBC, 21 October 2016.

28. Quoted in H. Francis and D. Smith, *The Fed: A History of South Wales Miners in the Twentieth Century*, London, Lawrence and Wishart, 1980, p. 457.

29. Ashworth, *History of the British Coal Industry, Volume 5*, p. 264.

30. See Victor Allen, *The Militancy of British Miners*, Shipley, Moor Press, 1981; and Tony Hall, *King Coal: Miners, Coal and Britain's Industrial Future*, Harmondsworth, Penguin, 1982.

31. For details of these developments see Arthur Scargill, 'The New Unionism' (interview), *New Left Review*, 1:92, July/August 1975; also Michael Crick, *Scargill and the Miners*, Harmondsworth, Penguin, 1985.

32. William Ashworth, *The History of the British Coal Industry, Volume 5*, p. 282.

4. From Heath to Thatcher

1. This reflected the concern felt for unity in 1944 by men who had seen the old Federation split asunder after the 1926 strike.

2. See Victor Allen, *The Militancy of British Miners*, Shipley, Moor Press, 1981, pp. 166–8. McGahey was the younger man and the obvious person to succeed Gormley after his retirement, and this was something the new president was determined to prevent. He introduced a rule change, placing an age limit of fifty-five on all candidates for national positions within the union, and stayed in post until the Scottish president passed that age. It was a decision he came to regret, as this change had, in his words, allowed 'the

genie [Arthur Scargill] to be released from the bottle'.

3. Tony Hall, *King Coal: Miners, Coal and Britain's Industrial Future*, Harmondsworth, Penguin, 1981, p. 175.

4. For a detailed account of these events see Arthur Scargill, 'The New Unionism' (interview), *New Left Review*, 1:92, July/August 1975.

5. Wilberforce Report, HC Deb. 21 February 1972, vol. 831, cc898–906. See also Richard Orme Wilberforce, *Reflections on My Life*, Durham, Roundtuit Publishing, 2003, pp. 77–85.

6. Keith Jeffrey and Peter Hennessy, *States of Emergency: English Governments and Strike Breaking since 1919*, London, Routledge and Kegan Paul, 1983, p. 235.

7. When he gave his public lecture at Durham University on 16 November 1979, Ezra was introduced enthusiastically by Sir William Reid as 'the man who loves coal!'

8. The Social Contract was an agreement between the government and the TUC to adopt economic and social policies favoured by the trades unions in exchange for voluntary wage restraint. It was intended to avoid the problems that had arisen with the previous incomes policy. See Roger Tarling and Frank Wilkinson, 'The Social Contract: Post-War Incomes Policies and their Inflationary Impact', *Cambridge Journal of Economics*, 1:4, 1977, pp. 395–414.

9. These Areas were in favour of a straight wage demand for £100 a week.

10. See E. P. Thompson, 'A Special Case', *New Society*, 24 February 1972, reprinted in E. P. Thompson, *Writing by Candlelight*, London, Merlin Press, 1980, pp. 65–76.

11. The Kent Area's attempt to stop the ballot on the grounds that the decision had already been decided by conference was overruled by Lord Denning, the Master of the Rolls, who famously judged that the conference may not have expressed the true wishes of the membership.

12. Average gross wages for underground workers increased from £84.80 in 1977 to £125.80 in 1979.

13. See William Ashworth, *The History of the British Coal Industry, Volume 5: 1946–1982 – The Nationalized Industry*, Oxford, Oxford University Press, 1986, p. 690, which notes that the index of reportable injuries also increased in this period from 1.01 in

1975–76 to 1.69 in 1982–83. For a discussion see T. Nichols, *The British Worker Question*, London, Routledge, 1997, p. 115.

14. Hall, *King Coal*, p. 238.

15. Denis Healey's proposals were resisted most strongly by Michael Foot, Tony Benn, John Silkin, Peter Shore, Albert Booth and Stan Orme. Kenneth O. Morgan, *Michael Foot: A Life*, London, Harper, 2008, p. 345.

16. Department of Trade and Industry, *British Steel Corporation: Ten Year Development Strategy*, Cmnd 5226, London, HM Stationery Office, 1973.

17. The speech was written by Peter Jay, his son-in-law. Jay himself noted that the speech was the one that Milton Friedman had 'most frequently quoted with approval of any delivered by any politician anywhere'. See Leo Panitch and Colin Leys, *The End of Parliamentary Socialism: From New Left to New Labour*, London, Verso, 1997.

18. Nicholas Ridley, *My Style of Government: The Thatcher Years*, London, Hutchinson, 1991, p. 3.

19. This was achieved through the Social Security Act 1980.

20. In 1975 the nationalised British Steel Corporation employed 280,000 workers; this declined over ten years to 54,000, a process that contributed to the major national strike of 1980. For details see C. McGuire, '"Going for the Jugular": Banner and the 1980 National Steel Strike in Britain', *Historical Studies in Industrial Relations*, 38, 2017: 37–78; also Ralph Fevre, *Wales is Closed: The Quiet Privatisation of British Steel*, Nottingham, Spokesman, 1989.

21. For details see A. R. Townsend, *The Impact of Recession on Industry, Employment and the Regions*, Beckenham, Croom Helm, 1983; T. Austrin and H. Beynon, 'Global Outpost: The Experience of Multinational Corporations in the North East of England 1968–1980', ESRC Working Paper, University of Durham, 1981; R. Hudson and A. M. Williams, *Divided Britain*, Chichester, Wiley, 1996; T. Dickson and D. Judge, eds, *The Politics of Industrial Closure*, London, Allen and Unwin, 1984.

22. House of Commons Debate, 6 May 1982, vol. 23, cc370–6.

23. T. Lane 'We're Talking about a Closure Movement', in A. Rainnie and J. Stirling, eds, 'Plant Closure: The Trade Union Response',

Occasional Paper, Newcastle Upon Tyne Polytechnic, 1982.

24. Hall, *King Coal*, p. 256.

25. Ben Curtis, *The South Wales Miners: 1964–85*, Cardiff, University of Wales Press, 2013, p. 171.

26. The resolution was moved by Tommy Bartle, the secretary of the Durham Colliery Mechanics' Association and the intellectual leader of the right (or moderate) wing of the NEC.

27. Michael Portillo, 'Britain Had to Change: She Had the Courage and Vision to Make it Happen', in *Observer* special issue 'Margaret Thatcher 1925–2013', 2013, pp. 8–9.

28. M. Thatcher, *Margaret Thatcher: The Downing Street Years*, London, Harper Collins, 1993:141.

29. Payments under the scheme related to the number of years worked for the NCB: generally, the older men (with longer service) would receive much higher payments, encouraging them to leave; however, given their age, they were less likely to find alternative employment. This outcome favoured the NCB (retaining younger, fitter workers) but not the local areas into which ex-miners were essentially 'pensioned off'.

30. Alvin Gouldner identified such arrangements as 'indulgency patterns': A. Gouldner, *Patterns of Industrial Bureaucracy*, Glencoe, Free Press, 1957.

31. For details see Phil Rawsthorne, 'Implementing the Ridley Report: The Role of Thatcher's Policy Unit During the Miners' Strike of 1984–85', *International Labor and Working Class History*, 94, Fall 2018: 156–201.

5. Conflagration: The State Against the Miners

1. Dean Hancock and Russell Shankland, miners in the Merthyr Vale Colliery in South Wales, dropped a concrete block from a bridge onto the taxi that was taking a miner to the colliery. The taxi driver, David Wilkie, was killed; and the men were convicted of murder and sentenced to life imprisonment. At the announcement of the verdict in May 1995, the 700 miners at the Merthyr Vale Colliery walked out. On appeal the convictions were reduced to manslaughter with an eight-year sentence.

2. This was the figure provided by the NCB to the Select Committee on Employment on 22 May 1995. The committee's report argued that the NCB's procedures amounted to 'summary treatment' that should be reviewed.

3. K. O'Donnell, 'Brought to Account: The NCB and the Case for Coal', *Capital and Class*, 26, 1985, 105–24.

4. Policy makers came to define coalfields by the pattern of *residence* rather than *jobs* in a way that was not helpful in the Durham context. For further discussion of these issues, with detailed maps, see our entry 'Changing Patterns of Mine Closures and their Social Consequences', on the Verso blog.

5. Ben Curtis, *The South Wales Miners 1964–1985,* Cardiff, University of Wales Press, 2013, p. 183.

6. Quoted in Ben Curtis, *The South Wales Miners 1964–1985,* Cardiff, University of Wales Press, 2013.

7. B. Curtis, *The South Wales Miners,* 191.

8. Arthur Scargill, *Miners in the Eighties*, Barnsley, National Union of Mineworkers, 1981, pp. 3, 5.

9. Obituary, *Guardian*, 12 January 2002.

10. Quoted in Martin Adeney and John Lloyd, *The Miners' Strike 1984–85: Loss without Limit*, London, Routledge, 1986, p. 57.

11. Meetings took place, usually twice a week, from the start of the strike in March until the end of October, when the National Association of Colliery Overmen, Deputies and Shotfirers (NACODS), the union of deputies and safety officers, agreed a revised system for consultation and agreement on pit closures with the NCB. The CMGC met just once a week thereafter.

12. For details of how this was managed within Number Ten see N. Jones, 'The Cabinet Papers: Misinformation and Cover-Ups', in G. Williams, ed., *Settling Scores: The Media, The Police and the Miners' Strike*, Nottingham, CPBF, 2014, pp. 3–25; J. Phillips, 'Containing, Isolating and Defeating the Miners: The UK Cabinet Ministerial Group on Coal and the Three Phases of the 1984–5 Strike', *Historical Studies in Industrial Relations*, 35, 2014: 117–41.

13. Ian MacGregor, *The Enemies Within: The Story of the Miners' Strike 1984–85,* London, Collins, 1986, p. 344.

14. Ibid., pp. 186–7.

15. In later life David Hart worked as political adviser to various Tory

Cabinet ministers and set up a variety of political organisations and groups described as 'right wing, patriotic or pro-American – not quite fascist, just lurid'. Edward Pearce, *Guardian*, 9 January 2011.

16. This rule related to 'Strikes and Lockouts' and allowed for disputes to take place officially within a particular Area if agreed to by the National Executive Committee.

17. H. Francis and G. Rees, 'No Surrender in the Valleys', *Llafur*, 1989, reprinted in H. Francis, *History on our Side: Wales and the 1984–85 Miners' Strike*, 2nd edn, London, Lawrence and Wishart, 2015.

18. Arthur Scargill, *Morning Star*, March, 1984.

19. MacGregor, *The Enemies Within*, 1996, p. 255.

20. MacGregor, *The Enemies Within*, p. 195.

21. Quoted in Harry Paterson, *Look Back in Anger: The Miners' Strike in Nottingham Thirty Years On*, Nottingham, Five Leaves Publications, 2014, pp. 56–7.

22. MacGregor, *The Enemies Within*, pp. 192–3.

23. CMGC, 14 March 1984.

24. On the same day, the NCB, drawing on the Employment Act, was granted an injunction against the Yorkshire NUM to prevent the deployment of flying pickets. This was ignored and, on 16 March, the NCB was granted leave to bring action for contempt. MacGregor, realising the potential for this to unify the labour movement behind the NUM, chose instead to ask for an extended postponement of the order. He was to see this use of the Employment Act as his one regret over his handling of the strike: 'we were wrong to even contemplate using the injunctive procedure . . . it could have been disastrous if it had been granted . . . as a rallying point for the whole trade union movement at a critical time' (MacGregor, *The Enemies Within*, p. 370).

25. CMGC, 27 March 1984.

26. W. J. Morgan and K. Coates, 'The Nottingham Coalfield and the British Miners' Strike 1984–85', Occasional Paper, Department of Adult Education, University of Nottingham, n.d.

27. For an account of one group of miners from Herrington in Durham see H. Beynon, 'What Happened to the Herrington Delegates', 1984, huwbeynon.com/publications; and for a full

account of the experiences of South Wales miners see Welsh Campaign for Civil and Political Liberties, *Striking Back*, Cardiff, WCCPL, 1985.

28. J. Coulter, S. Miller and M. Walker, *State of Siege: Miners' Strike 1984: Politics and Policing in the Coalfields*, London, Canary Press, 1984.

29. WCCPL, *Striking Back*, p. 95.

30. Ibid., p. 97.

31. D. Waddington, K. Jones and C. Critcher, *Flashpoints: Studies in Social Disorder*, London, Routledge, 1989, p. 91.

32. WCCPL, *Striking Back*, p. 97.

33. Thirty-nine men were arrested, charged with rioting and faced lengthy prison sentences. However, the trial of the first fifteen collapsed in the face of highly dubious police evidence, illustrated by thirty-one officers from fourteen different forces using the same complex phrases. Vera Baird, acting for the defence, described the police action as 'perverting the course of justice'.

34. There is no doubt that these negotiations represented the one point when the strike could have been settled, the NUM having lost little ground in its Areas supporting the strike and the government slightly on the back foot after worries over a dock strike. However, it is very unlikely that this would have been a final settlement with the NCB remaining attached (if secretly) to its plan to remove 25 million tonnes of capacity in the following two years.

35. These events form part of the narrative of the film and stage show *Billy Elliot*. For a detailed account see H. Beynon, 'The Strike at Easington', *New Left Review*, 148, 1985; and Keith Pattison and David Peace, *No Redemption: The 1984–85 Strike on the Durham Coalfield*, Newcastle upon Tyne, Flambard Press, 2010.

36. Gellhorn returned to Newbridge in the 1990s, courtesy of BBC Wales. What she found horrified her in a different way. Many of the people she had met during the strike had died, and 'while the people were spirited . . . the town now has everything going: youth unemployment, crime, vandalism, drugs. They were right. The sense of community is gone.' D. Devine, 'Martha Gellhorn at Newbridge', *Western Mail*, 28 November 2012.

37. D. Price and N. Butts-Thompson, eds, *How Black Were our Valleys,*

Bargoed, BBTS Publications, 2014, p. 113.

38. C. Jones and T. Novak 'Welfare Against the Workers: Benefits as a Political Weapon', in H. Beynon, ed., *Digging Deeper: Issues in the Miners' Strike*, London, Verso, 1985.

39. R. Turner, 'The Women who Joined the Pickets of the Miners' Strike', *Western Mail*, 19 March 2014.

40. Vin MacIntyre, personal reflection, in 'The Miners' Strike of 1984–85', *North East History*, 45, 2014: 159.

41. Siân James, 'From the Picket Line to the Palace of Westminster', in D. Alsop, C. Stephenson and D. Wray, eds, *Justice Denied: Friends, Foes and the Miners' Strike*, London, Merlin, 2018, p. 39.

42. Pat McIntyre, 'The Response to the 1984–85 Miners' Strike in Durham County: Women, the Labour Party and Community', Durham University, 1992.

43. Mary Stafford, personal reflection in 'The Miners' Strike of 1984–85', *North East History*, 45, 2014: 153.

44. D. Massey and H. Wainwright, 'Beyond the Coalfields: The Work of the Miners' Support Groups', in H. Beynon, ed., *Digging Deeper: Issues in the Miners' Strike*, London, Verso, 1985, pp. 149–69.

45. Bala Nair, personal reflection, in 'The Miners' Strike of 1984–85', *North East History*, 45, 2014: 15.7

46. Pat McIntyre, 'The Response to the 1984–85 Miners' Strike'. McIntyre also sees the NUM as having had responsibility here. She argues that by not going out beyond its own membership with the Campaign for Coal it lost the opportunity of developing a more progressive politics, instead allowing a slide back to the division between the industrial and political wings of the labour movement.

47. Francis and Rees, 'No Surrender in the Valleys'.

48. Raymond Williams, 'Mining the Meaning: Key Words in the Miners' Strike', *New Socialist*, March 1985, reprinted in Williams, *Resources of Hope*, London, Verso, 1993, p. 125.

49. Ralph Miliband, 'Class War Conservatism', reprinted in Miliband, *Class War Conservatism and Other Essays*, London, Verso, 2015.

50. Williams, 'Mining the Meaning', p. 122.

6. Of Managers and Markets

1. Tony Lane, 'Foreign Ships and Disorganised Trade Unionism: An Alternative Interpretation of the Defeat of Miners in 1984–5', *Work, Employment and Society*, 10:1, March 1996: 57–84.

2. M. Prior and G. McCloskey, 'Coal and the Market: Can BCC Survive Privatisation?' London, FT International Coal Report, 1988: 9.

3. House of Commons Energy Committee, 'The Coal Industry', London, 1985–1986: 18.

4. Gareth Rees, 'Regional Restructuring, Class Change and Political Action: Preliminary Comments on the 1984–85 Miners' Strike in South Wales', *Society and Space*, 33,1985: 389.

5. Ian Isaac, *When We Were Miners*, Maesteg, Ken Smith Press, 2010, p. 125.

6. T. Parker, *Red Hill: A Mining Community*, London, William Heinemann, 1986, p. 22.

7. Ibid., p. 21.

8. Work and Employment Research Unit, '(Mis)managing Horden', Durham University, 1985.

9. Decision letter from L. Stuart Shields QC, chair, independent review into the closure of the Horden Colliery, 28 January 1986.

10. Ian MacGregor, *The Enemies Within: The Story of the Miners' Strike 1984–85*, London, Collins, 1986, pp. 296–7.

11. Michael Atkin, 'The 1984/85 Miners' Strike in East Durham: A Study in Contemporary History', PhD thesis, Durham University, 2001, p. 262.

12. S4C, 'Y Streic: Cyscoed Cynheidre', 12 March 2014.

13. See Jonathan Renouf, 'A Striking Change: Political Transformation in the Murton Miners and Mechanics', PhD thesis, University of Durham, 1989.

14. For a discussion of how organisations can shift from indulgent to punishment centred modes see Alvin Gouldner, *Patterns of Industrial Bureaucracy*, Glenco, Free Press, 1957.

15. Payment also altered. As one man from Newbridge explained, 'when you went back to work, it was really degrading . . . before the strike we were all paid with a docket and pay packet on a

Friday but when they went back, we were paid by cheque. Well 99 per cent of the miners then didn't have a cheque book, you had to go around begging businesses which weren't taking any money, to change these £50 cheques.'

16. MacGregor, *The Enemies Within*, p. 373.

17. *Financial Times*, 28 June 1989.

18. See H. Beynon, A. Cox and R. Hudson, *Digging Up Trouble: The Environment, Protest and Opencast Coal Mining*, London, River Oram, 2000.

19. *Financial Times*, 24 July 1985.

20. In 1991, the European Commission had removed the restrictions on the use of gas for electricity generation. This allowed the development in the UK of a new generation of combined-cycle gas turbines (CCGTs), leading to new companies entering the sector and generating electricity for sale to the grid.

21. John T. Boyd Company, 'Independent Analysis of 21 Closure Review Collieries', London, 1993, and John T. Boyd Company, 'Independent Review of 10 Collieries under Consultation', London, 1993.

22. House of Commons Employment Committee, 'Employment Consequences of British Coal's Proposed Pit Closures', 1993: viii.

23. George Robson, 'The Gala Is About Our Heritage', in P. Crookston, *The Pitmen's Requiem*, Newcastle upon Tyne, Northumbria Press, 2010, p. 66.

24. Ibid., p. 66.

25. In order to encourage sales, the management decided to offer everyone who spent over £100 two free air tickets to Europe or the USA. It was a great success with increased sales of £30 million, but at a cost of £50 million. Tom Stevenson, 'Great Financial Disasters of Our Time: The Hoover Fiasco', *Independent*, 15 August 1998.

26. For a full account see D. Howell, 'The British Coal Crisis 1992–93', University of York Papers in Politics and Polity No. 2, 1996.

27. Betws was to close again in 1997.

28. This is discussed in detail in Chapter 14.

29. For details see H. Beynon, R. Hudson and A. Cox, 'The Decline of King Coal', Discussion Paper 1, Cardiff University, 1997.

30. Steven Fairclough, 'Coal Tips: Almost 300 in Wales Classed as

"High-Risk"', BBC News, 16 February 2021.

31. R. Hudson, F. Peck and D. Sadler, 'Undermining Easington: Who'll Pay the Price of Pit Closures?', Easington District Council, 1984.

7. Thatcher's Redundant Entrepreneurs

1. House of Commons Employment Committee, 'Employment Consequences of British Coal's Proposed Pit Closures', London, 1993, p. xix.

2. L. Mainwaring and V. Wass, 'Economic and Social Consequences of Rationalization in the South Wales Coal Industry', *Contemporary Wales*, 3: 161–85.

3. From July 1986 the company's name changed from NCB (Enterprise) Ltd to BCE (Ltd).

4. British Coal Enterprise, annual review 1986, p. 2.

5. British Coal Enterprise, annual review 1987.

6. *Observer*, 5 July 1987.

7. *Newcastle Journal*, 9 August 1988. This was not just an issue in the North East, nor was it new. In a parliamentary debate on 24 November 1986, Peter Walker, the energy minister, had claimed that BCE had created nearly 12,000 job opportunities in coal-mining communities. This was challenged in the House of Commons: was he 'aware that British Coal Enterprise is refusing to give any information or details about where these jobs are, what types of jobs they are, and what companies are being supported? Therefore, it has been impossible to evaluate what the impact in our communities of British Coal Enterprise will be. Many of us still do not see much evidence of its working.' House of Commons Debate, 24 November 1986, vol. 106 c12.

8. G. Rees and M. Thomas, 'From Coalminers to Entrepreneurs? A Case-study in the Sociology of Re-industrialisation', in M. Cross and G. Payne, eds, *Work and the Enterprise Culture*, Lewes, Falmer Press, 1991.

9. F. Ennis and R. Hudson, 'British Coal (Enterprise), Enterprise Agencies and Local Economic Regeneration', Report to the Nuffield Foundation, 1989, p. 9.

10. Rees and Thomas, 'From Coalminers to Entrepreneurs?'.

11. Ennis and Hudson, 'British Coal (Enterprise)', p. 32.

12. G. Rees and M. Thomas, From Coal-miners to Entrepreneurs? A Case-study in the Sociology of Re-industrialisation, in M. Cross and G. Payne (eds.), *Work and the Enterprise Culture*, Lewes: Falmer Press 1991.

13. British Coal Enterprise annual review 1996, p. 33.

14. Vickie Wass, 'Colliery Closure and the Re-employment Experiences of Redundant Miners', PhD thesis, Cardiff University, 1992. See also S. Monk, 'Retraining Opportunities for Miners Made Redundant', Report for the Coalfield Communities Campaign, Barnsley, 1996.

15. Vicki Wass, 'The Psychological Effects of Redundancy and Worklessness: A Case Study from the Coalfields', in D. Waddington, ed., *Coal Culture and Community: Conference Papers*, Sheffield, Sheffield Hallam University Press, 1993, p. 190.

16. Tony Parker, *Redhill: A Mining Community*, London, Heinemann, 1986, p. 35; and H. Beynon, R. Hudson and D. Sadler, *A Tale of Two Industries: The Contraction of Coal and Steel in the North East of England*, Milton Keynes, Open University Press, 1991, p. 52.

17. M. Thomas, 'Colliery Closure and the Miner's Experience of Redundancy', *Contemporary Wales*, 4/1, 1991: 55.

18. Beynon, Hudson and Sadler, *A Tale of Two Industries*, p. 50.

19. In our attempts to meet these men in 1999 we found that many of the addresses we were looking for had been boarded up or knocked down, and that many of the people we were searching for had moved away.

20. The Coalfield Communities Campaign was an all-party association representing more than eighty local authorities in the present and former coalmining areas of England, Scotland and Wales. It changed its name to the Industrial Communities Alliance (Alliance) in 2007.

21. Nerys Anwen Jones, 'Coal Was Our Life', PhD thesis, University of Wales, Bangor, 1996, p. 163.

22. Ibid., p. 217.

23. Ibid., p. 233.

24. Ibid.

25. Ibid., p. 239.

26. Tim Strangleman, 'Networks, Place and Identities in Post-Industrial Mining Communities', *International Journal of Urban and Regional Research*, 25:2, 2001: 253–67.

27. For a full discussion and account of the factory operations see Julian Hunt, 'From Despair to Where? Coal, Capital and the New Economy', PhD thesis, University of Wales, Cardiff, 2004.

28. Edward Fieldhouse, and Emma Hollywood, 'Life After Mining: Hidden Unemployment and Changing Patterns of Economic Activity Amongst Miners in England and Wales, 1981–1991', *Work, Employment and Society*, 13:3, 1999: 492–3.

29. Christina Beatty and Steve Fothergill, 'Registered and Hidden Unemployment in the UK Coalfields', Sheffield Hallam University, 1996. Fothergill was to become the Director of the Coalfield Communities Campaign and then of Alliance.

8. Sticking Together and Falling Apart

1. The goaf is the area in the mine from which coal has been removed and into which waste material is deposited as the face moves forward.

2. Anthony Jones, *Welsh Chapels*, Cardiff, National Museums and Galleries of Wales, 1984, p. 49.

3. See David Bean, *Tyneside: A Biography*, London, Macmillan, 1971, p. 182.

4. Peter Marris, *Loss and Change*, London, Routledge and Kegan Paul, 1974, and Peter Marris, *The Politics of Uncertainty: Attachment in Public and Private Life*, London, Routledge and Kegan Paul, 1981.

5. For a consideration of the impact of this on young men in Ebbw Vale see V. Walkerdine and L. Jimenez, *Gender, Work and Community after De-Industrialisation: A Psychosocial Approach to Affect*, Basingstoke, Palgrave Macmillan, 2012.

6. This is illustrated by a story told by Peter Heathfield, general secretary of the NUM, in 1983. It relates to a South Derbyshire miner whose wife was having a home confinement. The midwife was in attendance and the birth imminent when all the lights in the house went out. 'Put some money in the meter', was the cry.

Then, after some minutes of darkness, came the reply, 'Marge, where is the meter?'

7. M. Allen, 'Carrying on the Strike: The Politics of Women Against Pit Closures', PhD thesis, University of Manchester, 2001, p. 75.

9. Regeneration?

1. S. Jenkins, *Thatcher and Sons: A Revolution in Three Acts*, London, Allen Lane, 2006, p. 4.
2. Coalfields Task Force, 'Making a Difference: A New Start for England's Coalfield Communities', Department of Environment, Transport and the Regions, London, 1998, para. 3:12.
3. Ibid., para 1.2.
4. That this was based more upon hope than any understanding of economic processes was made clear by Jim Gill, commercial director of English Partnership. Speaking at a meeting at the Royal Geographical Society on 16 November 1999, he expressed deep uncertainty over the link. His worries were understandable and supported by a subsequent report, which concluded that 'the capacity of coalfield areas to make the most of employment opportunities on new site developments depends on the pace of the economic recovery.' House of Commons Public Accounts Committee, 'Regenerating the English Coalfields', HC 247, 10 March 2010.
5. ONE was abolished in 2011, its assets of land of land and property being consolidated into the Homes and Communities Agency. GONE was also abolished in the same year.
6. One North East, 'Regional Economic Strategy: Unlocking Our Potential', Newcastle on Tyne, 1999.
7. Philip Cooke and Kevin Morgan, *The Associational Economy: Firms, Regions and Innovation*, Oxford, Oxford University Press, 1998.
8. G. Rees and M. Thomas, 'Inward Investment, Labour Market Change and Skills Development: Recent Experience from South Wales', *Local Economy*, 9, 1994: 48–61.
9. ONE North East, 'Regional Economic Strategy: Unlocking Our Potential', Newcastle on Tyne, 1999. For a fuller consideration and

critique of this approach, see Ray Hudson, 'From Knowledge-Based Economy . . . To Knowledge-Based Economy: Reflections on Changes in the Economy and Development Policies in North East England', *Regional Studies*, 45, 2011: 997–1,012.

10. As of 2020, there were a few hundred jobs on Phase 1 of the NETPark development, and the preliminary earthworks for building work on Phase 2 are under way.

11. *Northern Echo*, 21 April 2006: 14.

12. The EU Objective 2 Programme: to promote the economic and social convergence of areas facing structural difficulties in the industrial and service sectors.

13. The RECHAR initiative (from the French: la reconversion des bassins charbonniers) aims to accelerate the economic conversion of those areas worst affected by the decline of coal mining through supporting the development of SMEs, financing vocational training for redundant miners or those threatened with unemployment and enhancing the environment of former mining areas.

14. East Durham Development Agency promotional material, n. d.

15. *Western Mail*, 12 December 1997.

16. Kenneth O. Morgan, *Rebirth of a Nation: A History of Modern Wales 1880–1980*, Oxford, Oxford University Press, 1981, p. 322.

17. Between 1998 and 2006, for example, warehouses made up 31 per cent of new commercial floor space development in coalfield areas as compared to 23 per cent nationally. Report by the Comptroller and Auditor General, 'Regenerating the English Coalfields', HC84 Session 2009–2010, paras 4.4 and 4.18.

18. James Wadwell, 'Coalfield Regeneration and Improving Best Practice', PhD thesis, Durham University, 2005.

19. Chris Mullin, *A Walk-On Part: Diaries 1944–1999*, London, Profile Books, 2011, p. 375. Dewhirst was also closing factories in Peterlee at this time.

20. C. Garner, 'North-East's Jewel Quickly Lost its Shine", *Independent*, 3 August 1998.

21. Daily Mail Online, 19 March 2017.

22. *Northern Echo*, 16 January 2004.

23. The Nissan plant is heavily dependent upon exports to the EU market, however, and this is at risk following the UK's exit from the EU.

24. F. Robinson, I. Zass-Ogilvie, M. Jackson, 'Never Had it So Good? The North East Under New Labour', St Chad's College, Durham, 2007, p. 9.

25. *Northern Echo*, 16 January 2004.

26. Mullin, *A Walk-On Part*, p. 390.

27. Tyne Tees News, 22 May 2012. Young's is a subsidiary of the Imperial group.

28. *Daily Telegraph*, 19 August 2006.

29. Cooke and Morgan, *The Associational Economy*.

30. *Western Mail*, 4 March 2016. GMB, 'Almost 600,000 Jobs Lost in Manufacturing', London, 2 June 2018.

31. As with Nissan in the North East, the reduced number of jobs and the feeling that the plant was vulnerable anyway became a factor in the vote to leave the EU from 1 January 2020.

10. 'Just Jobs'

1. Wales Development Agency, Annual Report, 1999, p. 23.

2. Coalfields Task Force 1998, p. 32.

3. This development was associated with a restructuring of banking in the nineties that shifted operations away from branch banking. Specialised offices managed the settlement of accounts, while call centres dealt with customer relations and the marketing of new products.

4. In the North East, the major urban centres of Tyneside and Teesside also proved attractive call centre locations to companies such as Barclaycard and British Airways.

5. For details see V. Belt, 'Women's Work and Restructuring in the Service Economy: The Case of Telephone Call Centres', PhD thesis, University of Newcastle upon Tyne, 2003.

6. *Sunderland Echo*, 28 July 2006.

7. Ibid.

8. BBC News, news.bbc.co.uk/go/em/fr/-/1/hi/england/ 2818567.stm.

9. Cited in Jonathon Warren, 'Living the Call Centre: Global, Local, Work-Life Interfaces', PhD thesis Durham University 2011, p. 162.

10. Quoted in Warren, 'Living the Call Centre', p. 174.

11. See *Call Centre Western Mail*, spring 1998.

12. James Bloodworth, *Hired: Six Months Undercover in Low-Wage Britain*, London, Atlantic Books, 2018, p. 163.

13. Ibid.

14. Peter Bain and Phil Taylor, '"An Assembly Line in the Head": Work and Employee Relations in the Call Centre', *Industrial Relations Journal*, 30:2, 1999: 101–17.

15. EE Employees Reviews in Merthyr Tydfil, indeed.co.uk, accessed 14 August 2018.

16. Stuart Tannock, 'Bad Attitude? Migrant Workers, Meat Processing Work and the Local Unemployed in a Peripheral Region of the UK', *European Urban and Regional Studies*, 22:4, 2015: 416–30; John Lever and Paul Milbourne, 'The Structural Invisibility of Outsiders: The Role of Migrant Labour in the Meat-Processing Industry', *Sociology*, 51:2, 2017: 306–22.

17. Tannock, 'Bad Attitude?': 6. Further quotations in this section, unless stated, are drawn from this source.

18. Ibid.: 8.

19. Lever and Milbourne, 'The Structural Invisibility of Outsiders': 312.

20. J. Salt and S. Millar, 'Foreign Labour in the United Kingdom: Current Patterns and Trends', *Labour Market Trends*, ONS, October 2006: 342.

21. Ian Fitzgerald, 'Working in the UK: Polish Migrant Workers Routes into Employment in the North East and North West Construction and Food Processing Sectors', TUC London, 2007; Ian Fitzgerald, 'Polish Migrant Workers in the North – New Communities, New Opportunities?', in Jo McBride and Ian Greenwood (eds), *Community Unionism*, Basingstoke, Palgrave Macmillan, 2009, pp. 93–118.

22. S. Dench, J. Hurstfield, D. Hill. and K. Akroyd, 'Employers' Use of Migrant Labour', Home Office Online Report 04/06, February 2006, homeoffice.gov.uk/rds/pdfs06/rdsolr0406.pdf.

23. Lever and Milbourne, 'The Structural Invisibility of Outsiders': 317.

24. Gareth Rees and Dean Stroud, 'Regenerating the Coalfields: The South Wales Experience', Bevan Foundation, 2004.

25. ONE North East, 'Realising Our Potential – The Revised Regional Economic Strategy for the North East of England', Newcastle on Tyne, 2002. This was a revision of an earlier document, 'Unlocking Our Potential', 1999.

26. Christina Beatty and her colleagues identified a jobs shortfall of 44,460 in South Wales and 33,840 in Durham at this time. See C. Beatty, S. Fothergill and R Powell, 'Twenty Years On: Has the Economy of the UK Coalfields Recovered?', *Environment and Planning A*, 39, 2004: 1,654–75.

11. The Fabric of Decline

1. John Campbell, *Nye Bevan and the Mirage of British Socialism*, London, Weidenfeld & Nicolson, 1987, p. 7.

2. Aneurin Bevan, *In Place of Fear*, London, EP Publishing, 1976 (1952), pp. 21–2.

3. One of us served as a member of the Durham Rural Community Council in the 1970s and 1980s and the issue of how best to think about the future of and policies for the former mining settlements, rural but deindustrialised, was a persistent challenge.

4. Martin Bulmer (ed.), *Mining and Social Change*, London, Croom Helm, 1978, p. 33. Emphasis added.

5. In the early years it was seen to be favoured with funding, at the expense of existing colliery villages that were left to run down. For details see Ray Hudson, *Wrecking a Region: State Policies, Party Politics and Regional Change in North East England*, London, Pion, 1989, pp. 211–326.

6. Government Office for the North East, 'Local Area Profile: Easington', Newcastle upon Tyne, 2007, p. 35.

7. Katy Bennett, 'Homeless at Home in East Durham', *Antipode*, 43:4, 2011: 960–85.

8. The housing association was modelled on the historic Aged Miners' Homes, set up by the Durham Miners' Association.

9. G. Anderson, 'Housing-Led Regeneration in East Durham: Uneven Development, Governance, Politics', PhD thesis, Durham University, 2015, p. 134.

10. A. Smith, 'Construction of Sustainability and Coalfield Regeneration', PhD thesis, Durham University, 2004.

11. Alexander Masters, 'Introduction', A. Clarke, *Gary's Friends*, Hove, West Pier Press, 2006, iv.

12. Yvette Taylor, 'Coalfield to Carpark Collection', Interview 016, quoted in Jon Lawrence, *Me, Me, Me? The Search for Community in Post War England*, Oxford, Oxford University Press, 2019, p. 212.

13. Ibid., Interview 017, p. 213.

14. Bennett, 'Homeless at Home': 960–85.

15. K. Bennett, H. Beynon and R. Hudson, *Coalfield Regeneration: Dealing with the Consequences of Industrial Decline*, Bristol, Policy Press, 2000.

16. See T. Marsden, P. Milbourne, L. Kitchen and K. Bishop, 'Communities in Nature: The Construction and Understanding of Forest Natures', *Sociologia Ruralis*, 43:3, 2003: 238–56. A. Smith, *Construction of Sustainability and Coalfield Regeneration* PhD Thesis, Durham University, 2004.

17. H. Beynon, A. Cox and R. Hudson, *Digging Up Trouble: The Environment, Protest and Opencast Coal Mining*, London, Rivers Oram, 2000.

18. M. Francis, 'New Choices for Women in Mining Areas', in R. Benn, J. Elliott and P. Whaley, eds, *Educating Rita and Her Sisters*, London, NIACE, 1999.

19. Steven Morris, 'Memorial Marks Six Bells Colliery Disaster', *Guardian*, 28 May 2010.

20. Jim Coxon, 'The Memorialisation of Mining in the Durham Coalfield', in Granville Williams, *The Flame Still Burns: The Creative Power of Coal*, London, CPBF, p. 38.

12. Tragic Outcomes

1. Mike Foden, Steve Fothergill and Tony Gore, 'The State of the Coalfields: Economic and Social Conditions in the Former Mining Communities of England, Scotland and Wales', Sheffield Hallam University, 2014, p. 16.

2. 'One in Six People in this Town is on Anti-Depressants. Is it, as

Local GPs Fear, Because They Get More Benefits?', *Daily Mail*, 28 June 2013.

3. *Durham Miner*, 1 December 2007: 8.

4. For example, Martyn Senior, 'Area Variations in Self-Perceived Limiting Long Term Illness in Britain: Is the Welsh Experience Exceptional, *Regional Studies*, 32:3, 1998: 265–80.

5. Christina Beatty and Steve Fothergill, 'Registered and Hidden Unemployment in the UK Coalfields', Sheffield Hallam University, 1996.

6. Christina Beatty and Steve Fothergill, 'Jobs, Welfare and Austerity: How the Destruction of Industrial Britain Casts a Shadow over the Present-Day Public Finance', Sheffield Hallam University, 2016, p. 8.

7. We have displayed this visually in map form on our Verso blog.

8. Bro Taf Local Medical Committee is the statutory representative organisation for GPs in the Local Health Board areas of Cardiff, Merthyr Tydfil, Rhondda Cynon Taff and Vale of Glamorgan.

9. M. Marmot, J, Allen, P. Goldblatt, T. Boyce, D. McNeish, M, Grady and I. Geddes, 'Fair Society, Healthy Lives (The Marmot Review)', Institute of Health Equity, London, 2010.

10. P. Townsend, P. Phillimore and A. Beattie, *Health and Deprivation: Inequality and the North*, London, Croom Helm, 1988, p. 90.

11. The lowest rates were in Guildford, Chichester and other towns in southern England.

12. Marmot *et al.*, 'Fair Society, Healthy Lives'.

13. 'Inequality in Health: Report of a Working Group (The Black Report)', DHSS, London, 1980.

14. Alastair McIntosh Gray, 'Inequalities in Health. The Black Report: A Summary and Comment', *International Journal of Health Service*, 12/3: 351.

15. Although similar in form, the measures used in Wales and England came to differ after devolution but remained broadly comparable.

16. Thomas S. Langner and T. Michael Stanley, *Life Stress and Mental Health*, New York, Free Press, 1963.

17. G. Williams, '"History Is What You Live": Understanding Health Inequalities in Wales', in Pamela Michael and Charles Webster, *Health and Society in Twentieth-Century Wales*, Cardiff, University

of Wales Press, 2006, p. 302.

18. Adrian Clarke and Alexander Masters, *Gary's Friends*, Hove, West Pier Press, 2006, pp. 104, 78.

19. Williams, '"History Is What You Live"', pp. 301–2.

20. Ibid., p. 302.

21. 'Saving Lives: Our Healthier Nation', Cm 4386, Department of Health, London, 1999, p. 12.

22. Ibid., p. 9.

23. He remembers with some pride that his grandfather Thomas Fallow was one of the miners arrested and imprisoned during the riot at Horden that led to the burning of the Big Club in 1910. See Huw Beynon and Terry Austrin, *Masters and Servants: Class and Patronage in the Making of a Labour Organisation*, London, Rivers Oram Press, 1994, p. 236.

24. Named after the pigeon crees where men would wait for their racing pigeons to return home.

25. J. Shucksmith, S. Carlebach, M. Riva, S. Curtis, D. Hunter, T. Blackman and R. Hudson, 'Health Inequalities in Ex-Coalfield/Industrial Communities', Improvement and Development Agency, London, 2010.

26. *Durham Miner*, 16 May 2017.

13. Monsters and Ghosts

1. DP 7, 2000, derived from 'Occupational Mortality', OPCS, 1991.

2. Arthur McIvor and Ronald Johnston, *Miners' Lung: A History of Dust Disease in British Coal Mining*, London, Routledge, 2007, p. 227.

3. Ibid.

4. Bumsang Yoo, 'Welfare Politics and the Social Policy of Coal Workers' Pneumoconiosis in Britain and South Korea', PhD thesis, Edinburgh University, 2019, p. 179.

5. Vic Allen, *The Militancy of British Miners*, Shipley, Moor Press, 1981, p. 291.

6. The DMA was severely criticised for this approach by some local Labour MPs, but it seems to have been widely accepted by the

members, with only a minority taking up the offer of reimbursement.

7. Quoted in David Temple, *The Big Meeting: A History of the Durham Miners' Gala*, Washington, TUPS Books, 2011.

8. *Durham Miner*, 1, 2007: 10.

9. Robin Rudd, 'Coal Miners' Respiratory Disease Litigation', *Thorax*, 53, 1998: 337. See also Clare Dyer, 'Miners Win Historic Battle for Compensation', *British Medical Journal*, 316:31, January 1998: 316–27.

10. 'Miners Win Historic Compensation Claim', BBC, 23 January 1998.

11. HL Deb 19 December 2000, vol. 620, 713–4.

12. Quoted in McIvor and Johnston, *Miners' Lung*, p. 305.

13. In 2007, average settlements in Durham were £9,289 and in South Wales £7,550.

14. 'Phurnacite Plant, Abercwmboi: Workers' High Court Win', BBC, 23 October 2012.

15. 'British Coal Coke Oven Workers: Widow Wins Court Battle', BBC, 15 August 2018.

16. Richard Fletcher, 'Taxpayers May Have to Dig Deep for Miners' Pensions', *Daily Telegraph*, 5 August 2008.

17. Rachel Heeds, 'Why You Should Care about the Miners' Pensions Scandal', *Huffington Post*, 26 September 2016.

18. Orgreave Truth and Justice Campaign, otjc.org.uk/about.

19. '#Deathofjustice Rally', Orgreave Truth and Justice Campaign event listing, 12 July 2017.

14. Building from the Past

1. J. Kelly and R. Bailey, 'British Trade Union Membership, Density and Decline in the 1980s: A Research Note', *Industrial Relations Journal*, 20:1, 1989: 54–61.

2. 'Trade Union Membership 2017: Statistical Bulletin', DBEIS, London, 2018.

3. H. Beynon, R. Davies and S. Davies, 'Sources of Variation in Trade Union Membership across the UK: The Case of Wales',

Industrial Relations Journal, 43:3, 2012: 200–21.

4. See Stephen Yeo, *A Useable Past: Cooperation and Education for un-Statist Socialism in Nineteenth and Twentieth Century Britain: Volume 2*, Brighton, Edward Everett Root, 2018; Hilary Wainwright, *A New Politics from the Left*, Polity, 2019.

5. In the second year of its operation, the mine was visited by David Waddington, David Parry and Chas Critcher, who produced an interesting assessment comparing the experiences of Tower with those at another buy-out at Monktonhall in Scotland. D. Waddington, D. Parry and C. Critcher, 'Keep the Red Flag Flying? A Comparative Study of Two Worker Takeovers in the British Deep Coalmining Industry, 1992–1997', *Work, Employment and Society*, 12:2, 1998: 317–49. Jane Parry's PhD thesis, 'The Changing Meaning of Work' (2000), included interviews with Tower workers as part of her consideration of responses to unemployment; this was later published in an article, 'The Changing Meaning of Work: Restructuring in the Former Coalmining Communities of the South Wales Valleys', *Work, Employment and Society*, 17:2, 2003: 227–46. Emma Wallis also conducted interviews with workers and managers at Tower for her PhD thesis, now published as *Industrial Relations in the Privatised Coal Industry*, Aldershot, Ashgate, 2000. Molly Scott Cato, the Green Party economist, included a study of Tower in her book *The Pit and the Pendulum: A Cooperative Future for Work in the Welsh Valleys*, Cardiff, University of Wales Press, 2004. See also Hywel Francis, *The Tower Story: Lessons in Vigilance and Freedom*, Tower Productions, n.d.

6. See C. Cornforth, 'Patterns of Cooperative Management: Beyond the Degeneration Thesis', *Economic and Industrial Democracy*, 16:4, 1995: 487–523.

7. Positive steps were taken at Monktonhall in the East Lothian and also at Thurcroft near Rotherham. In both cases the control of the coal market by unsympathetic electricity generators, combined with the dash for gas, proved too big an obstacle.

8. Weekes agreed to participate, but wanted no payment save for a pint of beer in the bar after the meetings had finished.

9. Waddington, Parry and Critcher, 'Keep the Red Flag Flying?': 335.

10. Under the privatisation arrangements set up by the government, Tower Colliery was part of a package that included five opencast mines. The managers were not interested in the opencast sites and needed the colliery to be taken out of the package – this could only be achieved by its closure.

11. This was confirmed by the survey of workers conducted by Emma Wallis, which found that the situation compared remarkably well with other post-nationalised mines, including the management buy-out at Betws. At Tower: 76 per cent responded favourably on the changed attitude of management; 41 per cent thought that the union had more influence than before; 83 per cent found overtime to be a voluntary commitment; and 74 per cent thought that safety standards had improved. In all, only 10 per cent considered that the takeover had not been a good thing. See Wallis, *Industrial Relations in the Privatised Coal Industry*, ch. 5.

12. Jack Lawson, *A Man's Life*, London, Lawrence and Wishart, 1932, p. 107.

13. *Durham Chronicle*, 18 July 1872.

14. David Guy, 'Preface' in David Temple, 'The Big Meeting: A History of the Durham Miners' Gala', Washington, Tyner and Wear, TUPS Books, 2011.

15. D. Wray, 'The Place of Imagery in the Transmission of Culture: The Banners of the Durham Coalfield', *International Labor and Working-Class History*, 76:1, 2009.

16. George Alsop, 'A Kind of Socialism', in Terry Austrin *et al.*, eds, *But the World goes on the Same: Changing Times in Durham Pit Villages*, Whitley Bay, Strong Words, 1979, p. 31.

17. David Ayre, 'Instinctive Socialism, in Terry Austrin *et al.*, eds, *But the World goes on the Same: Changing Times in Durham Pit Villages*, Whitley Bay, Strong Words, 1979, p. 8.

18. David Temple, *The Big Meeting: A History of the Durham Miners' Gala*, Washington, TUPS Books, 2011, p. 168.

19. Quoted in Carol Stephenson and David Wray 'Emotional Regeneration through Community Action in Post-Industrial Mining Communities: The New Herrington Miners' Banner Partnership', *Capital and Class*, 87, 2005: 192.

20. David Adamson, 'Social Segregation in a Working-Class Community: Economic and Social Change in the South Wales

Coalfield', in Guy van Gyes, Hans De Witte and Patrick Pasture, eds, *Does Class Still Unite? The Differentiated Workforce, Class Solidity and Trade unions*, London, Routledge, 2001.

15. The People Speak Out

1. These closures came about in spite of positive developments in a number of carbon capture and storage (CCS) schemes which had seemed to signal the possibility of a clean green coal future. Progress was halted when Chancellor George Osborne removed the subsidy, opening the door for the energy secretary, Amber Rudd, to renounce coal within the UK's future energy mix.

2. There was of course regional variation, with the North East and Wales recording the highest percentage at 10 per cent, and Greater London the lowest at 2 per cent. See C. Rhodes, 'Manufacturing Statistics and Policy', House of Commons Briefing Paper 01942, 10 January 2020.

3. Simon Jenkins, *Thatcher and Sons: A Revolution In Three Acts*, London, Allen Lane, 2006, p. 91.

4. Ethan B. Kapstein, 'Workers and the World Economy', *Foreign Affairs*, May/June 1996: 16.

5. *Guardian*, 1 October 2002, theguardian.com/politics/2002/oct/01/labourconference.labour14.

6. E. Engelen I. Ertürk, J. Froud, S. Johal, A. Leaver, M. Moran, A. Nilsson and K. Williams, *After the Great Complacence: Financial Crisis and the Politics of Reform*, Oxford, Oxford University Press, 2011, p. 148; and Dave Feickert, 'Arthur was Right by Instinct', *Guardian*, 11 February 2004.

7. Tom Crewe, 'The Strange Death of Municipal England', *London Review of Books*, 16 December 2016.

8. Weighing the reasons against having a referendum, Cameron is reported to have said: 'You could unleash demons of which ye know not.' See Tim Shipman, *All Out War: The Full Story of How Brexit Sank Britain's Political Class*, London, William Collins, p. xxi; and Craig Oliver, *Unleashing Demons: The Inside Story of Brexit*, London, Hodder and Stoughton, 2016.

9. F. Furedi, 'Brexit Pity Parties Show How Out of Touch Academia

Is', *Times Higher Education Supplement*, 14 July 2016.

10. See C. Barnard, '"British Jobs for British Workers": The Lindsey Oil Refinery Dispute and the Future of Local Labour Clauses in an Integrated EU Market', *Industrial Law Journal*, 38, September 2009: 245–77; Deborah Summers, 'Brown Stands By the British Jobs for British Workers Remark', *Guardian*, 30 January 2009.

11. These constituencies are Easington, Houghton and Sunderland South, South Shields, Washington and Sunderland West.

12. There is an echo here of Edward Thompson's account of discussions around the 1832 Reform Bill, when the slogan 'Equal suffrage' was, he argued, interpreted by the Durham miners as 'equal suffering'.

13. Alan Sillitoe, *The Loneliness of the Long Distance Runner*, London, W.H. Allen, 1959, p. 5.

14. Electoral Reform Society, *It's Good to Talk Doing Referendums Differently*, London, 2016: 39.

15. Balls's trajectory was part and parcel of the rise of a new political class lacking much in the way of real-world experience, Llew Smith's 'kids'. Typically moving from university to Parliament via a research job with an MP, building on family and personal contacts and linked closely with the mass media, this new cohort represented a rupturing of the old Party structure and brought about a significant change in the manner of government. This in turn had far-reaching consequences, exacerbated by underlying weaknesses in the new economy. Peter Oborne, *The Triumph of the Political Class*, London, Simon and Schuster, 2007.

16. Brought up in Cardiff, Jones was a graduate of the University of Sussex before becoming an officer for NUPE (National Union of Public Employees, later UNISON). She was made a life peer (Baroness Jones of Whitchurch) in 2006 and was in the Labour Party shadow team until 2015.

17. 'Corbyn was the victim of a carefully planned and brutally executed political assassination. He was never given a chance. Not by the bulk of Labour's parliamentary party and many officials, some of whom (we are now learning) campaigned harder against their elected leader than they did against the Tory government'. Peter Oborne and David Hearst, 'The Killing of Jeremy Corbyn', *Middle East Eye*, 5 June 2020.

18. 'Creating a Dedicated Fund for Coalfield Communities – State of the Coalfields 2019', Coalfield Regeneration Trust, 13 November 2019.

19. Laura Pidcock, 'Letter to the People I Represented', *Medium*, 18 December 2019.

20. Quoted in 'If Labour Doesn't Talk to the Voters It Lost, I Fear for the Future', *Guardian*, 24 January 2020.

21. 'Wishy-Washy Centrism Wrong for Labour, Warns Lord Hain', BBC Wales, 14 December 2019.

Conclusions and Reflections

1. Tim Shipman, *All Out War: The Full Story of How Brexit Sank Britain's Political Class*, London, William Collins, 2017, p. 587.

2. Raymond Williams, 'Mining the Meaning: Key Words on the Miners' Strike', in *Resources for Hope*, London, Verso, 1993, p. 123.

Index